Electro

News

Electronic Age News Editing

Harry W. Stonecipher
Edward C. Nicholls
and
Douglas A. Anderson

Nelson Hall nh Chicago

Library of Congress Cataloging in Publication Data

Stonecipher, Harry W.
    Electronic age news editing.

    Bibliography: p.
    Includes index.
    1.   Journalism—Editing.   I.   Nicholls, Edward C.
II.   Anderson, Douglas A.   III.   Title.
PN4778.S82   070.4′1   81–536
ISBN 0–88229–636–1 (cloth)   AACR2
ISBN 0–88229–779–1 (paper)

Manufactured in the United States of America

10   9   8   7   6   5   4   3   2   1

Contents

Preface

NEWSPAPER EDITING is changing. Mounds of copy paper, the paste pot, and scissors have been replaced by video display terminals in many newspaper offices. Editing tools are undergoing a constant transformation. Though computers have not replaced skilled, capable editors, they have altered dramatically the daily functions of these editors. In turn, today's students preparing for tomorrow's news editing careers are confronted not just with mastering basic editing techniques, but also with acclimating themselves to the new technology and an ever-changing society.

The purpose of this textbook is to help prepare students for jobs in this electronic age by combining a discussion of pragmatic, painstaking, editing skills with the philosophical and technological aspects of the craft. This book, then, focuses on the practicalities of day-to-day newspaper editing as well as on the social, political, legal and technological environments in which editors function. More specifically, the book:

1. provides an overview of the editing process by exploring the ethical and constitutional frameworks within which editors operate;
2. examines traditional copy-processing procedures, making use of practical examples;
3. discusses editing considerations when working with various types of copy;
4. deals with the importance of maintaining style and readability in newspaper copy;

5. places in perspective the effects of the new technology on traditional editing practices;

6. considers the many variables which affect news judgments;

7. provides examples and a discussion of headlines;

8. presents criteria for selecting, processing, and sizing news photographs;

9. examines the aesthetics of contemporary newspaper page design;

10. discusses the wire services, including insights into the working relationship between newspaper editors and the services;

11. reflects on the news-editorial hierarchy of daily newspapers and the concomitant inherent management pressures;

12. focuses not only on editing daily newspapers, but also on the demanding roles of nondaily and campus newspaper editors;

13. analyzes the effects of communication law on the editor within a practical and theoretical framework; and

14. investigates trends in electronic age news editing.

This book was written for journalism students who aspire to editing positions. Certainly no textbook standing alone can adequately prepare students for editing jobs and responsibilities. But, it can provide a solid supplement to essential practical experience. The authors, in fact, bring more than thirty years of newspaper and wire service experience and almost twenty years of college teaching to this project. In addition to drawing heavily from their varied backgrounds, the authors culled scores of newspapers for relevant examples, consulted hundreds of books and articles, surveyed some two hundred fifty weekly and daily newspaper editors for their opinions of and experiences with various aspects of newspaper editing, and conducted personal and telephone interviews with dozens of editors and photographers.

This is a book by journalists for journalists. Readers, however, will notice references to the news*man,* to *his* skills, to *his* responsibilities and to *his* tasks. Apologies are offered to anyone who might be offended. It was not the intention of the authors to take a sexist position; rather, this usage was adopted to avoid awkward, clumsy phrasing which could detract from the book's readability.

Many persons and organizations contributed to the research and preparation of this text. Though this list is not complete, formal thanks should be extended to The Associated Press for permission to quote liberally from *The Associated Press Stylebook and Libel Manual* and from other published AP materials; to United Press International for permission to use some of its material as examples; and to the University of Nebraska at Omaha (UNO) Faculty Senate Research Committee which provided funding for newspaper subscriptions, questionnaires and typing while co-author Douglas Anderson was on the UNO faculty.

Individuals who were particularly helpful through their insights and counsel in the preparation of various portions of this book were James Geladas, managing editor, Dubuque, Iowa, *Telegraph Herald;* Donald R. Seaton, publisher, and Burt James, former editor, the *Hastings* (Neb.) *Daily Tribune;* Barry Bingham Jr., publisher, William Ellison, director of news administration, and C. Thomas Hardin, director of photography, all of the *Courier-Journal* and *Louisville Times;* David Anderson, assistant photo editor, *Miami Herald;* Edward Seaton, publisher, *Manhattan* (Kan.) *Mercury;* Donald Tremain, still photographer, the Nebraska Educational Television Network; Carl Keith, night managing editor, Rudy Smith, photographer, and Donald Wright, copy editor, all of the *Omaha* (Neb.) *World-Herald;* Gene Pospeshil, photo editor, *St. Louis Post-Dispatch;* William Harmon and Dr. Robert Trager, Southern Illinois University; Associate Dean Milton Gross, University of Missouri; Dr. Michael Stricklin and Professor George Tuck, the University of Nebraska-Lincoln; Dr. Hugh Cowdin and Catherine Peterson, the University of Nebraska at Omaha; Professor William Korbus, University of Texas at Austin; Susan Eisert, picture editor, the *Washington Post;* Joseph M. Ungaro, vice president and executive editor of Westchester Rockland Newspapers, Inc., White Plains, N.Y.; the hundreds of weekly and daily newspaper editors who took the time to respond to survey questionnaires; and those newspapers, publications and individuals who gave permission to reprint examples. Credit for typing the manuscript goes to Kathie Lee, Omaha, Nebraska.

Special appreciation is extended to our wives and families for their patience and understanding during the months this manuscript was in preparation: Helen Marie Stonecipher; Marles, Brent and Lisa Jule Nicholls; and Claudia, Laura and Mary Anderson. To them this book is dedicated.

Chapter 1

News Editing in Contemporary America

CONTEMPORARY NEWSPAPER EDITING is a difficult calling. Gone is the day when editors and publishers could use their newspapers to simply foist prejudices off on an ill-informed, poorly educated readership. History has chronicled the idiosyncrasies of colonial and frontier editors who, through their publications, selfishly bugled personal, political, religious, and philosophical messages.

Today's newspapers, on the other hand, must be edited for the most intelligent, discerning readers in American history. These readers seek more than pictures, stories, and advertisements. They demand, through their buying habits, that newspapers be thorough, well edited, and responsible. Editors must be intelligent, fair, responsive, and responsible.

The constitutional bedrock upon which editors rely is the First Amendment. Essentially, it says that Congress shall not abridge freedom of speech or press. Significantly, however, the amendment says nothing about the responsibility of the press. In a legal sense, the First Amendment gives editors freedom to express their views and make news decisions—but it does not mandate responsibility in return. The U.S. Supreme Court has made this unambiguously clear.

In a 1974 case (*Miami Herald Publishing Co.* v. *Tornillo*), the Court unanimously held that a newspaper could not be compelled by the state to accept editorial replies. Recognizing the importance of exercising editorial judgment, Chief Justice Warren Burger said, "A responsible press is an undoubtedly desirable goal, but press responsibility is not mandated by the Constitution and like so many other virtues it cannot be legislated." Burger continued:

> A newspaper is more than a passive receptacle or conduit for news, comment, and advertising. The choice of material to go into a newspaper, and the decisions made as to limitations on the size of the paper, and content, and treatment of public issues and public officials—whether fair or unfair—constitutes the exercise of editorial control and judgment. It has yet to be demonstrated how governmental regulation of this crucial process can be exercised consistent with First Amendment guarantees of a free press.

In a concurring opinion, Justice Byron White emphasized that, "A newspaper or magazine is not a public utility subject to 'reasonable' governmental regulation in matters affecting the exercise of journalistic judgment as to what shall be printed." Still, White tempered his opinion by saying that, "The press is the servant, not the master, of the citizenry, and its freedom does not carry with it an unrestricted hunting license to prey on the ordinary citizen."

Justice William Brennan, in a concurring opinion in the 1976 *Nebraska Press Association* v. *Stuart* case, also stressed the danger of restraints from the judicial branch. He said: "The press may be arrogant, tyrannical, abusive and sensationalist, just as it may be incisive, probing and informative. But at least in the context of prior restraints on publication, the decisions of what, when, and how to publish is for editors, not judges."

Obviously, the press enjoys considerable constitutional protection. Media critics during the post–World War II years have, however, contended that the press—in return for this protection—must become increasingly responsible.

Four Theories of the Press

Fred S. Siebert, Theodore Peterson, and Wilbur Schramm more than twenty years ago explored the relationship between the press, the government, and the people in a classic book, *Four Theories of the Press*. The scholars summarized this multifaceted relationship through four systems—theories—that they labeled authoritarian, Soviet-communist, libertarian, and social responsibility. These philosophies are germane to contemporary newspaper editing practices. Though none of the labels precisely fits the current press-people-government relationship in the United States, elements of both the libertarian and social responsibility theories are recognizable in editing decisions made today.

From the writings of philosophers such as John Milton, John Locke, and John Stuart Mill, the libertarian theory was born. A reaction to the stringent authoritarian system—where the collective rights of the state were placed above individual liberties and where the state controlled, to a certain extent, the media—the libertarian theory evolved in the late seventeenth and early eighteenth centuries. Essentially, it places the emphasis on natural rights and individual worth.

Under the libertarian system, the press serves as a check on government; through the press, citizens discover truth. As a vast array of information is made available to the public, truth majestically rises to the top. Government exercises no control over the press. Rational, intelligent citizens discern truth from fiction; viable, strong newspapers survive and prosper. The courts occasionally intervene (when newspapers are charged under obscenity, privacy, or libel statutes), but the legislative and executive branches of government are not allowed to interfere.

The system flourished in less complex times, but the days of competitive-newspaper communities and sure access to the press are, in many instances, romantic recollections. As the number of American newspapers started to decline shortly after the turn of the twentieth century, people began to wonder if an adequate forum could be found to transmit divergent points of view. After all, media owners controlled their news columns; they possessed tremendous power. Government was unable to intervene. The courts served only a peripheral role. As this concern about newspapers adequately serving an increasingly complex and ever-changing society became more pervasive, a group was formed shortly after World War II to study the dilemma.

The Commission on Freedom of the Press, composed of scholars and philosophers, expressed dissatisfaction with the way some American media were carrying out the functions normally associated with a libertarian system. The fact of a decreasing number of media voices understandably raised the question of whether the press was providing a sufficient forum for the dissemination of information and debate necessary for a self-governing people.

Essentially, the commission reasoned that the press should exercise more responsibility—to insure that divergent views were aired—and if the press did not, the government could possibly be called upon to intervene. From the committee's report emerged what has been labeled the social responsibility theory of the press. Peterson capsulized its major premise:

> Freedom carries concomitant obligations; and the press, which enjoys a privileged position under our government, is obliged to be responsible to society for carrying out certain essential functions. . . . To the extent that the press recognizes its responsibilities and makes them the basis of operational policies, the libertarian system will satisfy the needs of society. To the extent that the press does not assume its responsibilities, some other agency must see that the essential functions of mass communication are carried out.

Naturally, the possibility of government intervention with the inner workings of the press evoked strong reactions. Legal scholar Zechariah Chafee, Jr. warned that the government should never come to be regarded as the guardian of free political debate. He said, "So much stress has been laid of late on various economic pressures and forces which warp mass communications that there is some risk that the American people will lose sight of the evils of a government controlled press." Chafee then cautioned that, "The meaning which our ancestors gave to liberty of the press, namely, freedom from the will of legislators and officials, is just as vital today as it was in 1791."

The situation is apparent; today's newspaper editors and owners enjoy considerable protection under the First Amendment—but repeated abuses of the freedom could erode it. A comment in the *DePaul Law Review* vividly emphasizes the role of newspaper executives:

> The directors of American newspapers thus exercise a powerful form of private censorship—a censorship traditionally associated with government and which forms the basis for the First Amendment protection from restraints on freedom of speech and of the press. The decision not to publish is characterized as an exercise of freedom of choice, freedom of expression or editorial discretion.

Contemporary newspapers play a large part in forming public opinion. The press is, indeed, a powerful institution.

Newspapers and Public Opinion

In today's complex world, Americans are no longer aware of everything that affects their lives by experiencing those things directly. This might have been possible a few generations ago, but it isn't possible any more. People now rely on the media to gather information, not only in city halls but also in state capitols, Washington, D.C., places around the world, and even in outer space—because what happens in these places affects our lives, our pocketbooks, our futures, and our very survival. Journalists must provide their audience not only with information but also with understanding.

A news editor faces the staggering responsibility of sifting through huge amounts of information which flow into his newsroom. He passes on a fraction of it—perhaps 10 percent or less—to his readers. The vast majority of information and opinions Americans possess is not based on direct experience but on secondhand information from the news media. In turn, this information is based on the judgments of a news editor—on what he has decided will be of value and what will not.

By selecting and displaying the news, an editor plays a crucial role in shaping the social reality for his readers. He structures thinking about that reality his readers have not experienced directly but which might profoundly affect their lives. This editorial role has been linked with the so-called agenda-setting function of the press.

Until the 1940s, the accepted wisdom was that the mass media—primarily newspapers at that time—were all-powerful. That is, they were capable, all by themselves, of manipulating and changing, virtually at will, the attitudes and behavior of their audience. This view was the result primarily of the apparent effectiveness of advertising and wartime propaganda in the earlier part of the twentieth century. But in the 1940s and 1950s, researchers discovered through a series of voting and leadership studies that the mass media do not have the kind of power unilaterally to change attitudes and behavior that they were originally thought to have. The media are best at reinforcing attitudes that already exist in the audience, and they are effective in creating new attitudes on new issues; but they are not very successful, all by themselves, in changing existing attitudes, especially on relatively serious issues like politics (in contrast to relatively trivial matters like choices between brand names). By 1960, the evidence was clear that the direct effects of mass communication on attitudes and behavior are minimal.

So, if the news media, as indicated above, play a crucial role in the formation of public opinion, then in what way are they crucial? According to research since 1960, the news media are most effective in creating awareness of issues, in providing information about the world and in indicating to their readers how much importance should be attached to an issue by the emphasis that the media place on it.

In other words, newspapers and other media shape perceptions of reality, structure thinking, and influence opinions by telling readers what they should be thinking *about*; newspapers are much more successful in these functions than they are in telling readers what they should be thinking—that is, what attitudes they should hold and what behaviors they should engage in. When the process reaches that point, other psychological and sociological influences—like value systems, preconceptions, families, friends, and peer groups—will probably be more important than the mass media.

Research indicates, in effect, that the news editor is more important than the editorial writer, though editorial writers, of course, also help set an agenda. Readers make judgments about which candidates to vote for and which positions to take on controversial issues primarily on the basis of what is in the news columns, not on what is on the editorial page. Most studies show that fewer than a third of all newspaper readers read the editorial page, but virtually all of them read the front page. It is on the news pages that the press—by creating awareness, providing information, and indicating what is important— sets the agendas for its readers; it is primarily here that elections and issues are won or lost.

If this were not the case—if elections and issues were in fact won primarily on the editorial page because of the news media's alleged power to manipulate public opinion and behavior (for example, voting behavior)—then the results of elections would be universally consistent with the positions taken by newspapers on their editorial pages. But we know, in one community after another, that this is not the case.

The power of the news editor is indeed considerable and so, obviously, is his responsibility.

Newspapers and Responsibility

Today's surviving daily newspapers, for the most part, are strong, robust institutions. But, as their numbers decrease, are owners and editors cognizant of their pervasive power? Do newspaper editors believe they have a responsibility to society? If so, what are they doing to meet this responsibility?

In *All the President's Men,* Bob Woodward and Carl Bernstein recounted some of their Watergate investigative procedures, which included gathering names of grand jury members. The reporters consulted the *Washington Post*'s library copy of the Federal Rules of Criminal Procedure. They found that grand jurors were required to take oaths to keep secret their deliberations. The burden of secrecy, however, appeared to be on the jurors. Nothing in the law seemed to forbid anyone from asking jurors questions, though the identities of grand jurors were to be kept secret. Using his ingenuity, Woodward gained access to and memorized names of the grand jurors. The reporters then questioned six of the jurors—to no avail. Only one even admitted to being on the grand jury. Another complained of harassment to prosecutors. The complaint was passed on to Judge John J. Sirica. Though the reporters were not singled out, Sirica warned against further investigations of this nature.

Reporters and editors often find themselves in compromising situations. Journalists technically might be within their legal rights. Ethical considerations are often more difficult to deal with—particularly when working on stories where there is a compelling need for the public to know.

A growing concern for media responsibility emerged in the post-Watergate period. Even the Rev. Billy Graham jumped on the bandwagon. During the annual meeting of the Southern Newspaper Publishers Association in 1974, he said that "newspaper publishers should make a crusade for moral and spiritual integrity." He emphasized that circulation and advertising growth should not be the only concerns of publishers. Graham said the "breakdown of morality calls for strong countermoves."

John B. Oakes, former senior editor of the *New York Times* and editor of its editorial page, pointed to changing citizen attitudes toward the press. He said public understanding and support of the First Amendment is weakening. Oakes cited the decreasing number of newspapers (the approximate 1,750 daily newspapers today is down from more than 2,000 at the turn of the twentieth century, even though the population has more than doubled) and the perception held by media critics that newspapers are forgetting their traditional editorial responsibilities while becoming totally business-oriented.

At a Frank E. Gannett Memorial Lecture in 1978, Oakes said: "I think that we of the American press would be living in a fool's paradise if we believed that we could continue to enjoy public support for our constitutional protection under the First Amendment, if we forgot our implied responsibilities under it, by allowing our credibility to be eroded or destroyed."

In his address to the 1976 convention of the National Conference of Editorial Writers, Oakes emphasized that "in this fantastically complex society in which we are living, no one can be an expert on all matters; but each of us by virtue of the position we hold—whether supreme boss of a small-town daily or a small but significant cog in a huge publicity empire—is capable of having some effect on the public policies of his community and country."

The growing concern over ethics in the 1970s was also apparent. The Associated Press Managing Editors Association, the American Society of Newspaper Editors, Sigma Delta Chi/The Society of Professional Journalists, The National Conference of Editorial Writers, and The Associated Press Sports Editors were among groups that revised existing codes of ethics—some of which dated back to the 1920s. This surge in rearticulating ethical standards has also been felt on the local newspaper level. In the summer of 1978, 150 managing editors were polled to determine if their newspapers had policies on ethics. Of those responding, 52 percent said their newspapers had written policies; 45 percent said their papers had oral policies. Only two newspapers said their newspapers had neither written nor oral policies.

Newspaper ethics encompass a broad spectrum. Policies of national organizations are very general. For example, a summary of The Associated Press managing editors code entails four broad areas:

Responsibility. Truth is the "guiding principle." Newspapers should "serve as a constructive critic of all segments of society" and should "vigorously expose wrong-doing or misuse of power." Newspapers should recognize the paramount importance of the public's right to know. Further, news sources "should be disclosed unless there is clear reason not to do so."

Accuracy. Newspapers should beware of inaccuracies and should be careful to admit all substantive errors. Errors should be corrected "promptly and prominently."

Integrity. Newspapers should not extend favors in the news columns to special interest groups or advertisers. The news columns should be objective, with editorials and opinion pieces clearly labeled. In addition, "concern for community, business or personal interests should not cause a newspaper to distort or misrepresent the facts."

Conflict of interest. Newspapers should accept nothing of value from news sources or others outside the profession. Political involvement, outside employment, and financial investments are areas which could create the appearance of conflicts of interest.

These guidelines go to the very heart of the issue; can a reporter or editor have an active involvement with news events and sources and still report accurately and objectively? Even if he can, will readers believe it? For example:

• Could an editor serve on appointive city boards, such as the parks and recreation commission, without compromising his news judgment?
• Should an editor chair a downtown community improvement council that might request tax dollars from the city for certain projects?
• Should the publisher, who claims detachment from his paper's news columns, serve on the city council or school board? Will his involvement directly or indirectly affect news coverage?
• Should an editor serve on a Chamber of Commerce industrial committee?
• Should the circulation manager, an individual who has no control over news content, be allowed to serve as a county commissioner?
• Should an editor move in social circles with elected officials or other city leaders? Will this affect his news judgment?

Obviously, answers to some of these questions are more clear-cut than others. Almost any community involvement by newspaper executives could raise eyebrows—no matter how innocent or well-meaning.

To be sure, codes of ethics are merely words on paper. The consensus is, however, that they have made an impact on newspaper practices. David B. Offer, former chairman of the Ethics Committee of the Society of Professional Journalists, said recently that the codes are working satisfactorily in most areas, although there is room for improvement. He cited newspaper travel departments where travel writers still accept free trips.

Many newspapers have taken additional steps to increase credibility: they have appointed ombudsmen to see that public complaints get acted on; they have displayed corrections prominently—often on page one; they have opened the letters column to as many writers as possible; they have surveyed persons who were subjects of news stories for their opinions on the fairness and accuracy of the articles;

and they have conducted surveys to help determine the types of information readers would like to see in the paper. In addition, local press councils have been formed to help bridge the gap between the public and the press.

Not surprisingly, this increasing concern over ethics and responsibilities has made an imprint in post-secondary journalism curriculums. In a recent survey conducted by the Associated Press Managing Editors Journalism Education Committee, all universities responding said their journalism schools or departments teach ethics. Some schools teach it as a separate course; many incorporate ethics into other classes.

News Editing—Now an Electronic Art

Newspaper editors, in addition to dealing with ethical questions on a philosophical and practical plane, must master traditional skills. These skills go beyond rearranging paragraphs, slicing superfluous words and changing "that" to "which." Editors do all of those things —and more; they write headlines, crop and size photographs, process and combine wire copy, and lay out pages. Indeed, editing requires intelligence, sound judgment, an understanding of the law, and, perhaps most importantly, the ability to work with others.

Editors must recognize their immense responsibility to their readers and their power as molders of public opinion. They should also wisely use their influence in choosing which stories to print, where to place them, what size headline to assign, which syndicated columnist to select, which political candidate to endorse, and which events to cover.

Today's editors must meet these and other challenges. The electronic editing age is upon us. Throughout most of the twentieth century, American newspaper editors have pounded manual typewriters, edited with soft-lead pencils, and cut and pasted copy. Computerization, however, has significantly altered the process for many newspapers; copy is now edited on computer terminals.

Contrary to what some might think, however, computers are not replacing editors in newsrooms. A national survey showed that good, skilled editors are more important than ever before. Efficient, masterful editing has been revitalized. John K. Murphy, of the *Portland* (Maine) *Press-Herald,* emphasized that his copy editors have more freedom with an electronic system. "It is making our copy editors regain skills which had been badly corrupted by years of handling [perforated] taped copy that for production reasons was virtually untouchable."

The managing editor of the *Grand Island* (Neb.) *Independent,* Al Schmahl, contends that good editors should thrive in an electronic newsroom. He said newspapers have been "wedded to wire service tape in the type-setting process but electronics gives everyone the opportunity to once again really edit their newspapers." Schmahl points out that editors "can change a word with a few key strokes, chop out a cumbersome phrase, tighten a loosely written article and still turn out an absolutely clean piece of copy. Nobody has to decipher your hieroglyphics."

Chapter 2

The Copy Editor

PAINSTAKING COPY EDITING is often termed a lost art. Encompassing far more than merely marking paragraph indentations or slicing superfluous words, skillful editing is indeed an art form. Editors must adroitly incorporate changes without destroying the tenor and style of each writer's work.

Important as it is, editing is an anonymous task. Seldom does one hear praise for editors who improve prize-winning investigative reporters' copy.

Though copy editors have been accused of hiding behind their typewriters—or video display terminals (VDTs)—while reporters fearlessly pound the pavement in pursuit of sensational stories, the copy desk is not a haven for the timid. Editors are often berated—sometimes aggressively stalked—by disgruntled reporters who claim their work has been butchered beyond recognition. These same copy editors, however, are seldom thanked when they save reporters from grammatical blunders or factual inaccuracies.

Work on the copy desk is not glamorous, but it is extremely crucial. The desk is often the last check point before a story is printed. Every paragraph, sentence, word, and letter must be intensely scrutinized. Every fact must be verified. While copy editors strive to produce the best possible editorial product, they must also work effectively and quickly under deadline pressure.

The goal of the copy editor is to improve every story. Editors should never rewrite; if copy requires that, it should be sent back to the reporter. Obviously, improving copy and insuring that it is objective, fair, and tasteful is no easy task. Possibly the challenge of copy editing—and the concomitant absence of recognition—explain why newspaper executives today claim there is a shortage of copy editors. Buster Haas of the *Dallas Morning News* said recently that copy editors "are in short supply and there doesn't appear to be any relief in sight." A total of 73 percent of the editors responding to an Associated Press Managing Editors survey said applicants for copy desk jobs are scarce. In a companion survey of journalism schools, it was found that only about 10 percent of journalism majors had expressed an interest in copy desk work.

Not surprisingly, the classified ad pages of *Editor & Publisher* are jammed each week with announcements of openings for copy desk positions. The job descriptions vividly illustrate that copy editing, though usually done with little fanfare, encompasses far more than catching spelling errors. A sampling of ads in one edition included these:

> We need someone who can fit competently into our high-quality, 6-member, major metro feature copy desk. The work is wide ranging and requires both innovative layout and kind but firm copy editing.

> A major metro in one of the Sun Belt's leading resort cities seeks a copy editor for lifestyles section. We want someone with a flair for headlines, ability to make copy sparkle, sound knowledge of modern layout techniques and potential for leadership.

> We're a major southern daily and want you if you're a first-rate, experienced copy editor who knows how to word edit, write headlines that grab readers and work quickly and gracefully under pressure. We prefer layout skills and VDT experience but your eagerness to grow and learn is more important.

> Wire editor for 17,000 daily. Experience with front-end system, layout, copy editing helpful, but we are willing to train for right person.

Obviously, jobs await most qualified journalists who aspire to copy editing positions. Certain basic skills, however, must be mastered before one is ready to competently fulfill this vital newspaper function.

The Copy Desk

Copy desks at most newspapers are horseshoe shaped; the slot person sits in the middle of the horseshoe and assigns stories to copy editors who sit around the "rim." Slot persons on newspapers which do not have electronic newsrooms receive copy from the wire editor, city editor, or news editor with penciled or verbal instructions as to length, headline size, and page position.

Fig. 2–1. Copy editors sat around the horseshoe "rim" and edited with pencils at the *Omaha* (Neb.) *World-Herald* before the newspaper converted to an electronic copy-processing system. (Photo courtesy of the *Omaha* (Neb.) *World-Herald*.)

The slot person then assigns the story to a particular editor on the rim—someone who might have special knowledge about the subject or who possesses the "old hand" expertise to handle a difficult story.

The copy editor can measure copy by one of two methods: he can count every line to determine an approximate length, or he can fold the copy in fourths, counting the lines in one quadrant and then multiplying by four to get the total lines and an approximate length. Individual newspapers have guidelines to estimate story lengths. At the *Washington Post,* for example, if a story is to be set for 13.9-pica columns in 8-point type, four and one-half wire copy lines or five and one-half typed lines equal one inch in type. If the body type is 9-point, three and one-half wire copy lines or four and one-half typed lines equal one column inch. Some copy editors even employ the space-age technology of the pocket calculator to compute length. Ultimately, however, it is the makeup editor or the printers themselves who "shrink the type" to fit the designated space.

Headlines are either counted in the copy editor's head or scribbled on a piece of scratch paper. (Headlines will be discussed in detail in chapter 7.) After the headline "fits" (when the characters have the proper count), the headline is written at the top of the copy along with page location, column width, and other special instructions for the composing room or "backshop." At many newspapers, headlines are typed or printed on separate half-sheets of paper and sent to the composing room.

Once an editor commits himself to a particular story, that story is usually his for the remainder of the shift. During the news cycle, editors are often handed confetti-follow-up stories or "writethrus" (wire service terminology will be discussed in detail in chapter 11) of earlier stories that might include new information. The editing challenge becomes formidable when new information is made available for developing stories over a long period; for example, as updates of the mass suicide in Jonestown, Guyana, in the fall of 1978 became available, copy editors were hard pressed to stay abreast of recent happenings.

Desk work is not as tedious as it might sound, however. Along with the work is the constant string of chatter among editors about the more unusual, funny, bizarre, or disheartening news of the day. Humor, puns, and Monday morning quarterbacking are common.

Copy editing procedures, though, are somewhat different on those newspapers which have converted to electronic newsrooms (the effects of the new technology on copy editing will be examined in detail in chapter 5). Telephones still ring; people still chatter; the humor isn't any better. But, in the new electronic newsroom, the insistent clatter of battered typewriters has been replaced by the "plock-plock-plock" sound of video display terminal (VDT) keyboards.

Electronic newsroom editors are likely more cautious than they were during cut-and-paste days. Most have even taken up the study of the stylebook again, some after a lapse of many years. No longer

Fig. 2–2. Though editing aids such as dictionaries, city directories, stylebooks, almanacs, old newspapers, and the like (foreground) are still found in electronic age newspaper newsrooms, manual typewriters are gone. Editors, like these at the *Omaha* (Neb.) *World-Herald*, process copy on video display terminals. (Photo courtesy of Rudy Smith, *Omaha World-Herald*.)

is there a proofreader to catch style and spelling errors. The responsibility rests squarely with the copy editor.

Copy editors in traditional newsrooms often blame proofreaders or printers when errors appear in print. These "typos," a term reaching back to the days of printers in backshops sweating over cantankerous Linotype machines, have been replaced with "newsos" in electronic newsrooms. When working with electronic copy processing systems, editors make their own errors and set them in "type." Thus, mistakes are called "newsos," reflecting their source more accurately.

Some editors who have moved from using pencil to high-speed electrons contend that the editing process has slowed considerably, even though the type—actually photographic film—is set more quickly using computers and VDTs.

In contrast to the old days on the rim, copy editors seldom receive hard copy (written on paper). Instead, they receive and edit stories on their terminal screens. The slot person still assigns copy editors certain stories; instead of penciling instructions, however, the slot person places the assignments and instructions in computer queues. Thus, editor Henion might have a queue named HEN. Though systems vary, this procedure is representative:

Coming to work, Henion signs on to his VDT by tapping HEN on the keyboard and pressing the sign-on button. The VDT then confirms he is ready to begin work by printing across the top of the screen:

QUEUE HEN SIGNED ON TC 00 TERMINAL 01

Editor Henion then presses the "director" button to see if any stories have been assigned to his queue or to work stories left there from the last time he was on the desk. The VDT shows him what is in his queue:

FILE DIRECTORY
(MSPC) (QL)
HEN (MSPC) (QL)
(MSPC) (QL)
BOOK-HEN 18:47 — 6/15/79 KBD E BOOK-HEN

This message tells the editor that he has correctly activated the machine, that it is HEN's file directory, and that there is one story in the queue—something about a book with the file name of BOOK-HEN. The story was put in his queue at 6:47 P.M., on June 15, 1979, by someone using a keyboard (KBD), and the story has either been looked at—"opened"—by someone or it has been edited (E). The tag line concludes with the file name again, just in case the first part of the line is mutilated (there are a variety of ways this can happen, resulting in a frantic search of backup systems looking for some kind of file name with the word "book" in it).

Henion then moves the blinking light called the cursor to the beginning of the file name, presses the "open edit" button and the story appears on his screen.

This entire process takes about fifteen seconds.

If there is nothing in his queue, Henion could look at the directories for other general desk queues—COP ("copy"), PAI ("page 1") and SHO ("shorts").

In the COP queue he finds this story:

AA5930-A15 WOMENAM—15:00-6/15/79 NWR SPI E 15
AA5930-A22 (QL) R 1stLD-WRITETHRU A5300 AM-WOMEN
LST LD-WRITETHRU (QC)

The number AA5930 is the story's file name; the A15 is the date. WOMENAM tells the editor the story is about women, that it was originally an AM or a morning story that is being rewritten, that it moved on the Associated Press wire at 3:00 P.M. on June 15, 1979, that it came off the news wire (NWR) and specifically from the "spike" queue (SPI). It is about fifteen inches long and this version is the first writethru of the earlier story.

Before assigning the story to his queue, the editor notes the file name on his copy desk log just in case the computer system "crashes" and everything on his screen is lost. With a file name recorded, he is assured that the story can be retrieved from the computer's backup system—unless that, too, flops.

After the editor has worked the story to his satisfaction, he presses the "end" button. At the top of his screen at the left will appear the story's file name. Opposite it at the extreme right will be a flashing word "close," which tells him the story is ready for assignment to the slot or to be set directly from his machine. And so it goes for additional stories during the news cycle.

Despite the emergence of electronic newsrooms, aspiring copy editors should still master traditional methods of marking and preparing copy. Not all newspapers have converted to electronic copy processing systems, and, besides, news releases from outside sources must still be contended with.

Preparing Copy

Editors use traditional editing symbols to expedite hard-copy processing. These symbols, though confusing to the novice, soon become automatic and form an effective means of communication between the newsroom and composing room. The most common symbols include:

New paragraph:	⌐The University of Nebraska Board of Regents voted today not to raise tuition rates for in-state students.
Capitalize the letter or letters:	⌐Henry Smith, editor of the school newspaper, is a native of butte, Mont.
Make the letter or letters lower case:	⌐An honors graduate of the university, John was a History major.

Insert a hyphen: Jones was a high stepping halfback.

Italicize the words: Summa cum laude, magna cum laude.

Insert a dash: Jack Nicklaus the tournament winner finished 17 strokes under par.

Run together the copy: This sentence should be joined.

Insert a letter, word or words: Thieves removed the paintings from a locked storage area where they were being kept.

Delete letters, punctuation or figures and don't close up the space (arc above only):   Cool weather in the 1980s will be followed by a worldwide warming trend for the rest of century.

Delete the letter and close up the space (arc above and below):   The state's presidential primary election will be next month.

Let the copy stand as originally written: He lives at 1111 E. Main Street.

The copy is correct as written: John Smyth is expected to win the mayoral race.

Delete the word and leave a space (arc above only):   The state's presidential primary election, which required a blanket-size type ballot in the last election, is expected to be even more complicated this time around.

Make a space: Gregg Jones hit a 15-foot jump shot to win the basketball game.

Transpose letters, words or phrases: The city library knows you are out there, hiding books that are overdue.

Make the copy conform to newspaper style. When using this symbol, or course, the editor assumes the typesetter is familiar with the stylebook. The symbol is ofen used to indicate that a word should be abbreviated:

⌊Bill Jones, 2222 W. Norwood (Street) witnessed the crime.

If the editor circles an abbreviated word, the typesetter should spell it out:

⌊Bill Jones, 2222 W. Norwood (Dr.) witnessed the crime.

This symbol is also convenient when editing copy that contains numbers. According to The Associated Press stylebook, numbers nine and below are spelled out, but numbers 10 and above are not.

⌊Bill Jones, 2222 W. Norwood St., Parsons, Kan., (twenty-one) years old, was sentenced to (5) days in jail.

End mark. The story is complete:

⌊If the sale is finalized, hospital officials expect the group to take possession of the property immediately.
(—30—)

Other editing suggestions:
• *Be precise.* Editors are constantly called upon to insert punctuation marks. These marks should be accompanied with a caret or circle to show specifically where they should be inserted. For example:

When the football game ended‸ the Mississippi rooters were discouraged. It was‸ after all‸ a heart-breaking loss. In addition, coach John Smith's job is in jeopardy. Smith, however, is philosophical about it. He said‸ "Remember, it's only a game."

● *Use a pencil.* The temptation always exists to edit with a pen, particularly when working with cheap copy paper, but since erasing is often necessary, editing should be done with pencil.

● *Make straight lines through deleted passages.* Don't scratch out the copy with bold strokes of the pencil. If the editor later decides that the copy should be reinstated, he can simply mark "stet" in the margin and the typesetter can still follow the original version.

● *Do not scrawl in the margins.* When inserting words or phrases, use the caret to guide the typesetter. Write the edited version neatly above the original. Don't stretch a long insert into and down the margin. If the insert is extensive, it should be retyped and pasted over the original.

● *Avoid excessive arrows and lines when transposing paragraphs or sentences.* If they are limited and clear, arrows are efficient shortcuts. But if they begin to look like the rough draft of a road map, retype the copy.

● *Don't split paragraphs from one page to the next.* Occasionally a story will be distributed to more than one typesetter. Problems are created if paragraphs are not completed on each page.

● *Above all, make changes clear to the person setting the type.* More time is wasted by having the typesetter puzzle over scribbled editing than is saved by the editor hurrying his markings.

Processing Copy

Once a story is edited, it must, of course, be properly marked for processing. Common, but necessary, directions include:

The "slug" line, which is placed in the upper right corner of the page, provides a key word to identify the copy. In this case, the story is about gasohol. The slug also indicates that Howard of The Associated Press wrote the story. The story is to appear on page 1 of Monday's afternoon edition.

Gasohol
Howard—AP
Front-Monday PM

If the story runs more than one page, subsequent pages must be marked as additions ("ads"). The second page is the 1st ad, the third page is the 2nd ad, and so on. The slug is also included on each subsequent page.

1st Ad-Gasohol
Front-Monday PM

Editors decide whether locally written stories or wire service stories will carry bylines. If the editor thinks the story merits a byline, he will mark it. In this example, the byline is to be centered (note the brackets on each side), the reporter's name is to be set in bold face type and his identification will be in 7-point type.

]By Mike Patterson[(BF)
Journal Staff Writer (7pt.)

This is an example of a centered byline for an Associated Press writer.

]By Edward Howard[(BF)
Associated Press (7pt)

Many wire service stories, like weather roundups, sports roundups, state road fatalities and the like, are not credited to an individual reporter. These stories are based on contributions from several sources at various locations. Thus, a credit line similar to this is often used.

]United Press International [
(BF)

When copy editors compile stories from both the Associated Press and United Press International—using the best material from each—a credit line similar to this is normally used.

]From Wire Services[(BF)

Additional information often becomes available after the original story has been sent to the composing room to be set in type. If it is a single paragraph, for example, the editor will label it as "Insert A." If subsequent inserts are made, they are labeled accordingly—e.g., "Insert B" and so on. The editor then must get a Xerox copy proof or galley proof of the original story and mark where the inserts should be placed.

Insert "A"
Gasohol
Front-Monday PM

If significant new information is made available which is important enough to write a new lead—beginning—to the story, the editor will mark it as a "new lead." He will then retrieve a copy of the proof

1st Lead
Gasohol
Front-Monday PM

or galley proof of the original story and mark it to show that a new lead is coming. He will then cross out copy in the original story that is being replaced.

Most newspaper copy editors will not mark column width for stories unless it differs from the newspaper's standard one-column size. For example, if the story is to fit in the newspaper's normal 14-pica columns, no column widths are marked. However, if the editor decides to emphasize a particularly important story, he might want to set it wide measure (more than 14 picas). In this case, the editor decided the gasohol story should be set a width of 26 picas.

set 26 picas

If an editor determines that a story is of extraordinary significance, he might want to set the lead paragraph or first two paragraphs wide measure and set the body type larger than normal. For example, the editor might decide to emphasize the lead two paragraphs by setting them 26 picas (instead of the normal 14 picas) and to use 9-point type, 1-point larger than the normal 8-point. The editor must, of course, mark the rest of the story to be set in regular column width and type size.

set 26 picas 9 point

If a story is written on more than one page, the editor must write "more" at the bottom of each page before the final page. This tells the typesetter that the story is not complete and that more copy is to come.

more

Once the editor has marked the copy properly, he places a headline on it, complete with size specifications. In this example, the gasohol headline is to be a 2-column, 48-point, 2-line headline. Some news-

2|48|2 Gasohol decision to face senators

papers code their headlines. For example,
a 2-48-2 might be a "B" headline.

Once a story has been edited and processing instructions written,
it would look something like this when sent to the composing room:

2|48|2
|Gasohol decision
|to face senators

|Gasohol
|Howard—AP
|Front—Monday PM

Set 26 picas
9 point

] By Edward Howard [(8F)
Associated Press (7pt)

LINCOLN--A decision on the future production of gasohol in Nebraska most likely will
come out of the 1981 Unicameral session.

That decision with be whether to fund
a program allowing authorization of up to (5)
grants that can total $500,000 each for cities,
counties or villages in the state to build
gasohol plants.   Set 14 picas
                  8 point

gasohol is a blend of (ninety) per cent
gasoline and (ten) per cent grain alcohol designed
to save oil resources while producing a market
for agricultural products.
                                          new

The 1979 legislature approved LB424 but
did not make an appropriation to fund the grants
intended in the legislation.

(Stet)

The state's Gasohol committee issued
guidelines for the local governing units willing
to apply for the grants for grain manufacturing
alcohol or storage plants. Guidelines were issued
in May by the panel known as the Agricultural
Products industrial Utilization Committee.

(more)

1st Ad - Gasohol
Front - Monday PM

Seven grant applications were received by the ~~newly formed~~ committee, but only (4) were approved. Those given priority for state subsidized grain alcohol manufacturing or storage plants were O'Neill, Hartington, Phelps County, and (Saint) Paul.

Gasohol Administrator Charles R. Smyth (CQ) said he expected the legislature to provide the grant money in the upcoming session.

"Barring another series of floods or some other disaster that would put a drain on the state treasury, I would anticipate approval of whatever grant amounts are okayed by the joint committee meeting," he told The Associated Press earlier this year. The joint meeting was held with the legislature's Agriculture Committee.

(-30-)

Chapter 3

Editing Copy

Once an editor—whether he works in a traditional newsroom or in an electronic newsroom—is well-versed in processing copy, he is ready to begin his most formidable task: improving every story he handles. Each article must be carefully scrutinized. Seldom does a story—even one written by an experienced reporter—cross the copy desk which cannot be improved. Copy editors should keep in mind several important questions when editing a story:

- Is it worthy of publication?
- Is it accurate?
- Is it fair?
- Does it make sense?
- Is the lead appropriate and concise?
- Does it contain all essential information?
- Is it developed properly?
- Are the transitions logical?
- Has the reporter made good use of direct quotations?
- Has the reporter attributed facts and quotations when necessary?
- Does the story contain superfluous words or phrases?
- Is it free of cliches and double meaning?
- Are there grammatical, punctuation or spelling problems?
- Are there possible legal ramifications?

Probably the most imposing challenge of copy editing is making sure the news story lead is appropriate and concise; the editor must delicately, yet forcefully, polish it.

Editing Leads

For decades, reporters and editors were schooled to get the five *W*s and *H* (who, what, when, where, why, and how) into the lead paragraph. This philosophy, however, has changed. Today's leads are streamlined, often focusing on only one or two of the most pertinent elements of the long-practiced formula. Other essentials are incorporated into subsequent paragraphs. This does not mean, of course, that editors are bound to one-sentence leads. Each lead is judged on its own merits.

An editor must work diligently to get the news into the lead and to emphasize the most significant, up-to-date facet of a story. (This

John Smith, director of campus security, told students today that the ~~discussed the horrendous~~ parking problem at State University ~~with interested students in the student center today~~.

"We hope the tight parking problem at present will become less acute as additional snow melts and the lots are completely cleared," Smith said, speaking at the student · enter.

~~He went on to say that the problem~~ is likely the worst it has ever been.

~~Smith responded to the students' questions at the request of~~ the Student Senate ~~which~~ sent a delegation to the Board of Regents meeting last week to protest the ~~acute~~ problem.

(-30-)

observation does not apply to feature stories in which the climax is delayed.) Reporters are well aware that the lead should be strong, forceful, and relevant. Still, they sometimes place the real lead deep within the story. The copy editor must find it and relocate it.

Reporters often fall into the trap of burying the real lead when writing about press conferences or speeches. The tendency is to summarize the topic of the speech—an easy assignment—rather than focusing on the most important element. Before the preceding story was edited, it was a good example of a "ho-hum" or "say nothing" lead.

After reading it, the editor quickly discovered that the real lead— the primary news element—was in the third paragraph. The campus security director had, after all, termed the university's parking problem the "worst" it had ever been. That's news!

The reporter and many readers likely knew in advance that the parking dilemma was going to be discussed. Of primary importance to the reader—the individual unable to attend the session—is what the speaker said about the problem. How bad is it? Are there alternative measures to ease the parking crunch?

A good guideline to follow is this: if the reporter could have written his lead before the event took place, the up-to-date news element has been ignored. Readers want to know what the speaker said today— they can check the general topic in advance of the meeting.

Here is another example of a "say nothing" beginning which, by efficient copy editing, is made into a relevant lead with news substance:

Chancellor Del D. Jones ~~spoke on~~ *said today that* State

University's new admissions policy ~~today at a~~

~~very special meeting of the Student Senate.~~

~~"The new policy~~ is an imperative if this

school is to attain its rightful place among the

nation's top flight institutions of higher educa-

tion." ~~he said.~~

~~Jones spoke at the special meeting in the~~

~~Student Center auditorium at the invitation of~~
Last week the Student
~~the Student Senate.~~ ~~The~~ Senate sent a delegation

to the Board of Regents meeting ~~last week~~ to

protest the new admissions requirements as unfair

to disadvantaged students.
Jones spoke today in the Student Center auditorium.
The new policy requires that entering

freshmen score in the top two-thirds on the American

College Testing (ACT) entrance exam and rank in

the upper half of their high school graduating

classes or that they score in the top 50 percent

on the ACT exam. ~~It was~~ approved by the Regents,
the policy
subject to review after two years. ~~It~~ will be

effective this fall.

-30-

Locating and honing the proper lead becomes more difficult when several newsworthy elements compete for attention. The following story was written for a daily newspaper's Thursday afternoon edition. As originally written, the lead contained a strong news element. However, time is a factor when editing for a daily newspaper. Note the following:

John C. Smith, 1111 E. Park St., accused of murdering two State University students, was captured without a struggle early Wednesday in the woods around Lake Pottawattamie after an all-night manhunt by the largest and most heavily armed force of lawmen in Sheridan County history.

Smith, who was either drunk or under the influence of drugs, was found asleep in a camper van in a campground near the lake at about dawn. The murderer was taken immediately to the Sheridan County Jail and shortly before noon Thursday was arraigned before District Court Judge Henry Jones on two charges of first-degree murder.

Smith, a 26-year-old construction laborer and drifter, who may have had a record of sex crimes in California, became the object of a grim and intensive manhunt Tuesday night.

In this story, a copy editor found reference to Thursday's (the day of publication) noon arraignment deep within the second paragraph. It is the most recent development. The man could not have been arraigned had he not been in custody. Details of the manhunt and capture are essential background, but since they were undoubtedly in the news Wednesday, they do not belong in the lead paragraph.

This story also posed legal and ethical questions. The phrase "who was either drunk or under the influence of drugs" is unsubstantiated hearsay without attribution; reference to "the murderer" is conjecture because no one has yet been convicted of the crime; and the unverified reference to the *possibility* of sex crimes in California is clearly irresponsible reporting and prejudicial. (Legal considerations of editing will be examined in detail in chapter 12.)

The editor, by eliminating the prejudicial passages and by finding the buried, logical lead, transformed the first paragraphs of the story into an accurate, concise lead:

> John C. Smith, 1111 E. Park St., was arraigned Thursday before District Court Judge Henry Jones on two charges of first-degree murder.
>
> Smith, a 26-year-old construction laborer and drifter, became the object of an intensive manhunt Tuesday night.
>
> He was captured without a struggle early Wednesday in the woods around Lake Pottawattamie after an all-night manhunt by the largest and most heavily armed force of lawmen in Sheridan County history, according to law enforcement officers.
>
> Smith was found asleep in a camper van in a campground near the lake at about dawn.

Editors must also be alert to localize stories. Quite often, a report from the nation's capital will mention a local or state official in the body of the story. Involvement of the state official is not of particular interest to most readers around the country. The role of the state official, however, is of primary importance to his constituents. When an editor receives a national wire story which mentions a local man, it often can—and should—be made the lead. Assume the following story was received by a Colorado newspaper:

> WASHINGTON (AP)—The nation's governors, meeting here today, voted 36-14 to endorse President Reagan's proposed welfare reform package.

The vote, split largely along party lines, is expected to carry considerable influence as the House considers the complex proposal tomorrow.

The most vociferous proponent of the measure was Colorado Gov. John Jones. Jones said the present program is badly in need of overhaul and action should be taken immediately.

Jones said the President's plan was "vastly superior" to the present system.

Jones' colleagues praised him for leadership in the endorsement process.

Another staunch backer of the proposal was . . .

Without extensive editing or rewriting, the Colorado copy editor should localize the lead to make it more relevant to his readers:

WASHINGTON (AP)—The nation's governors praised Colorado Gov. John Jones today for providing leadership which led to an endorsement of President Reagan's welfare reform package.

Governors from all 50 states, meeting here, voted 36-14 to endorse the proposal.

The vote, split largely along party lines, is expected to carry considerable influence as the House considers the complex proposal tomorrow.

Jones said the present program . . .

Once an editor has located and streamlined the appropriate lead, he is ready to edit the remainder of the story. Generally, it is wise to quickly skim a story to get a feel for it. An editor is then in a better position to edit for content and organization.

Inclusion of Essential Information

An editor should not get so caught up in streamlining the lead, dotting i's, inserting commas, and editing out superfluous words, quotations, and phrases that he overlooks the content of the story. Most readers, at one time or another, have waded through a fifteen-paragraph story, only to feel frustrated that the writer did not provide enough information to make the article meaningful. Essentially, the editor should always ask himself: Does the story make sense? After all, a news story can be grammatically flawless and powerfully written without providing essential facts to make the account comprehensible. An editor should determine if additional information is necessary. The need for more details or background is apparent in stories which have been in the news for an extended time or in the coverage of court cases. The following article illustrates incomplete reporting:

WINCHESTER, Tenn. (AP)—A federal judge dismissed a $6 million damage suit against NBC today, saying there was no evidence the network was negligent in airing a film called "Judge Horton and the Scottsboro Boys."

Mrs. Victoria Price Street, now 70, said the film suggested she lied in her testimony at the trials. The defendants, known as the Scottsboro boys, were convicted and sentenced to a total of 130 years in prison.

After four days of testimony, U.S. District Court Judge Charles Neese ruled that "there is no evidence of any fault against NBC."

The reader needs to know more about the original trial—but not in such detail that it detracts from the flow of the current news story. Notice how the inclusion of one additional, concise paragraph provides the necessary link:

WINCHESTER, Tenn. (AP)—A federal judge dismissed a $6 million damage suit against NBC today, saying there was no evidence the network was negligent in airing a film called "Judge Horton and the Scottsboro Boys."

Victoria Price Street had filed the suit, accusing the network of defaming her by broadcasting the film depicting the trials of nine black men accused of raping her and another white woman 46 years ago.

Mrs. Street, now 70, said the film suggested she lied in her testimony at the trials. The defendants, known as the Scottsboro boys, were convicted and sentenced to a total of 130 years in prison.

After four days of testimony, U.S. District Court Judge Charles Neese ruled that "there is no evidence of any fault against NBC."

Story Development

Writing done under deadline pressure is often disjointed. The organization of lengthy stories should always be critically examined. Even if the reporter has capably compiled the facts, this does not necessarily mean the story is well constructed. Editors must help the story flow logically from lead to conclusion. Transitions, whether they be words, phrases, sentences, or even paragraphs, are necessary to cement a story, and the editor should make sure the article is properly organized. The following story, which evolved from a court appearance, contains several related parcels of information: the actual court appearance; background on the young man charged and on his father's state government position; details of escalating rape statistics in the city; and references to emotionalism surrounding the litigation.

Note the poorly organized original draft and how common sense editing makes the story more readable:

John E. Jones, 16, 2222 W. Washington St.,
pleaded innocent this morning in Douglas County
District Court to charges of kidnapping and raping
a 14-year-old girl.

~~The alleged incident occurred~~ last Nov. 18.
~~Jones was~~ ordered ~~to be~~ held in jail on
Jones
$300,000 bond ~~by~~ District Court Judge Henry Smith.
Under state law, Jones can post 10 percent of the
amount in cash and be released. Jones' father is assistant state attorney general
Only once, when the judge asked him for his
address, did Jones speak. ~~He was calm and stood~~
~~silently as the charges against him were read aloud.~~

Jones was arrested last week after detectives were given information by one of his (Jones')
acquaintences.

This is the third time Jones has been
charged with criminal offenses.

The rape ~~of the girl~~ was the fifth in the
last three months in University City.

Police spokesman Stanley Reed said, "We
don't have an epidemic on our hands, but it is
bordering on that."

Reed said the department was becoming
increasingly concerned with rapes in the area.

insert at end of story

School records at Southeast High School
show that Jones dropped out of school at the end

1st Ad-Jones trial

of his freshman year. He was described by one
guidance counselor as "shy and reserved."

~~Jones' father is currently serving as an
assistant state attorney general.~~

The possibility of a prior restraint being
issued against press coverage of the trial was
suggested by Jones' attorney, Richard Johnson, but
Judge Smith said he hesitated to take such "drastic
measures."

"There are several procedural safeguards
available to the accused," Judge Smith said.
"Therefore, I think it would be highly improper
of me to gag the press."

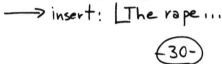

——> insert: [The rape...

—30—

Quotations and Attribution

Editors can streamline copy by making sure quotations are properly used and verbose direct quotations are boiled down. As editors scan copy for style, they should determine whether quoted passages add or detract from the way the story reads. Some quotations are not uniquely phrased and could be more simply said without quoting; direct quotations should be used when the statement is particularly vivid—not merely on routine comments. Reporters are sometimes tempted to let their sources write the story—to quote them extensively—instead of weaving paraphrases, transitions, and direct quotations into a smoothly flowing article.

An example of a routine quotation: "We will arrive at a conclusion concerning this all-important zoning issue at our next regularly scheduled meeting," said City Councilman Michael Walters. An editor should paraphrase it: The zoning issue will be settled at the next meeting, City Councilman Michael Walters said.

Direct quotations are wasted on matter-of-fact comments. However, assume Councilman Walters had said: "I'm fed up with haggling over this zoning issue. No matter what, I'm going to see that we settle this problem once and for all at our next meeting." The fervor of the statement removes it from the routine and makes it worthy of direct quotation.

In addition to seeing that direct quotations are not wasted on ho-hum material, editors must also be aware of rambling passages. In most instances, these long quotes can be cut to the minimum or para-phrased without destroying their intent. For example, when District Court Judge David Brown was asked about the possibility of closing a preliminary hearing to the press, he said:

> I think it would not be necessary to issue a restraining order. We definitely have a constitutional confrontation between the Sixth Amendment rights of the accused and the First Amendment rights of the press. I have complete confidence, however, in the ability of the press to function in a socially responsible manner. Our nation was founded on the premise that the press would occupy an es-teemed role in our society.

Without sacrificing the essence of the quotation, an editor could pare it:

> District Court Judge David Brown said he would not issue a re-straining order. Brown pointed to the "constitutional confrontation" between the rights of the accused and the rights of the press. How-ever, he said he had "complete confidence" that the press would "function in a socially responsible manner."

Editors should also watch for direct quotations which sound suspect. This often occurs in sports copy. After a team which was a four-touchdown favorite lost a game in the last ten seconds on a sixty-seven-yard run by a halfback who later admitted that he stepped out of bounds, a sportswriter talked with the losing coach and reported this:

> "Though we were big favorites and lost the game on a disputed call by an official, I feel our young men represented themselves and their school admirably," the coach said. "Despite giving up 36 points to a well-coached winless team that was averaging only one touch-down a game, I feel our defensive unit gave a herculean effort."

Not even successful gentlemen football coaches like Penn State's Joe Paterno or Nebraska's Tom Osborne are that diplomatic. Realistically, the quote is highly unlikely. Most contrived direct quotations are not so easy to spot. However, they do occur.

Reporters who cover the same events or public figures on a regular basis are also sometimes prone to put words into sources' mouths. An editor once received a telephone call from a city councilman. The councilman said he was calling to compliment the newspaper's city hall reporter. "I know I'm not a good public speaker," the councilman said. "But your reporter cleans up my grammar and makes my statements sound great." Though the public official meant well, the editor had some choice words for his reporter. An editor should insist on accurate and honest direct quotations.

When working with quoted passages, another important consideration is how attribution is given. If more than one person is quoted in a story, editors should be sure attribution is given preceding the quotation when a second speaker is introduced. Otherwise, his words could be mistaken for those of the other speaker. An example:

> Miller, Democratic candidate for the office, commented on his platform. "Minority rights will be uppermost in my goals if elected," he said. "Although the Constitution guarantees every citizen his rights, much work must be done to insure those rights."
>
> Lewis, opposing Miller in the campaign, said he will concentrate on keeping taxes under control. "Taxes are the main problem this year, as I see it," he said. "Other problems will have to wait."

The reader should not have to work his way through several complete sentences before he is told who the speaker is. Note how confusing the following story was before it was edited:

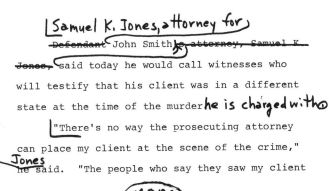

```
there on the night of the shooting are mistaken--

or they have bad eyesight.  Or, possibly, they

just may be lying." ⌐Prosecuting attorney Michael G. Johnson took a different view⌐
         ⌐"Anybody who gets up on the witness stand

and swears under oath that the suspect was in

another state at the time of the murder is taking
                                          he said.
a very serious risk of committing perjury, We

have six witnesses who saw Smith leave the murder

scene and their descriptions of him are accurate

in every detail." prosecuting attorney Michael

C. Johnson said.
```

Attribution should also be varied for smooth reading and should be as unobstrusive as possible. A simple "said" will usually suffice; seldom do people "huff," "puff," "moan," "grin," or "exclaim." Generally, they merely say it. Plugging "he said" into every sentence quoted, however, is both wordy and annoying. The reader should be aware of who is speaking, but not strangled with the fact.

If two consecutive paragraphs are quoted, attribution at the end of the first should be sufficient to alert readers as to who is speaking. For example:

"I've had great times at Central High. I've seen kids through quite a lot here, and I have come to care about what happens to them," Jones said.

"But sometimes you have to move on."

Cora Smith, principal of Central, spoke highly of the history teacher of seven years.

Superfluous Words

Few, if any, stories are ever written that copy editors cannot cut. Slicing superfluous words is a task often associated with copy editing. Though trimming copy is not the only function of editors, it is essential. Skillful cutting requires experience and common sense. Seasoned editors react instinctively to cluttered sentences or wordy phrases, but they are careful not to eliminate essential information.

With little effort, a copy editor trimmed these stories:

The Rev. Patrick O'Byrne, ~~an Irish Catholic~~
~~priest,~~ will ~~soon be~~ attempting to revitalize the
girls athletic program at Wahoo Neumann ~~after a~~
~~decade of tremendous success at Hastings St. Agnes~~ ⊗
~~where he~~ |O'Byrne helped mold eight consecutive Class C
state championship track teams **at Hastings St. Agnes**

~~If past experience is an indication, the~~
~~Wahoo school will soon become a state contender for~~
~~track honors. It is anticipated that Father O'Byrne~~
~~will make the Wahoo team competitive quickly.~~

~~It is a well-known tradition in Nebraska~~
~~that Father O'Byrne is a molder of strong track~~
~~teams. His reputation has gained national promi-~~
~~nence;~~ he is on the U.S. Olympic committee.

~~Special~~ examples of his success are many:
he coached Nancy Kindig, 1975 pentathlon champion
in the U.S.-Soviet Union junior girls dual track
meet; he helped mold Miss Kindig into a 19-5 long
jumper and a :10.1 low hurdler; and his ~~pet~~ **St. Agnes** 440-
yard relay team set a midwestern age-group record
in 1975.

(-30-)

~~His proteges have set many new records during~~
~~his coaching tenure. His personal charm and ability~~
~~to relate to athletes are believed to be prime~~
~~ingredients in his success.~~

TOPEKA, Kan. **Kansas educators will watch closely** ~~Educators throughout the~~
~~Sunflower State will keep close tabs on a unique~~
~~experiment~~ as five northwestern ~~Kansas~~ counties
try to establish a joint vocational school district.

~~One of the~~ **LA** major aims of the ~~ambitious~~
venture, which will offer ~~vocational~~ programs

(more)

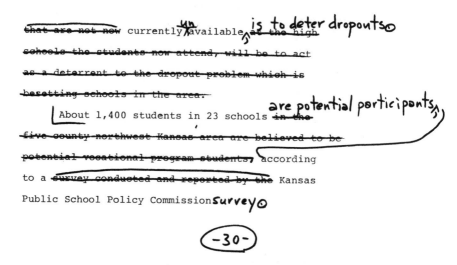

Clichés and Double Meanings

Clichés, jargon, and slang often work their way into news stories, but sports stories are the most susceptible. Sportswriters and sports writing have matured considerably during the past decade, though there is likely still more informal writing than most editors would like.

Don Duncan of the *Tacoma* (Wash.) *News-Tribune* and former vice chairman of the Associated Press Managing Editors sports committee recently explored the use of clichés in sports stories. He said there is a "new breed of boys in the press box—college-educated, anti-hero, weaned on 'just the facts, Ma'am.' " But clichés have not disappeared.

On the contrary, though "oblate spheroids, horsehides, and casaba melons have been dispatched to that Great Cliché Bin in the Sky," clichés still abound. Duncan formulated a comprehensive list, complete with an explanatory guide. Included were: "come to play," "coachable kid," "play hurt," "we'll have a lot to say about who wins it," "they wanted it more than we did," "we played with intensity," "found the crease/seam in the zone," "quicker off the ball," "it was a real war out there" (similar to "real donneybrook" or a "pier-six brawl"), "a game of inches," and of course "fleet-footed/gazelle."

Editors should guard against extreme informality entering news and sports columns. The following account of a high school football game is obviously going a bit far:

> Bladen crushed Trumbull 77-6 in an eight-man nonconference football battle royal here Friday night.

The outcome, never in doubt, was not surprising as Bladen upped its record to 6-0.

Bladen, ranked first in the state, was led by all-state candidate sophomore sensation Billy "scatback" Ewing. The talented Ewing, a 6-0, 175-pound package of dynamite, rambled roughshod inside and outside the Trumbull defense for four touchdowns and 223 rushing yards.

The sophomore dazzler's most electrifying run came on a 56-yard double reverse. He took the handoff, eluded the defensive end with a swivel-hipped movement that would have put the late Elvis Presley to shame, avoided a linebacker behind the inhumanly brutal block of his offensive right tackle, and outran the sluggish Trumbull secondary into the promised land.

" 'Scatback' is a major college prospect, there's no doubt about that," his coach, Bobby Booster, said.

This story is beyond reasonable editing. A request for a concise re-write should result in a story like this:

Bladen, the state's top-rated eight-man football team, crushed Trumbull 77-6 Friday night in a nonconference clash.

The victors, behind the 223 rushing yards of sophomore Billy Ewing, raised their record to 6-0. Ewing scored four touchdowns. His longest run came on a 56-yard double reverse.

Bobby Booster, Bladen coach, labeled Ewing a major college prospect.

Editors must also be alert to phrases which have double meanings. Election eve writing is often done under pressure, as this quotation from one newspaper's morning edition indicates: "Daub, the Republican challenger, hoped to stay close to Democrat Cavanaugh in the early returns and *nip him in the end*." Recognizing that Daub should set his sights elsewhere, an editor altered the phrase for the evening edition: "Daub, the Republican challenger, hoped to stay close to Democrat Cavanaugh in the early returns and *catch him at the wire*."

Use of Profanity

Guidelines on the use of profanity in news columns vary with individual newspapers; copy editors should be certain they understand management policy. Very few, if any, newspapers assume an ultra-liberal stance and generally allow the use of four-letter words and obscene or lewd descriptions (whatever they may be) when quoting sources directly. Some newspapers strictly forbid the use of four-letter words, no matter how germane to the story. Most papers assume a middle-ground. The *Washington Post*'s stylebook, for example, points to the philosophy of a "family newspaper" and reminds its editors and reporters that, "profanities and obscenities should not be used in a story unless something significant would otherwise be lost. The test should be 'why use it?' rather than 'why not use it?'" The *Post*'s stylebook gives two examples of vivid profanity which "reflects a mood or frame of mind that can be conveyed in no other way": John F. Kennedy's reference to steel executives as "sons of bitches" and John Dean's reference to "screwing" the Nixon administration's enemies. Still, even with "mood" or "frame of mind" direct quotations, the *Post* draws the line at "hard-core obscenities" and suggests use of the *s - - -* form. Obviously, copy editors should check with supervising editors when uncertain of newspaper policy regarding use of profane words or obscene descriptions.

News Releases

Some news releases are exceptionally well-written; much of the meaningful news that appears in newspapers each day comes from them. Professional public relations practitioners are attuned to the needs of the media; their copy is likely to be free of excess puffery, propaganda, or exaggeration. Conversely, releases distributed by not-so-professional practitioners may include hyperbolic adjectives about client firms, excessive quotations by company executives, editorial comments mixed with facts (e.g., "This *ingeniously designed* irrigation pipe goes on the market next week") and even poorly disguised advertising copy within the release itself (e.g., "The event promises to be one that every person will enjoy—so bring the entire family").

Editors soon learn which agencies, corporations, or institutions disseminate releases that require considerable editing. Conscientious copy editors, at any rate, must always thoroughly inspect and edit news releases. The following release, for example, required considerable editing:

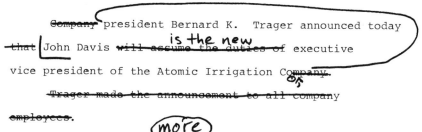

~~President~~ Trager ~~, who worked his way to the company's top spot after starting as a mail clerk 35 years ago,~~ praised Davis' record of the past 18 years.

~~"Mr. Davis, who has been with us for 18 years, is a prized and valued employee. He has worked his way into the executive ranks through diligence and hard work. If I were to describe Mr. Davis with a single adjective, it would be 'diligent.'~~ We all feel that he will do an outstanding job in his new position," Trager said.

~~Atomic Irrigation Company started operations in~~ University City in 1910. It has since grown into one of the largest, most efficient suppliers of irrigation equipment in the country.

A special center-pivot irrigation system, patented by the company in 1954, has paved the way for the company's exceptional record during the past two decades. Company president Trager was, in fact, part of the ~~team which developed the ingenuous center pivot system.~~

Davis is married and the father of three children. He was graduated from State University with an engineering degree.

-30-

Besides checking credibility of news releases, accuracy of detail, superfluous words, jargon, story completeness, and the like, copy editors must be watchful of grammatical errors, punctuation and spelling mistakes, and general stylistic considerations.

Grammatical Pitfalls

Unique usage questions arise each day when working the copy desk. Editors should, of course, refer to style and reference books when they are not sure of proper editing. Though the following list is not nearly complete, copy editors should be alerted to these grammatical problems commonly shared by reporters:

Subject-verb Agreement

Subject-verb disagreement is one typical grammatical error. Some problems are relatively simple: "Jones walk that way daily" should read "Jones walks that way daily." Other subjects cause more difficulty. In the sentence "A group of spectators gathers for the performance," *group* is the subject—not spectators—and so the verb must agree with a singular subject, not a plural one. Because of the prepositional *of spectators,* writers often become confused.

Another problem with subject-verb agreement arises with use of the word *couple.* If the word is used to refer to the two objects or persons individually, it takes the plural verb: "The couple *are* driving to St. Louis for *their* honeymoon." However, if the word is used to mean a unit of two, the singular verb form (and pronoun) should be used, as in "A couple of months *is* all that will be needed, he reported."

Editors must also be mindful of subject-verb agreement in sentences where the subject is separated from the verb by several words. When writing under deadline pressure, an easy mistake to make is breaking a sentence up with a clarifying phrase only to forget what subject was used. Thus, errors such as: "The suspect, allegedly identified for police by relatives, are being held without bail." It should read, "The suspect, allegedly identified for police by relatives, *is* being held without bail."

Run-on Sentences

Run-on sentences are another common problem. Run-ons are sentences which contain two or more actual sentences without proper separation. An example: "Teen-age runaways are a continuing problem, they are the result of many difficulties the problem stumps most parents." This conglomerate contains three potential sentences. Run-ons can be corrected in three ways—by inserting a semicolon between the two units; by adding a comma followed by a conjunction; or by separating the parts entirely into two sentences. The preceding example could be corrected by making it read: "Teen-age runaways are a continuing problem; they are the result of many difficulties. The problem stumps most parents." Or, it could be written, "Teen-age runaways are a continuing problem. They are the result of many difficulties, and so the problem stumps most parents." Sometimes, run-on sentences are the result of wordiness and can be rephrased to correct two problems at once: "Teen-age runaways, a continuing problem, result from many difficulties. The problem stumps most parents." However the error is corrected, it must be altered; run-on sentences slow the reader down, and they often confuse.

Dangling Modifiers

A grammatical error which is sometimes difficult to catch is that of dangling modifiers. These occur when a phrase used to begin a sentence is not followed by a subject, or when the subject is not correctly connected to the phrase or modifier. An example would be, "After rounding the curve, the road abruptly ends." The sentence is illogical because, since the subject is *road,* the road should carry all the action of the sentence. But obviously, the road is not rounding the curve—something else is. To correct this, a rewrite is necessary. After the curve is rounded, one finds the road abruptly ends" takes care of the problem, as does, "The road abruptly ends after the curve."

No hard and fast rules exist for correcting dangling modifiers. They are relatively unique and so must be corrected individually. Editors must simply be alert for errors of this kind.

Relative Pronouns

Relative pronouns are another source of writing errors. Three, in particular, are sometimes confused—who, which, and that. But a simple set of rules should allow for easy editing. *Who* refers to people, *which* to objects, and *that* may refer to either people or objects. One can correctly say "the man *who*" or "the man *that*"; either "the car *which* was allegedly stolen" or "the car *that* was allegedly stolen" is correct. One cannot say, "the man *which*" or "the car *who.*"

Punctuation Pitfalls

Another area of writing which creates many editing headaches is punctuation. Punctuation often causes journalists, particularly the inexperienced writers, more trouble than other aspects of writing, though punctuation is in many respects the most mechanical element of the writing process. While it is of utmost importance that the journalist has something to say, it is also important how the story is structured and punctuated if the message is to be communicated effectively to the reader. The copy editor plays an important role in checking and remedying faulty punctuation.

One of the problems facing the journalist is that practices regarding punctuation vary so widely, with authorities sometimes differing among themselves. In regard to punctuation, the Associated Press tells its staffers, "Think of it as a courtesy to your readers, designed to help them understand a story." The AP stylebook notes, however, that a mandate of this scope inevitably involves gray areas. For this reason the AP stylebook's punctuation entries have been labelled as "guidelines" rather than designated as rules. Such guidelines, however, should not be treated casually, AP warns.

The wire service stylebooks provide numerous basic guidelines for punctuation under at least twelve separate entries—the apostrophe, colon, comma, dash, elipsis, exclamation point, hyphen, parentheses, period, question mark, quotation marks, and semicolon. The AP stylebook, for example, devotes three columns to some of the most frequent questions raised about the use of commas. Specialized uses of the comma are treated in such separate entries as "dates" and "scores." Finally, for more detailed instructions, users of the stylebook are referred to sections on "The Comma" and "Misused and Unnecessary Commas" in the "Guide to Punctuation" section in the back of *Webster's New World Dictionary*.

The *New York Times* manual treats punctuation under separate entries, similar to the wire service stylebooks. The *Washington Post* devotes chapter 9 of its *Deskbook on Style* to punctuation. E. L. Callihan's *Grammar for Journalists* treats punctuation in chapter 17. Most standard grammar books available to a copy editor might also serve to supplement newspaper style manuals. A few books treat punctuation solely, for example, Harry Shaw's *Punctuate It Right!* (1963) and George Summey Jr.'s *American Punctuation* (1949).

Generally, news style requires less punctuation than does a more formal literary style. The rule in news style usually is, if a punctuation mark is not needed for clarity, don't use it. For example, although the comma is generally used to separate elements in a series, the comma is usually omitted before the conjunction in a simple series. The journalist would write, "The flag is red, white and blue." The student copy editor, like his professional counterpart before him, should study each stylebook entry dealing with punctuation and become familiar with the guidelines under the appropriate entries, noting any cross references to related materials. Only then will he be fully prepared to treat his readers "courteously," providing them with the guideposts they need to better understand what they read.

Though the copy editor will often find himself scurrying to the stylebook to check a unique punctuation problem, he will soon become accustomed to some errors which are made repeatedly by a large percentage of writers. Some common errors a copy editor should be alert to include the following:

Colons and Semicolons

Confusion between colons and semicolons is very common. Some writers have evidently never been shown the correct use of semicolons, so it is up to the editor to know their use. One use in particular is abused by a large percentage of writers. The semicolon *should not* be used to signal a list. A common practice, but a bad one, is illustrated in the following sentence: "The organization hopes to achieve several goals; improved communication between women and the City Council, extended special programming for women and general rapport between itself and the town." Instead, a colon should introduce the list: "The organization hopes to achieve several goals: improved communication between women and the City Council; extended special programming for women; and general rapport between itself and the town." (Note that when a colon is used for this purpose and the items of the series are more than a few words long, semicolons are used to separate items within the series.)

Punctuation with Direct Quotation

Another area to watch is punctuation with direct quotation. The rules governing this are: commas and periods are ALWAYS enclosed within the quotation marks; colons and semicolons follow the quotation marks; question marks and exclamation points must be judged according to whether they belong to the quotation or the surrounding sentence; commas end the quotation if attribution follows; capitalization is used as usual to begin a sentence.

Commas and periods are always enclosed within quotation marks. This is a hard and fast rule—no exceptions. Thus, the following example is wrong: "I am looking forward to it". This should read, "I am looking forward to it." Likewise, this is incorrect: "I'd swear to it", he said. No matter how the comma or period is used, it should be placed inside the quotation marks. Just as steadfast is the rule for colons and semicolons. These will belong to the structure around the quotation and will always be placed outside the quotation marks. This situation will rarely be seen in journalistic writing; an example, however, is: Johnson explained his "one big botch": "There it was, staring me in the face."

With question marks and exclamation points, the rules are more complex. These must be judged individually. The editor must determine whether the punctuation semantically attaches to the quotation or the surrounding sentence. The following examples correctly illustrate this principle:

Some may ask, "What's the use?"

How could the governor "beg the question"?

Why does every story end "and they lived happily ever after"?

"Will the tradition continue?" asked the visitor.

In each case, the punctuation was determined by the meaning of the sentence—if the quotation itself asks a question, the question mark appears inside the quotation marks; if the sentence which contains the quotation asks a question, the question mark falls outside the quotation marks. If an exclamation point is used, the same principle applies.

Periods are also sometimes misunderstood by reporters when working with direct quotations. Sentences like this are not unusual: "I will do my best." he said. However, they are wrong. One period, no more, should appear in a sentence, whether it contains a fully quoted sentence or whether it is simply a prose sentence. The proper punctuation for the preceding example is as follows: "I will do my best," he said. The general rule, then, is that if no obvious punctuation is called for, such as a question mark, then a comma is used to separate direct quotation from attribution. The exception to this comes when the quotation, whether it be an entire sentence or a phrase, flows with the surrounding structure without any punctuation. For example: "His response of 'I don't know' didn't answer the question." In all cases, the clarity of the passage should be the final test.

Sometimes, lengthy passages are quoted and broken into two or more paragraphs. If this occurs and attribution neither ends one paragraph nor begins the next (thus breaking up the quoted copy), no quotation marks are used to end the paragraphs until the last paragraph. For example:

"The two most important things I've learned as a reporter are speed and accuracy.

"The dictum of 'accuracy, accuracy, accuracy' is equally important today as it was when Joseph Pulitzer was a publisher."

Capitalization with direct quotations is fairly simple. If the quotation begins the sentence, capitalize; if it doesn't, don't. Example: "I can't understand what happened," he said. "Plans just don't always work out."

Spelling Pitfalls

One of the growing complaints of newspaper editors is that journalism graduates lack the requisite of language skills needed to perform their professional duties adequately. The one skill often singled out as being in shortest supply is a proficiency in spelling. Many schools of journalism are now working toward identifying and remedying grammar, punctuation, and spelling deficiencies; others are attempting to screen out students lacking basic writing skills, denying them entrance. The problem, of course, reaches beyond any failure of college English and journalism professors. It has been argued that many students reaching college campuses have not had enough instruction in grammar, punctuation, and spelling. They desperately need more practice to make up for the hours they did not spend writing in their elementary and secondary school years.

News-editorial majors in schools of journalism who are found deficient in one or the other of the basic writing skills need to engage in self-instruction to improve their deficiencies. A number of sources are available. Callihan's *Grammar for Journalists,* for example, devotes a chapter to the basic rules of spelling. Chapter 18, entitled "Correct Spelling is a 'Must' for the Journalist," also lists more than sixteen hundred words commonly misspelled. A list of hundreds of misspelled words is also incorporated into the new wire service stylebooks for the guidance of staffers.

Such manuals as the *New York Times* stylebook follow a similar plan, although the words listed may vary, and the spelling may vary where usage allows a choice in spelling. The copy editor is well advised to turn to his stylebook first to check out the spelling of a troublesome word.

The dictionary also should be used more frequently. Among wordsmiths, of course, the choice of a dictionary is itself controversial.

Webster's Third International, the backup source for the new wire service stylebooks, for example, is criticized by some because it has adopted too many colloquialisms and pays insufficient attention to formal usage. (For further information about spelling and use of dictionaries, see entries under appropriate headings in the AP stylebook.) One important consideration, however, is that some dictionary should be centrally located in every newsroom, and its frequent use should be encouraged.

Though editors can refer to appropriate stylebooks or dictionaries when puzzled about proper spelling, they should work diligently to cultivate their own spelling skills. An editor, for example, should master several homonyms which come up very often when reading copy:

Its/it's. The difference here is in usage. The easiest way to remember which of this pair to use is by answering the question, "Does it mean 'it is'?" If it does, then *it's* should be used—this is a contraction, like isn't or can't. If the word called for does not mean "it is," then no apostrophe is needed.

Affect/effect. Affect is a verb; *effect* is a noun. The distance the sun is from the earth *affects* the temperature on the earth. But, what an *effect* a few miles makes on the clothing we wear.

To/too. These are so far apart in meaning, it's surprising they are so often confused. *To* is a preposition, as in "He went *to* the station" or "I don't want *to* (go)." *Too* is an adverb. It has the same meaning as "also" or "very." For example, "Mary walks *too* slowly, *too.*"

Their/there. These, also, are different parts of speech and are quite dissimilar in meaning. *Their* is a third person possessive pronoun. "*Their* parents were notified." *There* is an adverb, as in "We went *there* yesterday" and may also be used for an impersonal construction such as "*There* was no one home at the time."

Whose/who's. Whose is a pronoun. "John Jones, *whose* car it was, survived." *Who's,* like *it's,* is a contraction. It stands for *who is,* as in *"Who's* responsible for that?"

Beyond these few frequently confused words, spelling errors are as individual as anything else in writing. If an editor looks up every word that seems questionable, that is all that can be asked.

Besides the "physical" problems editors must watch for—such as grammatical, punctuation, and spelling errors—are some broader, stylistic considerations that affect the readability and attractiveness of copy. Editors should be careful, at the same time they read for "flow," of a writer's style. Unless it is simply poor writing—awkward, wordy sentences—an attempt should be made to preserve the general style of the story. Editors, then, must be careful not to edit their style into writing for no reason.

Chapter 4

News Style and Readability

GOOD WRITING, one authority has noted, is a question of using the English language in a way that will achieve the greatest strength and the least clutter. Simplicity and an avoidance of clutter are paramount to both news style and readability. William Zinsser, writer, editor and critic for the *New York Herald Tribune* for thirteen years and the author of *On Writing Well,* notes that one must strip down his writing before he can build it back up. One must place greater emphasis upon the essentials. A carpenter, for example, must first be able to saw neatly and drive nails proficiently before he proceeds to beveling and cornicing. A good carpenter knows through experience that if the rafters are not properly sawed and assembled and if the nails are not secured, the house will collapse. Likewise, if the syntax is rickety and if the verbs are weak, the journalist's sentences and paragraphs will fall apart.

If the primary function of news writing is to communicate one's understanding of an event or issue to an audience, an often heard definition, the importance of writing with clarity and precision is even further emphasized. It is said that the journalist's primary concern should be to express, not to impress. The journalist, if he is to communicate his understanding of an event or issue to an audience effectively, must leave it to the literati to impress readers with the beauty and profundity of their rhetorical embellishments. While the journalist, as any writer, must gain the attention of readers if he is to be read, his primary goal must be to write as comprehensibly as he can. Good grammatical usage is of course involved if the journalist is to write clearly. Consistency and uniformity in style is also involved —consistency within a given news story, among the different departments, and from issue to issue of the newspaper. Choice of vocabulary, word and sentence length, and various other components of readability formulas are also important, particularly if the writer is striving to reach a mass media audience.

It is the copy editor's job to attain and maintain the clarity of style and level of usage needed to safeguard the elements of readability demanded for effective communication. Every newspaper has a certain style—a unique identity—which distinguishes it from its competitors. Most journalists write with a certain style which tends to set off their work from others. This journalistic style, once acquired through experience, may carry over into other areas of writing, according to one empirical study of the selected writing of eight literary figures, four of whom had served journalistic apprenticeships. It was found that the writing of former journalists Stephen Crane, Theodore Dreiser, Ernest Hemingway, and John Hersey, for example, was characterized by a more compressed syntax, by clear and active word choice, and by concrete, objective detail. The control group of non-journalistic writers in the study was made up of Henry James, Edith Wharton, Thomas Wolfe, and Truman Capote.

The writing from various departments of the newspaper likewise may differ in various stylistic characteristics; the news page may be more bold and straightforward, the editorial pages more analytical and formal, the sports pages more casual and chatty. But the hallmark of newspaper style, if not grammatical usage, is consistency. Such consistency in news writing has been fostered through the use of various stylebooks which set out rules and guidelines in such areas as capitalization, abbreviation, punctuation, spelling, and the use of numerals.

The Role of Stylebooks

Associated Press (AP) and United Press International (UPI) first worked toward developing a common writing style in the late 1950s. Hundreds of newspapers, forced to grapple with different spelling, punctuation and abbreviations in stories from the two wire services had clamored for more uniformity in style. These early handbooks for AP and UPI staffers were subsequently adopted as the official stylebook and usage manual by hundreds of newspapers. The wire service stylebooks also became important reference sources in scores of journalism schools. Though the style manuals were updated jointly in the late 1960s, new needs and new questions arose during the 1970s which called for additional revisions. In 1977, after a two-year effort, both AP and UPI published completely revised and greatly expanded stylebooks.

While the old wire service stylebooks had drawn heavily from *Webster's Second International Dictionary,* the 1977 stylebooks are based upon *Webster's New World Dictionary of the American Language,* Second College Edition, published by the William Collins-World Publishing Co. *Webster's Third International* is recommended by the wire services as the source for information not found in the stylebooks, or *Webster's New World.* Among other backup sources are the *Columbia Lippincott Gazetteer of the World* and the *Congressional Directory.*

The foreword of the AP stylebook sets out the purpose of the revised stylebook: "Make clear and simple rules, permit few exceptions to the rules, and rely heavily on the chosen dictionary as the arbiter of conflicts." Style rules, it is noted, seldom please everyone, since journalists approach style questions with varying degrees of passion: "Some don't really think it's very important. Some agree that basically there should be uniformity for reading ease if nothing else. Still others are prepared to duel over a wayward lowercase." The stylebook editors encountered all three types in their revision efforts, and, they point out, "in their special ways, all were helpful."

While hundreds of newspapers have adopted the wire service stylebooks as their own, many newspapers have developed their own stylebooks or stylesheets. The *New York Times* has its *Manual of Style and Usage,* a hardcover book of 231 pages. The 1976 revised edition, the latest and greatly expanded successor to more than seventy-five years of *Times* style guides, has a market far beyond the staff of the *New York Times.* The *Washington Post's* less forbidding *Deskbook on Style* takes a topical approach to various stylistic elements as well as such subjects as ethics, newspaper law and fairness, taste and sensibilities, good writing and correct usage, and useful reference books. Most urban newspapers have stylebooks of some type; many smaller newspapers have supplemental stylesheets which deal with local style, depending upon the wire service stylebooks as their general guide.

There are other generalized style and usage books which are often found on a copy editor's bookshelf. A classic work in this area is Theodore M. Bernstein's *The Careful Writer: A Modern Guide to English Usage* (1965) and a more recent Bernstein book, *Dos, Don'ts and Maybes of English Usage* (1977). Bernstein, a consulting editor of the *New York Times,* is considered an authority on the use of the English language. Another authoritative reference is H. W. Fowler's *Dictionary of Modern English Usage* (1965). An even more timeless classic is *The Elements of Style,* first published in 1935 by William Strunk, Jr. The third edition, published in 1979, is co-authored by E. B. White, who contributed the final chapter entitled "An Approach to Style," one of the best concise statements on style ever written.

Rules for Abbreviation

A constantly pursued goal in both newswriting and copy editing is brevity—brevity in the choice of words, in sentence length, in paragraph length, and in the selection of significant details to include in the news story. News style, as might be expected, employs greater use of abbreviation than does more formal writing, primarily in the interest of the economy of valuable column space.

The months of the year, for example, are abbreviated by AP and UPI if accompanied with a specific date and if formed by six or more letters. Seven months fall into this category. In a numbered address, three of the most common thoroughfare designations (avenue, boulevard, and street) are abbreviated in news writing. State names, when used in conjunction with the name of a city, town, village, or military base, are generally abbreviated. Exceptions are the six states which contain five letters or less, plus the two states outside the continental United States. In more formal writing such words would not be abbreviated.

Commonly used titles placed before names are generally abbreviated. So are courtesy titles, legislative, military, and religious titles. Numerous other special forms call for abbreviation in many stylebooks. In company names, for example, such words as company, corporation, incorporated, and limited are usually abbreviated. The names of organizations, particularly governmental bureaus and agencies, are often abbreviated, sometimes by initial letters which form acronyms which themselves may become words. Associated Press warns, however, that the too frequent use of acronyms may produce "alphabet soup" which tends to clutter news copy.

In tabulations the use of abbreviation may go even further to fit copy to space restrictions. Abbreviations also may be used more freely in headlines than in news stories. This is true, for example, even in the *New York Times.* A journalist, particularly a copy editor, needs to become familiar with the rules affecting abbreviation in the AP or UPI stylebooks and with any other stylebook his newspaper employs. The rules aren't difficult; with use, they soon become second nature.

Use of Numerals

Another common news style element tied to the desirability for brevity is the use of figures (arabic numerals) or letters (roman numerals) to express statistical information rather than spelling out the numbers in words or phrases. The use of numerals, while basic to most manuals of news style, often becomes unnecessarily involved and complex in the rule making. The general rule that numerals below ten (both cardinal numbers—1, 2, 9—and ordinal numbers—1st, 2nd, 9th) are spelled out while those of ten or above are designated by figures is a good starting point, but only that. Numerous special uses and exceptions to this general rule have developed in the interest of consistency and readability.

The AP and UPI stylebooks, for example, indicate that cardinal numbers are used exclusively in designating specific street addresses, ages, betting odds, the number of congressional districts, course numbers, dates, dimensions, election returns, formulas, handicaps, heights, highway and route numbers, latitude and longitude, page numbers, percentages, proportions, ratios, room numbers, scores, serial numbers, sizes, speeds, telephone numbers, and years. While dimensions, formulas and speeds are always designated by figures, distances below ten are spelled out, for example, "He drove four miles." Temperatures are given in figures except for zero, which is always spelled out. Casual numbers, even those above ten, are generally spelled out, for example, "Thanks a million." Likewise, except for casual references, figures are used to designate sums of money. For amounts of more than a million dollars, AP and UPI style calls for numerals up to two decimal places with the zeros to be dropped in the interest of brevity. The general rule of spelling out figures below ten is often waived in the case of their use in headlines or tabular matter. Even the *New York Times* makes such an exception.

Problems with Capitalization

The general rule, according to the AP and UPI stylebooks, is to avoid unnecessary capitals, and therein lies the problem. When are capitals unnecessary? Most stylebooks and manuals would indicate that capitalization is generally less necessary in news writing than in most other types of composition. Indeed, some newspapers use the so-called down style, which eliminates virtually all capitalization except for proper names and proper nouns. A school designation such as *Roosevelt High School,* for example, in down style would become *Roosevelt high school.* Such usage, of course, departs radically from the general rules of formal English usage and sometimes leads to countless discussions and arguments by copy editors over which capitals should be "knocked down" and which should be retained. The swing in recent years is back to a modified down style. This modification is reflected in the newly revised AP and UPI stylebooks.

The common nouns in such proper names as Democratic *Party,* Mississippi *River* and Fleet *Street,* for example, are capitalized; but when the common nouns stand alone in subsequent references, they become the *party,* the *river,* and the *street.* AP and UPI also capitalize words that are derived from proper nouns and still depend upon them for their meaning, such as *American, Christian,* and *Marxist.* Words that are derived from proper nouns but no longer depend on them for their meaning are not capitalized—words such as *french fries, herculean, pasteurize.*

The principal words in the titles of books, movies, plays, poems, operas, songs, radio and television programs, works of art, and periodical and newspaper names are capitalized. The principal words, according to AP and UPI, include prepositions and conjunctions of four or more letters. Articles of fewer than four letters are capitalized if they fall either first or last in the title. This general rule also applies to newspaper headlines, unless a down style is being deliberately used.

The Problem with Sexist References

One of the toughest "state of the language" questions the wire service editors faced in making revisions for the 1977 stylebooks was the matter of courtesy titles for women, i.e., the use of Mrs., Miss, and Ms. Both services reportedly put the issue to member newspapers. Ten options were developed and sent to editors for consideration, ranging from dropping all titles to retaining the more traditional forms. Since usage of courtesy titles for women was found to vary widely, and since the traditional forms were found to remain the norm on many newspapers, both AP and UPI agreed that the titles Mrs., Miss, and Ms. are not to be used on first reference when the first and last name of a woman are used. One exception to the rule would be if a married woman's first name cannot be determined, then Mrs. can be used—for example, Mrs. John Smith. By contrast, Mr. is not to be used in any reference for a man unless the title is combined with Mrs.—for example, Mr. and Mrs. John Smith.

Only on the sports wires do the new AP and UPI stylebooks advocate completely eliminating courtesy titles for women, a change that became a source of some controversy because of the apparent inconsistency of such a rule. The rationale offered for "last-naming" women on the sports pages was because of the more informal nature and tone of sports news, and because of the fact that such a precedent was set for men involved in sports news long ago. Titles may still be used for women in wire service sports news where such titles are needed to distinguish among persons of the same last name.

On the news wires, however, courtesy titles will continue to be used for women on second reference, following the woman's preference as to the use of Mrs., Miss or Ms. The stylebooks offer general guidelines for making such a determination, cautioning that if a woman prefers Ms., her marital status should not be included in the story unless it is clearly pertinent. By contrast, the *New York Times* stylebook allows the use of Ms. as an honorific "only in quoted matter, in letters to the editor and . . . in passages discussing the term itself." The *Times* stylebook devotes five columns to the use of Mr., Mrs., and Miss along more traditional lines.

An outgrowth of the concern over courtesy titles in the wire service stylebooks has been the inclusion of several new entries on sexism in news writing. Under the topic of "women," for example, the AP stylebook notes:

> Women should receive the same treatment as men in all areas of coverage. Physical descriptions, sexist reference, demeaning stereotypes and condescending phrases should not be used.

The entry also points out that news copy should not assume maleness when both sexes are involved, should not express surprise that an attractive woman can be professionally accomplished, and should not gratuitously mention family relationships when there is no relevance to the subject. Also, the same standards should be used for both men and women in deciding whether to include specific mention of personal appearance or marital and family situation. In other words, treatment of the sexes should be evenhanded and free of assumptions and stereotypes.

The reporter and copy editor striving to avoid sexism in news copy may also turn to numerous other sources dealing with the problem. McGraw-Hill Book Company, for example, has published guidelines for equal treatment of the sexes in an effort to avoid sexist references by staff members and authors in McGraw-Hill publications. Scores of sexist references in the portrayals of men and women are given with suggested alternatives to such sexist language.

Fighting Against Common Errors

Good English usage, like style, is a primary goal of most newspaper stylebooks. Usage refers to habitual or preferred practices in grammar, punctuation, spelling, word selection, etc. The wire service stylebooks deal extensively with usage; so do most newspaper stylebooks, as well as countless other references and manuals cited previously in this chapter. Strunk and White's *Elements of Style,* for example, sets out eighteen elementary rules of usage and composition. Bernstein's *Careful Writer* and *Dos, Don'ts and Maybes* treat hundreds of entries in alphabetical order in much the same format as the wire services, except that most of Bernstein's explanations are more detailed. A copy editor needs to become familiar with these portions of his newspaper's stylebook.

The AP stylebook, for instance, lists hundreds of words with cautionary notes about how they should be used. In general, AP notes, any word is acceptable which has a meaning that is universally understood, unless it is either offensive or below the normal standards for literate writing. Guidance on the acceptability of words is provided in the AP stylebooks under various entries, including "Americanisms," "colloquialisms," "dialect," "foreign words," "jargon," "special contexts," "vernacular," and "word selection." *Webster's New World Dictionary* should be used to sort out definitions unless the stylebook itself restricts use of the word.

If the dictionary cautions that a particular usage is objected to by some, or if the dictionary uses the description "substandard" to identify the word as below the norms for literate writing, a copy writer should beware of its usage in such a sense. One approach taken by

Associated Press in revising its stylebook was to incorporate into the manual a list of the fifty most common errors in news writing as compiled by the AP Writing and Editing Committee.

While style rules and guidelines are primarily intended to assure consistency of spelling, capitalization, punctuation, and abbreviation, usage entries deal more with the manner in which words should be employed, or, where there is a choice, urges the preferred usage. In discussing usage, the *New York Times* manual points out, for example:

> The intent is to give preference to that which safeguards the language from debasement: to maintain, for instance, distinctions like that between "imply" and "infer"; to avoid faddish neologisms like the verbs "host" and "author", while also avoiding a cliché like "crying need"; to shun slang and colloquialisms in inappropriate contexts, but to use them without self-consciousness when the context is appropriate.

The appropriateness or inappropriateness of various usages is, of course, often arguable. Despite their concerted efforts to establish uniformity, AP and UPI in a number of instances could not agree on usage. No solution could be found except to go their separate ways. For instance, UPI is less rigid when it comes to the use of the dictionary, allowing the use of more slang and colloquial expressions than AP. Another example of disagreement: UPI will allow "media" to be followed by a singular verb; AP requires a plural verb. UPI will allow *"Who* do you wish to see?" The AP requires *"whom."*

The Stylebook as Reference Source

While style and usage are unquestionably the chief purposes of most newspaper stylebooks, as such manuals grow in size they also tend to encompass more and more factual and reference materials. Louis D. Boccardi, AP executive editor, points out in the foreword of AP's 1977 revision that

> as work progressed we became convinced that while style would remain the chief purpose, there were many factual references we should include to make things a bit easier for busy editors. So we have a Stylebook, but also a reference work.

The most obvious reference-type material in the AP stylebook is the abbreviated libel and privacy manual in the back of the book and the two-page bibliography of books and other sources used in the preparation of the book. But, a number of the regular entries are also more informational than style or usage related. Under the "earth-quake" entry, for example, the difference between the Richter and Mercalli scales is explained, such related terms as "temblor" and "epicenter" are defined, and six "notable quakes" (noted for both their magnitude and amount of damage they caused) are listed. Under the heading "weather terms" are definitions used by the National Weather Service for blizzard, gale, cyclone, and hurricane, as well as twenty other weather terms. In the UPI stylebook, by contrast, weather terms are defined, but they are under separate, alphabetical entries scattered throughout the manual.

Both wire service stylebooks include dozens of metric entries with conversion charts and other helpful definitions. The AP stylebook, while noting that there are no hard-and-fast rules on when metric terms are relevant in a news story, sets out two guidelines to cover questions likely to arise as metric measurements gain increased acceptance in the United States. UPI, on the other hand, decided against providing guidelines on the use of metric terms because such information was considered to be a policy matter beyond the general scope of the stylebook.

A comprehensive newspaper stylebook is therefore more than a set of rules or guidelines intended to assure consistency of spelling, capitalization, punctuation, and abbreviation. It is also a manual of usage, dealing with the manner in which words are employed. Finally, a stylebook serves as a handy reference manual, containing useful definitions and factual information to aid the busy copy editor.

Editing for Readability

Clarity of thought and expression are to readability what consistency of form and precision of diction are to style and what word choice and correct grammar are to usage. But, as one authority on readability has noted, clarity of thought must precede clarity of style. Writing clearly and succinctly requires that the journalist be able to cut through surface details and get to the essence of a complex happening or issue in the news. Complex events and issues must also be treated in language that the reader can understand. Wisdom, it is said, goes arm in arm with simplicity; embellishment only causes confusion. The journalist needs first to understand fully the happening or issue he is reporting upon; he then needs to communicate that understanding to his readers, choosing words that his readers will understand, using as much specificity as his craftsmanship allows, and being as direct and straightforward in his approach as the subject permits. When he says what he has to say, he should stop.

Robert Gunning, a former consultant for UPI and author of *The Technique of Clear Writing,* has developed what he calls the "Ten Principles of Clear Writing." They are:

1. Keep sentences short.
2. Prefer the simple to the complex.
3. Prefer the familiar word.
4. Avoid unnecessary words.
5. Put action in your verbs.
6. Write like you talk.
7. Use terms your reader can picture.
8. Tie in with your reader's experience.
9. Make full use of variety.
10. Write to express not impress.

These principles are all designed, Gunning says, to "take the fog out of writing" and are each treated in a separate chapter. Gunning's "fog index" formula, based upon the number of syllables in words and the number of words in sentences, is one of a number of readability indexes used by newspapers, magazines, and book publishers to determine the difficulty of writing. The "fog index," in turn, is tied to the level of education.

Rudolf Flesch, formerly associated with AP and the author of several books on language and writing, including *The Art of Readable Writing,* developed his "reading ease" formula more than thirty years ago. Through the years, the Flesch test has stimulated lively discussions and roused the ire of both reporters and copy editors. The "reading ease" formula, similar to Gunning's "fog index," is based upon the number of syllables per 100 words and the average number of words per sentence. A sentence of about 17 words (each with 1.47 syllables) is considered standard. "Reading ease" scores, the result of certain multiplication, addition, and subtraction, fall into five categories, ranging from easy to very difficult. Sentences of 25 words (each with 1.85 syllables) are considered difficult.

In 1972, a sample of eighteen stories from AP and UPI, matched as to subject, were measured for readability, using the Flesch formula. UPI stories in the sample rated from standard to very difficult. Sentence length averaged 27.60 words with 1.68 syllables per word. The AP stories ranged from standard to difficult. Sentence length averaged

23.06 words and 1.61 syllables. Only two of the stories within the entire sample had a sentence length at or near 17 words. The study's conclusion: Both AP and UPI could make "significant improvements" in readability. It was noted, however, that today's newspaper readers may be more sophisticated than were readers when Flesch developed his "reading ease" formula in the 1940s. Results of the study may not be as bad as the scores indicate.

The most comprehensive evaluation of various readability measurements, along with an annotated bibliography of 482 publications dealing with the subject, is George R. Klare's *Measurement of Readability* (1967). Klare notes that one of the natural areas of application of readability formulas and research would seem to be newspapers and other mass media. Certainly a lack of readability in the media poses a direct communication problem, since the need for readability increases with the size and variability of the intended audience. Klare discusses a number of formulas in addition to those of Gunning and Flesch—most more complex, a few simpler. The predictability of the simpler tests, however, has been demonstrated to be almost as great as the more complex formulas, some of which require the time-consuming use of a word list in determining the test score.

Readability tests, it should be pointed out, are not necessarily writing formulas—they are not intended for that purpose. Readability focuses on the reader's ease of understanding, his comprehension or lack of comprehension which is linked to the style, and the manner of writing. A readability formula is a means of rating a piece of writing after it has been written. There are certain principles of writing, however, which have been linked to readability. As noted above, Gunning identified ten principles of clear writing. Klare discusses three general concerns or principles of readability which are linked to how a message is written.

1. Concern with the selection of words, particularly in terms of the frequency of their use and consequent familiarity. In practice, the words used may be classified as to (a) length, (b) derivation —Anglo-Saxon rather than Latin, (c) use—in common meaning rather than unusual, and (d) concrete or definite, rather than abstract.

2. Concern for sentence construction, particularly in relation to length of sentences. Two other characterizations are also of concern: (a) sentences that contain few prepositional phrases, and (b) sentences that have few compound constructions.

3. Concern that the style used is high in "human interest," i.e., the inclusion of "personal" words and sentences.

These concerns for clarity and readability should challenge the reporter and copy editor alike. The effective application of these principles of readability must also be related to the educational level, motivation, and experience of newspaper readers. Concern for clarity and comprehension, it should be noted, go hand in hand with concern for consistency in style and the correctness and appropriateness of usage.

Chapter 5

The New Technology

Y OUNG EDITORS ENTERING newspaper newsrooms for the first time likely will not see the tools of an editor's trade which date back for decades. But editing veterans still recall such things as heavy, black copy pencils, sloppy glue pots, dripping containers of rubber cement, clacking typewriters which always need a new ribbon. and the not-so-muted roar of wire service Teletypes.

These editing tools are still found in a few American newspapers—but the number is rapidly declining. They have been replaced at most newspapers by nearly soundless electronic keyboards attached to television tubes flickering white letters on black—or sometimes green —backgrounds. The standard typewriter keyboard is still there, but there aren't any ribbons to change, nor carriages to bang from left to right. There's just the VDT, or whatever other name editors apply to it.

The VDT, which stands for video display terminal, is the new tool of today's technology. On it, editors and reporters can perform all the functions they used to perform with the aid of pencils, paste pots, scissors, and typewriters. As for typewriters, even the portable variety is disappearing from press boxes and other away-from-home-base reporter locations.

Portable terminals can now be carried by reporters and used wherever there is a telephone. The story is simply written on the portable electronic unit and a transmitting device enables the reporter to send the signals of his words over the telephone line directly into the newspaper computer. From there, the copy from the remote location can be processed as though it were written at the newsroom desk.

Teletypes, those 1940s-era printers which ever so slowly pounded the wire service stories into the newsrooms at sixty-six words per minute, have been replaced by telephone lines hooked to newspaper computers. The boxes of paper which used to feed through the Teletypes to record the incoming material are gone. Instead, editors call the stories to VDT screens and read them there. In some cases, small, quiet, modernistic printers which emit a low buzz rather than a loud roar are used to make print-outs, or paper copies, of stories. Sometimes the same type printers are used to make a brief directory, or index, of copy entering the computer system. Complete stories, however, are usually printed on such devices only at the specific instructions of the editors.

The most basic uniformity of these new electronic systems is that they are designed to permit reporters to write their stories, edit them, and put them into storage. From there, editors are able to view the stories on another VDT screen, edit them, write headlines, and transmit them to the composing room. The editor's transmission to the composing room sends the edited, headlined story to a phototypesetting unit which justifies the copy (adapts it to the required column width) and puts it on photographic printing paper. From there, the copy is pasted up on a layout, a photo of it is made and an engraving is ultimately produced to put the entire page on the press.

Equipment is being developed which will permit an editor to lay out his page on a television screen and transmit the dummy (design blueprint of the page), showing all the copy locations, headlines and the like, to the paste-up person in composing. Technology may eventually allow VDT layout to be produced in a single step from a phototypesetting unit, with no manual paste-up required. So, what does it all mean to the newspaper and, more importantly, to the editors and reporters who use the VDT equipment daily?

It means virtually total editorial room control over the finished product. There is no longer a chance for composing room personnel to make spelling, grammatical, or other errors in the copy they are setting. Indeed, as Dr. Michael Stricklin of the University of Nebraska-Lincoln said: "The main point of text editing systems seems to be that editorial people now are responsible for both the physical quality *and* the creative quality of the product." Of course, this control also means there is no one in the composing room to catch and correct the errors made in the newsroom. It also means that no proofreader—green eyeshade or not—checks galley proofs, printed sheets with individual stories on them, before the copy is finally engraved and sent to the press.

Some editors are likely to say introduction of VDT equipment in the newsroom will speed up editing. However, a 1978 survey of electronic newsrooms in Idaho, Utah, Montana, and Wyoming conducted by Larry Kurtz, former Associated Press bureau chief at Salt Lake City, showed the opposite to be true. Kurtz found that the editing process was slowed by use of VDTs. He attributed this to three factors: the need for greater mechanical dexterity than paper and pencil editing; the need for closer scrutiny of copy in the newsroom since there are no proofreaders in the composing room; and the increase in editing of wire service copy. Stricklin has pointed out, however, that "the evidence available comparing the speed and ease of VDT vs. pencil editing is so conflicting that no agreement exists on which is better. Reporters seem to be more pleased than editors. Indeed, the VDT seems to be showing up basic differences in the two jobs in ways we haven't thought of before."

In the pre-computer era, wire service copy generally arrived at newspapers accompanied by a perforated, justified tape which could be fed through typesetting equipment. Altering wire service copy was difficult and time-consuming, since the tape was rendered useless by a good editing job. With computer editing, however, perforated tape no longer accompanies wire service copy. Editors can and do "open," or call to their VDT screens, more and more wire service stories and do the same kind of intense editing they perform on their own reporters' stories. No longer does a typographical error made by a wire service operator appear in every daily using the story. Most of those dailies now are able to catch and correct the error.

Basic VDT Commands

Newspaper work calls for constant on-the-job training. An editor, it seems, no sooner learns the functions of a given newspaper's program—the instructions and responses by which the computer system works—when he needs to comply with a revised program or even a new computer system. New computers, or front-end systems—the type of VDTs on which newsmen do their work—featuring ever-expanded performance capabilities, are constantly being introduced. Still, as one journalist has pointed out, the change from one front-end to another, though it requires an adjustment, is no worse than changing from one city editor to another.

While the programs, appearance, arrangement of keyboard controls, command language, and the like may differ from newspaper to newspaper, there are a number of constants. Basic controls—commands given by newsmen through certain VDT keys—are common to most systems. An examination of a VDT shows that the newsman using it can perform certain tasks regardless of the manufacturer, though the instructions he gives to accomplish the tasks may vary from model to model.

A VDT is simply a typewriter keyboard, accompanied by a number of control keys located above, below or beside the typewriter keyboard. The "paper" is a television screen, sometimes fairly large, sometimes rather small, but usually able to "roll up" or "roll down" to permit longer stories than the number of lines immediately visible on the screen. Normally, there are controls behind, below, or sometimes inside the cover of the VDT which permit newsmen to adjust the focus and brightness of the screen. Just like on a television set in a home, the picture on the screen can roll or get totally out of focus. Also just like on a home television set, the machine has horizontal, vertical, and centering devices to restore the proper images.

The control keys vary by name, more than by function, from model to model. Generally, there are control keys permitting newsmen to:
- Open files, or stories.
- Scroll the material on the screen up or down.
- Close files to store material.
- Move the cursor—a dot of light that appears where the next character is to be added or removed from the screen—left, right, up or down.
- Insert specific typesetting or computer language symbols.
- Delete characters, words, sentences, or paragraphs.
- Insert characters, words, sentences, or paragraphs.
- Move copy from one position in a story to another. Sometimes copy blocks, sentences, words, or paragraphs can be moved only up or down, not both ways.
- Set margins, or width, of copy.
- Justify copy.
- Clear the screen, or a portion of the screen.

Fig. 5–1. Journalists at electronic copy-processing newspapers such as the *Omaha* (Neb.) *World-Herald* edit articles on video display terminals. (Photo courtesy of Rudy Smith, *Omaha World-Herald*.)

● Put the unit on-line or off-line. When on-line, copy can be transmitted from the screen to the newspaper computer. When off-line, it cannot be so transmitted.

• Send copy either to the computer or to a printout device to make a paper copy of the material. In some smaller newspapers, the VDTs are not hooked up to the newspaper computer. Instead, the VDTs individually produce a recording or tape of the material on the screen and this material is then hand-carried to the composing room to be fed into a typesetting device or a computer.

Sometimes, one key can perform a number of functions; on other units, combinations of command keys can be used to master certain functions; and on still others, there is a different key for almost every command. Each newspaper has its own manual, or, at least, a manual from its front-end system manufacturer, explaining the use of the various control keys.

Reporters, Editors, and Queues

Nearly every system has a number of different queues, or files, into which various members of the staff file copy. In some cases, where the number of queues is small, various staff members are simply assigned certain codes to use on their stories, and the output of a number of individuals may go to a single queue. There, however, one individual's work can be grouped through the use of his code sequence. For example, one reporter may put a name from the sequence T200 through T299 on his various stories, while another reporter places his copy in the same queue with the sequence T300 through T399.

On some newspapers, such as the *Omaha* (Neb.) *World-Herald,* each reporter and editor has his own queue, taken from the individual's name. In addition, the *World-Herald,* like many other newspapers, has a backup computer system with different names for each of those queues. In the case of the Omaha newspaper, the backup queues are named by reversing the main system queue letters. Thus, for example, John S. Smith might have a main system queue named JON, while his backup system queue would carry the designation NOJ.

The reason for the secondary, backup system at various newspapers is simply to preserve copy that might otherwise be lost when the primary system fails or is shut down for a variety of possible reasons. It is insurance that the efforts of an entire staff won't be lost. On many newspapers, individual reporters and editors have access only to a limited number of the various queues which exist, while the managing editor and city editor might have access to all the queues.

In addition to queues for various members of the staff, queues also may exist for various incoming news or feature wires. For example, a newspaper receiving a single, slow-speed, sixty-six word per minute Associated Press wire might have just one queue for AP copy. But a large, metropolitan daily with a multiplicity of AP and UPI wires, along with various feature wires, might have numerous wire queues. There might be, for example, a queue for AP advances, one for AP domestic news, one for AP foreign news, one for AP financial news, one for AP regional news, and so on. Similar arrangements might be made for varying types of UPI copy.

The newspaper computer is able to sort the flow of incoming wire copy automatically into various queues, thanks to adoption of standardized coding of wire service copy, called the American Standard Code for Information Interchange (ASCII). (Details of the coding system are discussed in chapter 11.)

To prevent the newspaper computer from overloading, automatic kills, or purges, are sometimes assigned with varying time frames to the individual queues in a given system. In some systems, kills are accomplished only on a manual basis with specific instructions from editors. Some computer systems have a specific limit on the number of items which can be dumped into a given queue. When that limit, say 120 stories, is reached, the computer automatically kills out the oldest item when a new item flows into the queue.

In other systems, the kill or purge is based on a set time limit applied to a queue. A wire service queue might be set to kill anything twelve hours old, for example, while a reporter's queue might be set not to kill anything without a specific command to do so. Usually, there is a provision within the system to permit a reporter or editor to tell the computer not to purge a particular item or a number of items from the queue, irrespective of time or volume limits placed on the queue. This is done simply by sending the computer an instruction to hold the item or items involved until told to dispose of them.

Of course, if a queue is on a time-limit kill system, the more copy placed on hold, the quicker the system will tend to fill up. On a volume limit system, the more that is placed on hold, the faster freshly input material will be killed to hold the file within the set limits. The advantage of being able to hold material in a queue indefintely is fairly obvious. If a reporter is covering an involved court case, which may take days, weeks, or months to be completed, he can store pertinent information about the case until the entire matter has been resolved. This permits the reporter to quickly open up basic information needed in his continuing reports from the computer memory, rather than having to look it up in the newspaper morgue, or his own clip or note files and retype the material each time it is needed.

Looking up information stored in the computer is not as difficult as it may sound. If the individual knows the queue arrangements of his newspaper—that is, if he knows what kinds of copy are sorted into which queues—he can simply take a directory of the involved queue and identify the number or name under which the desired item is stored. From there, it's just a matter of telling the computer, via the VDT keyboard, to open the story on the individual's screen.

Directories usually are available in two forms—short and long. A short-form directory generally lists a single line of information about the stories in the queue, while a long-form directory can run up to three or four seventy-character lines of copy. A short-form directory of a specific queue—say the AP regional queue—in a given system might look like this:

```
17000 0181 15:45 04-07 PM-NPPD-LES, 200 LINCOLN, Neb.
17010 0236 15:49 04-07 PM-FFA, 230 GRAND ISLAND, Neb.
17020 0050 15:51 04-07 PM-Fonner Races, 50 GRAND ISLAND
etc.
```

The first column is the number or name under which the item is stored. The second column is the exact wordage of each item, in the examples above, 181, 236 and 50 words, based on a count of 6 characters per word. The third column is the time at which the item entered the system, in military terms, beginning with 00:01 for one minute after midnight and on through 23:59 for 11:59 P.M. The fourth column gives the date, April 7 in the examples above. Finally, the directory lists the cycle designation, PM in the examples, key-word of the story, wordage estimate of the editor who transmitted the item, and the first few characters of the story.

As can readily be seen, the short form index doesn't tell an editor much about the items listed. The keywords help, but in the case of the item slugged FFA, for example, even that is of little help. Some editors might know the FFA stands for Future Farmers of America, but others surely would not know that. Thus, the long directory can provide more meaningful information. An example of a long-form directory of the same AP regional queue, might look like this:

17000 0181 15:45 04-07 PM-NPPD-LES, 200 LINCOLN, Neb.
(AP)—The Nebraska Public Power District has filed a report with
the Lancaster County Court contending that
17010 0236 15:49 04-07 PM-FFA, 230 GRAND ISLAND, Neb.
(AP)—Some 500 members of the Future Farmers of America are
expected to gather in Grand Island this weekend to
17020 0050 15:51 04-07 PM-Fonner Races, 50 Grand ISLA
ND, Neb (AP)—Fonner Park race results Saturday: 1. 6 furlongs;
Daisy Mae 40.20, 20.60, 9.60; My Baby 10.20 8

The editor has considerably more information to work with from
the long-form directory and can more readily, at least in some cases,
decide which stories he would or would not want to open for a complete examination. In the examples shown above, there is a sports
story included in the regional queue, as might be the case at a small
newspaper carrying only a single wire service queue. At a larger newspaper, the sports copy would be listed in a sports queue rather than
the regional queue, assuming the larger newspaper's computer was set
to sort material according to service level designators rather than according to the initial alpha character (the *1* in the examples above)
on the items. (Service level designators are discussed in chapter 11.)

Movement of Copy

Once an individual has learned how to locate copy within a given
newspaper's system and how to operate the control functions of the
system, and once he has mastered the computer vocabulary of the
system, he is able to write or edit copy with ease. For purposes of
illustration, assume a hypothetical front-end system on the *Daily
Example* has ten terminals for reporters, two for the copy desk, one
for the chief copy editor and one each for the wire editor and managing editor. Not all fifteen VDTs have access to all queues. The reporters' VDTs are restricted to queues containing their own copy,
while all five VDTs assigned to the copy desk and editors have access
to all queues.

Reporter queues at the *Daily Example* are assigned names R01
through R20, a numerical sequence by which each reporter has one
assigned queue. Each reporter-designated VDT is shared by two individuals. The other queues consist of R21 for the incoming single-
circuit wire service, R22 for the two copy-desk editors, R23 for the

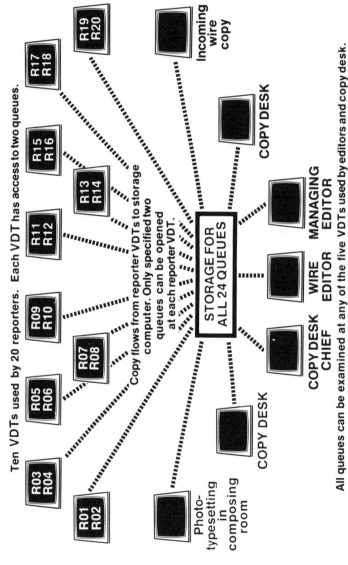

Ten VDTs used by 20 reporters. Each VDT has access to two queues.

R17 R18
R19 R20
R15 R16
R13 R14
R11 R12
R09 R10
R07 R08
R05 R06
R03 R04
R01 R02

Copy flows from reporter VDTs to storage computer. Only specified two queues can be opened at each reporter VDT.

STORAGE FOR ALL 24 QUEUES

Incoming wire copy

COPY DESK

MANAGING EDITOR

WIRE EDITOR

COPY DESK CHIEF

COPY DESK

Photo-typesetting in composing room

All queues can be examined at any of the five VDTs used by editors and copy desk.

Fig. 5–2. Reporters and editors of the hypothetical *Daily Example* would process copy with a front-end electronic system which would look something like this. (Drawing courtesy of Doug Knutzen, *Omaha World-Herald*.)

copy-desk chief and R24 for use by the editors in storing material to be held for later use.

The 20 reporters on the *Daily Example* each write all of their news stories on the queue assigned to them. Each has the ability to place any number of items on hold on those queues, and copy is killed or purged from their queues on a twenty-four-hour cycle, meaning that anything more than twenty-four hours old is automatically destroyed by the computer. The wire-service queue, R21, is set to eliminate any copy not placed on hold by an editor in the same twenty-four-hour time cycle. Queues R22, R23, and R24 are set not to permit the computer to automatically kill copy. Anything killed on these queues must be killed by instruction from an editor.

There is no need for the reporters on the *Daily Example* to tell the copy desk when they have finished writing a given story, unless, of course, there's a need or desire to have an editor make an immediate check of the story. The copy desk chief routinely takes directories of what is on file on the reporter's queues, assigns the stories as they come in to one of the copy editors for processing, and, by adding instructions at the top of the individual stories, tells the copy desk editors what size headline to put on the story.

The copy desk editors, each working from queue R22, take directories of that queue and open those stories assigned to them, write the headlines according to the instructions given by the copy desk chief, and then send the edited, headlined version of the reporters' stories to queue R23. As they write the headlines, giving the computer instructions for type size and number of columns, the computer automatically tells the copy editors the count of the headline and rejects the headline if it is too long. From this information, the copy editors can determine whether to try to stretch the headline so it will count closer to the assigned length, or whether they must cut it down to make it fit within the assigned length. (Headlines will be discussed in chapter 7.)

The copy desk chief keeps tabs on queue R23. As they are edited, headlined stories come onto the queue. The copy desk chief can double check those he wishes by opening the stories on his VDT, or he can order the computer to send the copy along to the photo-typesetting equipment in the composing room. Once sent to photo-typesetting, that device sets the headline in the assigned format and the body type in the assigned width and prints out the material, ready for paste-up, on photographic paper. Working from the dummy supplied by the copy editor, personnel in the composing room paste up the copy and prepare the individual pages for engraving, and, ultimately, the presses run.

Copy from the ten VDTs assigned to the reporters can be moved by the copy desk chief to queue R22, which can be opened by the copy-desk editors, the copy-desk chief, the wire editor, or the managing editor. The five editors also can send copy back on any of the twenty reporters' queues, R01 through R20, to be reworked by the original writer. The wire service queue, R21, can be read only on the VDTs assigned to the wire editor, copy-desk editors, copy-desk chief, and managing editor. Nothing can be sent to that queue except by the wire service, but anything from the wire service queue can be transferred to any other queue at the newspaper.

Suppose, for example, there's been a train derailment thirty miles from the community in which the *Daily Example* is published. A reporter from the *Daily Example* has been assigned to write the story for the newspaper. Meanwhile, the wire service has also transmitted a story concerning the derailment. The copy-desk chief, for example, can cull the derailment story from the wire service report and send it on the queue being used by the *Daily Example* reporter who is handling the story. The reporter can open the wire service story on his screen and take from it whatever material he may want for use in his own story, such as a comment from a railroad official in another city who was contacted by the wire service.

When the *Daily Example* reporter has welded his story together with the desired information from the wire service, he can send the story back to the copy desk for processing. After doing so, the reporter may decide to instruct the computer to place the story he has written on hold so it will not be killed in twenty-four hours. That way, he will still have it at hand in case there are later developments in the case—say, an investigator's report in a few days, or word of when the rail line will be reopened in a day or two. With the material stored on his queue and held there, the reporter will have the facts of the story at hand when he goes to write his follow-up piece. When the story is finally completed, perhaps days later, the reporter can eliminate the story from hold on his queue.

Meantime, however, assume that the managing editor has in mind a story about the number of derailments occurring in the region in recent months but has not yet assigned that story to a reporter. The managing editor has been storing all the stories that have come along in the past few months on derailments on queue R24, which automatically holds the information until told to kill it. Information on queue R24 can be sent to any other queue whenever the managing editor gets around to assigning a reporter to do the overall derailment story.

Of course, the system could be designed in such a way that everyone, or a selected group, could have access to R24 at any time. The *Daily Example*'s system is oversimplified, leaving out queues and VDTs for assignment to the women's department, editorial page and sports department, for example. But it is illustrative of how a system might work at a given newspaper.

Trouble Shooting

Computers, like people, aren't perfect. While they may not have the Monday morning blues, a headache, or an upset stomach, computers sometimes act as though they do. When that happens, the newsmen working with the computer systems may develop those human symptoms. A basic understanding of how a newspaper's computer system works is essential if a newsman is going to succeed in heading off some of the worst problems of a failing system. The editor or reporter doesn't have to be a technical genius or a part-time computer expert, but he does have to be able to react to minor irritants which have a way of becoming major problems if left untended. Again, each system varies, but there are some basic troubleshooting tips that should be helpful in most systems.

Newsmen often overlook the obvious when trying to figure out a problem with the computer system or the VDT. If the screen suddenly goes blank on a VDT, there's at least a chance that someone knocked loose the electric plug to it, or perhaps there's simply an overloaded circuit. If there's still a cursor light on the screen, but the copy has vanished, a newsman may have accidentally pushed a control button to erase the screen, or he may have inadvertently told the VDT to roll the copy up, leaving the visible portion of the screen empty.

When garble or strange symbols suddenly begin appearing on a VDT screen, it could be some type of interference with the line. The copy on the screen doesn't always have to be lost by permitting the garble to gradually write over it, destroying the story. At times, the VDT can be switched to off-line so that nothing—not even garble—can come onto the screen from the computer system. In this case, saving the copy from incoming garble may be as simple as moving the cursor to the bottom of the story where the garble would not interfere with what is already on the screen.

The most common computer problem probably isn't the computer's fault at all, but is rather a faulty command given by the newsman. The computer may reject an improperly worded command, snapping back with a phrase appearing on the screen, such as "ILLEGAL COMMAND." Or, the faulty command might destroy the copy on the screen if, for example, the newsman hits a control key to clear the entire screen when, in fact, he meant only to delete a word or a line.

Many times, there is a control on the keyboard named "reset" or something similar. When the screen begins doing strange things, striking the reset key can often stop the problem. The same control key can sometimes be used to stop an inadvertent transmission of copy from a VDT to the computer or another queue. In such cases, it's often necessary then to put an "end of message" signal into the system to totally terminate the copy which was interrupted when the reset button was pressed. Then the newsman is free to begin again and properly transmit the item when ready.

In some systems, there are indications that problems are coming. For example, the computer may begin responding very slowly to commands given it. Often, this is due to an overload of copy. The condition may be corrected by manually purging material no longer needed from various queues. Occasionally, the system will appear to freeze up, with the computer rejecting virtually all commands. This may occur because some command given the computer was erroneous or incomplete. A careful check of the VDT screen and a recall of what instructions have been given to the computer can often provide the key to what command must next be given to remedy the situation.

An unexpected halt of the computer system can leave a newspaper unable to receive incoming wire copy at crucial times. Such system halts are not uncommon, but they usually are not of long duration. A backup computer may solve the problem if a newspaper has one and is able to switch incoming material to the backup computer.

If, however, a power failure has rendered both the primary and backup computers inoperable, all still need not be lost. A battery-operated tape-recorder can be set up to record the incoming wire sounds and when the computers are functional again, this material can be played back into the computer through a spare input port, a receiving device on the computer. Wire service signals are nothing more than tones which are translated back into copy when the stories are called to VDT screens or sent to printing devices.

Judicious use of backup computers to store important copy can save the day if something happens to the memory of the main computer. Of course, the backup system usually does not have the capacity of the main computer, and overuse can create additional problems by overloading the backup system. When a specific piece of copy cannot be located, even though it's almost certain it should not yet have been affected by the automatic kill system, it's possible that another newsman has, for one reason or another, given the item a new name.

Some systems have a provision for locating such items. For example, if the newsman is looking for story T8090, which was slugged "house fire," he may be able to instruct the computer to search all queues to find an item carrying that keyword even without knowing the proper number it carries. If a system is not so designed, a newsman can ask any of his colleagues who may have had an interest in the particular item if they renamed it. This saves a lot of problems if the inquiring newsman is lucky enough to find someone who renamed the item.

Most newspapers have the ability to make a printed copy of material from their computer system, and sometimes a missing story can be located on a printout and be reinput by retyping it into the system if need be. Various systems present newsmen with differing problems and differing potential solutions to those problems. A good understanding of the individual newspaper's system and its capabilities is essential to deal with specific problems in specfic systems.

As technology improves, it is likely that many of the problems which plague today's computer systems will vanish, though new troubles may replace them. As Lawrence G. Blasko, deputy director of communications for the Associated Press, noted in a review of recent technology: "Our present state of the art in computers compares roughly to the state of aviation at about the time of the Wright brothers. And it is useful, if not necessarily comforting, to remember that the first few decades of pioneering in the air were marked by discomfort, crashes and disasters as well as by steadily increasing benefit."

Chapter 6

News Judgments

Editors who make scores of decisions daily on what is or is not going to be published in their newspapers can attest to the difficulties inherent in making news judgments. It is doubtless true that experience is the best teacher in the process of learning how to make sound news judgments, but it is equally true that editors can and indeed must know how to serve their audiences and be willing to accept the responsibilities of being fair and objective when selecting news for publication.

No newspaper has unlimited space in which to print every possible scrap of news. Even if it did, no newspaper would be likely to print all the information available to it. Very simply, some news or feature copy is not relevant to readers in certain locations. What is news in Johnson City, Tennessee, may not be news in Logan, Utah. The reason is apparent—the public in Johnson City may be interested in or concerned about news that can directly or indirectly affect them, but readers in Logan may not be affected in any way by the same information. This, then, is where the difficulty of deciding what is news in a given city surfaces.

Editors make news judgments constantly. Stories are rejected or printed based on various news values. The process is, however, often less than scientific. News judgments come into play several times while a single story is processed. For example, an editor initially decides whether an event is worthy of coverage. If he determines it is, he must assign a reporter. If he thinks the story has great significance (his opinion), he might assign the most respected reporter on the staff. If he thinks the story may be of little consequence, he might assign a less experienced reporter. After the reporter covers the event, he must decide which statements or points to include in the story. He determines which are newsworthy and which are not. After the reporter completes the story, an editor puts it in final form for publication. He could strip it of several direct quotations that the reporter felt were extremely newsworthy, or he might alter the lead—thus putting a totally different emphasis on the story. The editor might then decide the story belongs on page one—or he may conclude it should be placed on page twenty-seven. The editor then determines if the story should have a bold, multicolumn headline or a small, one-column headline. Even the composing room personnel could conceivably enter the process. They could misplace the story and, before it is located, allow the deadline to pass. Or, in this electronic age, a computer could simply swallow the story and the frustrated editor not have time to locate it.

Editors as Gatekeepers

Publication decisions are based ostensibly on news values. Like charging fouls in basketball, they are judgment calls. They are subjective, not objective. Subjectivity in making news decisions has led communication researchers to label editors who control the flow of news "gatekeepers." They open the gate to let certain news stories into the paper; they close it to keep other news stories out.

Sociologist Kurt Lewin first envisioned persons as gatekeepers in 1947. He saw key individuals in any chain of social action as having the ability to hold or release goods within that chain of action. Gatekeepers were described as those in special positions to determine what goes in the chain, or what stays out.

Application of the principle to newspaper editors doesn't take much imagination. Editors, because of their position, determine what subscribers read. David M. White was the first to actually study the process by which an editor selects the daily news—which stories get in the paper and which stories stay out. Through various replications of the original case study, researchers have found "Mr. Gates" living at news desks around the world. Although his situation may change along with the technology, the basic story selection process is still often his "best guess," albeit an educated one usually grounded with years of experience, "dictates" from more powerful gatekeepers such as publishers, and input from readers.

Communication researchers Richard R. Nicolai and Sam G. Riley took a broader view of the gatekeeper function in a 1972 study. They identified both editors and readers as gatekeepers. Each individual selects or rejects information from his environment and subjectively selects that information about himself that will be projected to other people.

Editors, too, are limited in their gatekeeping power by the quality of gatekeepers working for them as sub-editors, correspondents, and reporters. The news services from which editors choose stories are limited in like fashion by a similar network of gatekeepers, each one subjectively choosing from a universe of facts and stories. Each editor's view of the world, then, is only as broad as is allowed him by the scope of stories presented by the networks or gatekeepers he depends on to advise him.

Though there are no specific rules governing news values, editors, consciously or unconsciously, often rely on news factors or elements to make decisions. Carl Warren, in *Modern News Reporting,* for example, lists eight "elements of news": immediacy, proximity, prominence, oddity, conflict, suspense, emotions, and consequence.

Serving the Audience

Before an editor can make intelligent judgments—even subjective ones—on what should be printed in his newspaper, he should have a broad knowledge about the audience he serves. First, he must know the circulation area. If the Air Force Academy sends a press release which contains names of graduates and hometowns, the mere mention of a circulation-area community tells the editor the story has local relevance. The editor must also know political, social, and economic facts about the community, county, area, and state. The editor should know what topics are of interest to the audience he serves; he has to know the industries that have an immediate or less direct impact on his audience.

The Union Pacific Railroad, for example, is the largest employer in North Platte, Nebraska. Thus, any news involving the Union Pacific is of interest to many readers of the *North Platte Telegraph.* At the same time, news of the railroad industry in general is of interest to those readers for the same reasons. In Billings, Montana, on the other hand, the Union Pacific is not a major railroad in the area served by the *Billings Gazette*, but the Burlington Northern, with a major installation at Laurel, Montana, not far from Billings, is quite important to the area's economy. Thus, news about anything involving the Burlington Northern is of specific interest to *Gazette* readers, as is general railroad industry news, though not necessarily news of the Union Pacific in particular. The *Omaha World-Herald*, which serves readers throughout the state of Nebraska, where both the Burlington Northern and Union Pacific have major economic impacts, would likely cover in detail news of either railroad.

Editors acquire the necessary knowledge of their coverage areas by the day-to-day contacts they and members of their staff have in the community. Some suggest that editors be joiners—actively taking part in as many community groups and organizations as possible. Others suggest that editors should not do so in order to avoid potential conflicts of interest. We offer no guidance here on which is the better choice, but we do note that it's not necessary to belong to organizations to have knowledge of them. Routine contacts, coverage of activities, and continuing efforts to remain aware of the newspaper's coverage area can keep editors well informed.

Serving the newspaper's audience, however, isn't as simple as merely selecting relevant news stories. Editors must also provide a range of coverage, including spot news, features, sports, opinion pieces, news analysis, market and financial news, and, of course, syndicated columns on such topics as health, advice, and gardening, along with comics and crossword puzzles.

All of these things compete for space in a daily newspaper, and, to some extent, all belong in a daily newspaper. How much material can be provided and how varied the daily menu of offerings is in a given newspaper depends, of course, on available space. An 8,000 daily circulation newspaper which averages 12 pages obviously cannot provide the range of coverage that a 300,000 daily circulation metropolitan newspaper with 96 pages can. Even metropolitan newspapers can't provide as varied a menu for their readers in a Monday paper of 36 pages as they can in their grocery-ad-fattened Wednesday edition of 120 pages.

The important factor is to balance the package as well as possible to provide readers with the best of each category within the limitations of space. News of the community of publication certainly deserves emphasis, as does news of the state of publication. But readers also have to know what's going on nationally and internationally. They not only want to know how the local high school basketball team came out the night before, they also want to know what's going on in the National Basketball Association, at the state universities, and at area colleges.

Many newspapers prepare a daily budget which lists local and area stories which are likely to materialize for publication. This is an excellent way to help editors determine space requirements for local copy and to avoid gaps in coverage because someone forgot to assign a reporter to a particular story which is developing off a regular beat. Story selection, however, is not limited to local and area copy. Editors must also decide which wire service stories to publish.

Selection from Wires

Dozens of wire service stories pour into even the smallest daily newspapers each day. (The wire services will be discussed in chapters 10 and 11.) At metropolitan dailies, the total runs well into the hundreds from either the AP or UPI alone. Where both services are used, the number doubles and the copy from supplemental services, such as the New York Times services, Reuters, etc., further increases the load. Ultimately, the amount of advertising governs the number of pages published and the size of the news hole (the amount of space left after advertisements, the editorial page and comic pages are dummied). Into that space, editors must judiciously fit the copy most likely to appeal to their subscribers.

How Does an Editor Make Those Selections?

To begin with, both major wire services and some of the supplemental services provide daily digests, or budgets, for the AM and PM newspaper cycles (budgets will be discussed in detail in chapter 11). The digests list the top dozen or so stories from around the world. In addition, AP and UPI provide daily state digests listing top stories from a given state for each cycle each day. These informational listings tell editors what the wire services consider to be the prime stories of the day. Generally, a newspaper editor will select his front page stories—other than local page one material—from the digests. In addition, there are sports digests to help guide sports editors, and, for those newspapers subscribing to financial wires, there are financial news digests.

Naturally, major spot news stories can break after digests have been transmitted. In such cases, the wire services usually send advisories outlining briefly what coverage by way of stories and photos can be expected on the late-breaking stories. The bulk of the stories provided to newspapers each day by the wire services is, of course, not listed on the wire service digests. Selections from this material pose more difficult choices for editors.

What Does an Editor Look For?

First, an editor seeks out fixture materials that his newspaper routinely runs to satisfy its readers. Fixtures include items such as a selected stock list, livestock markets of importance to area ranchers, futures markets, weather and temperature tables, stories and forecasts, perhaps state auto fatality reports, and the like. Still, there remains a substantial volume of copy to choose from and a fairly substantial news hole to be filled. This is where the concept of local news comes in. In this context, the term local news means, quite simply, any news that is of direct interest to a given community. It does not mean only news originating in the community or about persons from the community.

Stories originating from the statehouse dealing with property tax assessments would have a local impact in the editor's community and might be termed local news. But, a story about a new complex of state offices in another community at the opposite corner of the state may have no direct relationship to the editor's community and, thus, may well be passed.

Similar judgments can be made on world news. An editor thoroughly familiar with his own community will be more adept at making decisions on what news from elsewhere has direct local impact. Of course, not all the news chosen for publication in a given newspaper has direct local impact. Many decisions must be based on the newspaper's philosophy on how it should serve its community.

If the newspaper believes it should be a newspaper of record, that is, a newspaper that tells its readers about every matter of significance no matter where the news is from, then far more national, international, and statehouse news must be chosen for publication.

Another newspaper may see its role as one of providing intense regional news coverage for its readers, while leaving it to other media to provide the readers with more national and international coverage. At such a newspaper, an editor's selection of material is likely to lean far more to state news and feature copy. Other factors complicate the decisions. Both the basic wire services and the supplemental services received by newspapers provide a wide selection of feature material, some of it of considerable length and much of it moved in advance.

The editor then must make plans as to when, what, and how much of such material to use, as well as deciding on the flow of daily copy. Usually, decisions on the use of advance copy are made days before publication, and much feature material is used on inside pages of the newspaper—pages which often are sent to the composing room, or processed by the editors on electronic equipment, well in advance of publication.

Selection of feature material, like that of spot news material, is based at least in part on the interests of a given community and the role of a given newspaper. A newspaper in Florida, for example, might not have much interest in a lengthy feature about the winter hardships faced by Mormon pioneers when they crossed Nebraska on the Mormon Trail. But newspapers in South Dakota, where residents experience harsh winters, and in Utah, where the Mormon church is based, most likely would have more interest in such a story. Likewise, a particular local newspaper might not have much interest in a story about tourism in Tunisia. But, if a local organization recently sponsored a tour to Africa, including a visit to Tunisia, the story might have more interest in the community.

In addition to the problem of selecting which stories a newspaper should print out of the multitude of different stories available, an editor whose newspaper receives both AP and UPI wires faces additional decisions. Suppose there's a plane crash in another state in which 122 persons are killed. Obviously, both wire services will have stories on the crash. What does the editor choose to use?

His decisions are likely to be governed primarily by three factors —speed of delivery, completeness of the story, and quality of the writing. If the editor's newspaper is close to deadline and one wire service lead arrives ten or twenty minutes before the other wire service lead, the editor is most likely going to select the first lead received. This, of course, is one reason for the wire service dictate that its newsmen strive always to be first. However, if both leads arrive about the same time, the editor has a better possibility of choosing which to use on the basis of completeness and writing quality.

Of course, time permitting, an editor may choose to use elements of both stories and combine them into a single story to furnish his readers a more comprehensive story than either wire service story would provide alone. For example, the UPI story might include some dramatic quotes from eyewitnesses to the crash which are not in the AP story, but the AP story includes pertinent information about the plane having had mechanical difficulties on its last two flights while the UPI story makes no mention of the problems. An editor should then combine the stories and provide his readers with the more complete information, as well as the quotes.

But, suppose the UPI story had the quotes from eyewitnesses, while the AP story had only the basic information that the plane had crashed, with no quotes. In that case, an editor likely would choose the UPI story for publication. If the newspaper had a later edition and the AP's follow-up lead included fresh information on the cause of the crash along with quotes and other new material while the UPI story was not updated with the new material, the editor could, of course, choose to switch stories for the later edition.

No set rules exist on selection of wire service copy applicable to every newspaper. But there are some generalizations to consider:
● Is there any local interest in the story?
● Does the story fit within the philosophy of what the newspaper should be reporting?
● Can the story be processed in time to meet the edition deadline?
● Is one wire service story superior to the other in terms of completeness and quality of writing?
● Would a combination lead better serve the readers?

Responsibility of Editors

Editors should strive for balance and fairness in news coverage, not just in a given story or on a given day, but over the long range as well. If a newspaper, for example, prints only good things about a particular local industry or organization, while failing to report problems or shortcomings, readers may become suspicious of the veracity of everything printed in the newspaper. Credibility of the newspaper would suffer. Trust is the greatest asset a newspaper can generate among its readers.

It is simply not fair for a newspaper to talk to a disgruntled city employee about problems at city hall without also giving the officials involved a chance to explain their version of the problem or comment on the gripes of the disgruntled employee. There are usually more than two sides to a story, and the newspaper must make an honest effort to search out all pertinent viewpoints. While the disgruntled employee and the mayor may have disparate views on the problem at city hall, the city council or the city manager may have yet another view.

It is not fair to run a story saying that John Doe was arrested for drunk driving and then not print the story when the charge is dismissed for lack of evidence. Nor is it fair to make an error of fact in a story and, upon learning of the misstatement, fail to correct it or bury the correction which ultimately is run. If the story deserved page one play when it was wrong, the correction probably merits page one, not page twenty-nine, play as well, assuming the error is significant. Some newspapers solve this problem by having a fixed position in the newspaper for making corrections. Others attempt to run corrections in the same position and with the same size headline as the original, erroneous story appeared.

Whatever method is selected, the editor should make every reasonable effort to set the record straight, as quickly as possible and in such a way that readers will be aware of the correction. Corrections, when they must be run, should be straightforward and matter-of-fact, not apologetic. Neither should they be flippant or satiric. A simple way of handling such situations is that dictated by the Associated Press stylebook which advises editors to use a straight assertion at the start of a correction that a previous account was in error, as in: "The Associated Press reported erroneously on Feb. 27 that. . . ."

"In no instance," the stylebook cautions, "shall the story say *the Associated Press is glad to make this correction* or *regrets the error* or any similar phrase."

Ideally, no newspaper should have sacred cows—subjects which, for whatever reason, are treated with great care or simply not considered fit for publication. Often, such situations involve pet projects of publishers or organizations to which the publisher or editor of a newspaper belong. On the other hand, editors need not go overboard in reporting on problems in such organizations if similar information about other organizations would not likely be reported. Balance and fairness are the keys.

Chapter 7

Headlines

NEWSPAPER READERS OFTEN take headlines for granted. Subscribers don't realize the assiduously careful, frequently frustrating word-doctoring that goes into almost every headline. Creating effective headlines is a formidable challenge. It is, in fact, one of the essential functions performed by copy editors.

Headlines have undergone a metamorphosis. Contemporary examples that so pointedly summarize the important elements of each story have little in common with headlines that graced eighteenth, nineteenth, and early twentieth century American newspapers. Most pre–Civil War newspapers resembled the classified ad pages of today's publications. Headlines were limited to one-column captions or labels; they were broad descriptions of general subject matter. When George Washington died in 1799, the *Times and District of Columbia Daily Advertiser* paid homage to the nation's first president with a one-column label headline barely larger than the story's body type. The headline simply said GEORGE WASHINGTON. Headlines were confined to a single column for most of the next century.

In 1860, for example, the *New York Times* carried stories about the upcoming presidential election in the top left column on page one. These stories were routinely labeled PRESIDENTIAL. The headline was the same, day after day. During post-election coverage, stories were often merely labeled THE ELECTION. Though they never exceeded one column, multideck headlines were being written at about this time. (Decks stand alone; they supply the reader with supplemental information that is not part of a continuous flow from a preceding line.)

On March 6, 1861, the *Times* carried a multideck headline over a story which focused on Abraham Lincoln's new administration:

HIGHLY IMPORTANT NEWS

THE NEW FEDERAL ADMINISTRATION

The Cabinet and its Confirmation by the Senate

What Is Thought of the Inaugural Address

A 15-deck headline in the *Philadelphia Inquirer* that heralded the assassination of President Lincoln was even more dramatic:

MURDER
of
PRESIDENT LINCOLN!

His Assassination Last Night,
While at Ford's Theatre
in Washington!

J. WILKES BOOTH THE
SUPPOSED MURDERER

THE PISTOL BALL ENTERS
HIS BRAIN!

THE ASSASSIN IN HIS PRIVATE BOX

The Murderer Leaps Upon the Stage
and Escapes

A HORSE IS WAITING FOR HIM

MR. LINCOLN DYING AT MIDNIGHT

The Farewell of His Family

SAD AND SOLEMN SCENES

ATTEMPT TO KILL SEC'Y
SEWARD!

His Bedchamber Entered by the
Villain

HIS WOUNDS THOUGHT TO BE MORTAL

Assistant Secretary Seward
also Fatally Stabbed

TERRIBLE EXCITEMENT IN WASHINGTON

During the newspaper circulation battle between William Randolph Hearst's *New York Journal* and Joseph Pulitzer's *New York World* in the 1890s, multicolumn and banner headlines were used extensively for the first time. On Feb. 17, 1898, the *Journal,* in all-capital letters, stretched a banner across the width of the front page which proclaimed:

DESTRUCTION OF THE WARSHIP MAINE
WAS THE WORK OF AN ENEMY

Three years later, on Sept. 13, 1901, the *Buffalo Evening News,* in contrast to the single column, multideck treatment newspapers gave President Lincoln's assassination, announced in huge, bold letters which consumed all eight columns:

PRESIDENT DEAD!

Directly under the banner was this deck:

William McKinley Passed Away at the Mil-
burn Home from Effects of Cowardly
Assassin's Bullet

The all-capitals banner and multicolumn headlines, complete with verbs, became increasingly entrenched during the World War I years. On June 18, 1917, the *New York Herald* bugled:

AMERICAN SOLDIERS ARE LANDED IN FRANCE
READY TO JOIN ALLIES ON THE BATTLE FRONT

Newspapers use banner headlines today, though seldom in all-capitals. Melodramatic decks, however, have all but disappeared. Contemporary headlines are predominantly multicolumn; they focus directly on a news or a feature peg. Strong verbs convey the action; captions and labels are, for the most part, a thing of the past.

Purposes of Headlines

Today's newspaper headlines are not merely ornamental; they are functional. Among other things, headlines should:
● *Brighten the appearance of the page.* Nothing is drabber than

column after column of body type. The vast sea of grayness is difficult to read. One need only compare the classified ad pages of today's papers with a well-designed news page to realize the sharp contrast. (Newspaper design is discussed in chapter 9.)

● *Provide a quick summary of the news.* The hurried newspaper reader often has time to only‹skim a page. Accurate, forceful headlines, under these circumstances, can give readers the thrust of the story in a nutshell.

● *Rate news for importance.* Headline size serves as a rating system to indicate the relative importance of each story. If, for example, a story has a four-column, bold headline, the reader can assume that, at least in the opinion of the copy editor, it is significant. On the other hand, if a story has a one-column headline set in type hardly larger than the text, the reader can conclude it is of less importance.

● *Entice subscribers to read the story.* When news story headlines are strong and vivid, they will often entice hurried subscribers to read the story. If the headline over a feature story is bright and clever, the reader might be subtly coaxed to read the article.

● *Represent the personality of the newspaper.* Stodgy, gray newspapers which contain many single-column, multideck headlines have a different air—personality—than do contemporary newspapers which have opened themselves up to multicolumn, bolder headlines.

Type Faces and Point Sizes

Selection of headline type requires considerable care. Type is generally categorized according to *family*. Common families, many of which are named after their designer, include Bodoni, Futura, News Gothic, Century, Tempo, and Vogue. There are hundreds of others. There are several variations of type within each family; the most common variations are roman and italic faces (italic type faces are characterized by their slanted letter shapes). Thus, by using both roman headlines and italic headlines, papers can provide variety in appearance without mixing families.

One of the country's leading typography experts, Edmund Arnold, in his book, *Ink on Paper,* emphasizes that selection of type is indeed important. The function of type, according to Arnold, "is solely to convey information, easily, quickly, and clearly." Arnold lists characteristics that should be sought when selecting a type face: (1) It should be *invisible* (the reader "should easily grasp entire words and phrases without being aware of the letter forms"); (2) It should have a *pleasant texture*; (3) It should have *proper proportions*; (4) It must be *appropriate* (many faces, Arnold points out, have "strong feminine or masculine connotations"); and (5) It should have *typographic harmony* (a hodgepodge of headline type families on a page can be confusing to the reader, thus newspapers should keep their selection of type in the same family). Arnold, in fact, wrote that "to have to shift mental gears between Bodoni and Metro slows down reading as much as gear-shifting slows down driving."

Type faces are measured by point size. There are 72 points to the inch; 12 points equal 1 pica; 6 picas equal 1 inch. Type comes in a variety of sizes within each family. Generally, newspapers use headlines at specifically spaced intervals between 12 points and 72 points. Sometimes for news stories of significant magnitude, however, newspapers will use 84-point or even 96-point type. Most body type for news stories is 8-point to 10-point.

Roman and italic faces of the Bodoni Bold family used by the *Hastings* (Neb.) *Daily Tribune*:

This is 12 point italic
This is 12 point

This is 18 point italic
This is 18 point

This is 24 point italic
This is 24 point

This is 36 point italic
This is 36 point

Fig. 7–1. This chart illustrates various headline point sizes. (Courtesy of the *Hastings* (Neb.) *Daily Tribune*.)

48 point italic

48 point

60 *italic*

60 point

72 *italic*

72 point

Fig. 7–1 *(cont.).*

Basic Headline Styles

Headline forms vary greatly but there are several basic styles.

Headlines Set in All-Capital Letters

Many newspapers used to print headlines in all-capital letters. Though this practice has tapered, some newspapers continue to use all-capital headlines.

PRIMARY GIVES CONSERVATIVES IN IOWA A BOOST

Fig. 7–2. All-capitals headline. (Courtesy of the *Des Moines* (Iowa) *Register.*)

Headlines Set in Capital Letters and Lower Case Letters

Some newspapers use headlines in which the first letter of all words, except articles and conjunctions, is capitalized. Remaining letters are set in lower case.

Mark Lane and People's Temple: Cult's Defender Now Attacks It

Fig. 7–3. Headline with the first letters of all words in capitals with the exception of the conjunction. (© 1978–79 by The New York Times Company. Reprinted by permission.)

Headlines Set in Predominantly Lower Case Letters

Most newspapers in the decade of the 1970s converted to a headline style in which only the first letter of the first word of the headline and first letter on proper nouns are capitalized. Remaining letters are lower case. The primary reason for this style is increased readability. People are used to reading text in which only the first letters of the first words of sentences and first letters of proper nouns are capitalized. Thus, it is reasoned, headlines should follow this style as well.

State wants to add 600 homes
to program for foster children

Fig. 7–4. Headline set in lower case with the exception of the first letter of the first word. (Courtesy of the Louisville *Courier-Journal*.)

Step Headlines

Lines in step headlines are the same length but they are staggered. Subsequent lines in multiline heads are each indented from the left. Newspapers using this headline style today are in the minority.

Sheriff's Old Home Town
Ain't What She Used to Be

Fig. 7–5. Step headline. (Courtesy of the *Omaha* (Neb.) *World-Herald*.)

Inverted Pyramid Headlines

The *New York Times* is one of the few newspapers which continues to use inverted pyramid headlines. Each line in an inverted pyramid headline is shorter than the preceding one and is centered.

AYATOLLAH STEPS UP PRESSURE ON REGIME TO BOW OUT IN IRAN

OUTLINES A NEW CONSTITUTION

Defying Prime Minister Bakhtiar, He Asks 'Brothers' in Military to Join Him and 'Be Free'

Fig. 7–6. Inverted pyramid deck headline. (© 1978–79 by The New York Times Company. Reprinted by permission.)

Deck Headlines

Deck headlines are also used less frequently today. Information which supplements the primary headline is written as a deck.

Federal Hiring Rules Frustrate Employers

Other Firms Back Sears On Lawsuit

Fig. 7–7. Deck headline. (Courtesy of the *Omaha* (Neb.) *World-Herald*.)

Flush Left Headlines

Flush left headlines are common in most contemporary newspapers. The first word on each line of a multiline headline is set even with the left side of the column. Lines are not necessarily even on the right side, though they often are. Contemporary newspapers which emphasize horizontal design (see chapter 9 for details) use many one-line multicolumn headlines which are set flush left.

Movie of 'Roots' causes sensation during showings in South Africa

Fig. 7–8. Flush-left headline. (Courtesy of the Louisville *Courier-Journal*.)

Standing Headlines

Newspapers which carry regular items, like letters to the editor columns, athletic league standings, public record columns, news digests, personal columns, and the like, regularly place the same headline over them each day. This not only aids readers, but it also can facilitate page design.

for the record

Fairmount Results   **NBA Standings**   **College Tennis**

Fig. 7–9. Standing headlines: "For the record" (courtesy of the *St. Louis Post-Dispatch*).

Jack Anderson

Drug agents make hash of job

Fig. 7–9 *(cont.)*: "Action Editor" (courtesy of the *Omaha* (Neb.) *World-Herald);* "Jack Anderson" (courtesy of the *Columbia* (Mo.) *Daily Tribune).*

Special Headline Styles

Headlines which depart from basic patterns are special in terms of appearance and effect. These special headlines convey the essence of the story, just as basic headlines do, but they also bring extra attention to themselves. Only exceptional stories should be given special headline treatment.

Kickers

Kickers are set in smaller type and appear directly above the headline. Normally, kickers are ½ the type size of the headline (if the headline is 36-point type, the kicker is 18-point type). Kickers are often underscored with a thin rule. Also, if headlines are set in roman type, kickers are generally set in italic type. Conversely, if the headline is italic, the kicker is roman.

A kicker is ordinarily about one-third to one-half the length of the headline. Most newspapers favor kickers which extend one-half the column width of the headline. If, for example, the headline is three columns, the kicker would stretch about one and one-half columns. Kickers are used to supplement headlines—but they should not bear the brunt of supplying the main information of the story. Also, kickers should never carry attribution for headlines. Kickers are often expendable when making up a page. Thus, copy editors should not put qualifications or attribution in kickers. If composing room personnel eliminate the kicker when they make up the page, the headline would have to be rewritten to make sense. Or, worse yet, the headline could be published and not make sense.

Proposal would cut 18 positions

Hearing on firemen's budget held

Fig. 7–10. Kicker headline. (Courtesy of the Louisville *Courier-Journal*.)

In addition to providing supplemental information, kickers enhance page aesthetics. Graphics purists contend that kickers should not be used at the tops of pages since there already is white space there. Rather, they think kickers should be used in the middle and lower levels of the page as a design element. Still, many newspapers routinely place kickers at tops of pages.

Hammers

Hammers are, in essence, reverse kickers. Instead of being set in smaller type like kickers, hammers are set in larger type than headlines. Like the blow from a hammer, the headline's hammer word or phrase is an attention grabber. Obviously, all stories cannot be treated this way. At some newspapers, the hammer is routinely twice the size of the headline (if the hammer is 72-point italic type, the headline is 36-point roman). At other newspapers, the hammer type size is about 1½ times larger than the headline. If, for example, the hammer is 72-point italic, the headline is 48-point roman. The Louisville *Courier-Journal* uses this chart:

Format	Point Size
C36H	36 pt. roman and 24 pt. italic
C36XH	36 pt. italic and 24 pt. roman
C42H	42 pt. roman and 30 pt. italic
C42XH	42 pt. italic and 30 pt. roman
C48H	48 pt. roman and 36 pt. italic

Fig. 7–11. Hammer headline format sizes. (Courtesy of the Louisville *Courier-Journal*.)

C48XH	48 pt. italic and 36 pt. roman
C54H	54 pt. roman and 42 pt. italic
C54XH	54 pt. italic and 42 pt. roman
C60H	60 pt. roman and 42 pt. italic
C60XH	60 pt. italic and 42 pt. roman
C72H	72 pt. roman and 48 pt. italic
C72XH	72 pt. italic and 48 pt. roman

Fig. 7–11 *(cont.)*.

Hammers take various forms:

Beeware

These carpenters build a lot of trouble for you

By LINDA STAHL
Courier-Journal Staff Writer

Listen. Hear the muted buzzing? Well, don't shudder with terror. It isn't the approach of the South American killer bees. Not yet.

But if you live anywhere in Indiana, or in some parts of Kentucky, and are standing close to wood — especially redwood or cedar — you're probably listening to the sound of bee reproduction. And in this case reproduction means destruction.

In Indiana, record numbers of female carpenter bees are drilling perfectly round holes willy-nilly into wooden objects such as picnic tables, patio decks and the trim on houses. They don't discriminate between a new garage and a broken-down shed. They just want wood.

While unusually high populations of the bees have emerged in Indiana in the last week or so, they haven't been out in such force in Kentucky.

As of Friday, a University of Kentucky entomologist said carpenter bees

See THESE BEES
Back page, col. 2, this section

Fig. 7–12. Hammer headline. (Courtesy of the Louisville *Courier-Journal*.)

Side-Saddles

Side-saddle headlines, instead of appearing above stories, are placed at the left. Side-saddles are often used at the tops of inside pages when advertisements leave but a few inches for news space. Side-saddles are also utilized to create white space on news pages. Thus, they are not limited exclusively to placement on tops of inside pages. Side-saddles are usually written as one-column, multiline headlines, though they could be a column and a fraction in width, depending upon makeup style. Stories with side-saddle headlines are often bordered.

Gallup Poll

Survey shows more approve of president

By GEORGE GALLUP
Director, American Institute of Public Opinion

PRINCETON, N.J. — President Carter's fortunes have taken a slight turn for the better, after a four-month slide in popularity, according to the latest Gallup survey taken May 19-22.

Of those asked "Do you approve of disapprove of the way Carter is handling his job as prsident?", 44 percent said they approve, while 43 percent said they disapprove.

The current figure represents a five-point gain in approval from the presi-

dent's low-point in mid-April. Between mid-April and the latest survey, 41 percent of those questioned said they approved of Carter's performance. In December 1977, the approval rating was 57 percent.

The latest survey also showed Carter has the strong approval of 16 percent of those questioned. That is an increase of two points since the previous survey, but still four points below his showing in the November 18-21 survey.

Of those questioned, 28 percent gave Carter their mild approval while 20 per-

Fig. 7–13. Side-saddle headline. (Courtesy of the Louisville *Courier-Journal.*)

Counting Headlines

Since each newspaper headline must fit a designated space—be it one column, two columns, or more—the headline must be "counted" accurately. It takes practice to become adept at counting headlines (assuming that one does not work at an electronic copy processing newspaper where a computer does the counting). Unnecessary delays are created when headlines—each letter, space, numeral or symbol—are not counted properly and the headline consequently does not fit the designated space.

Though each newspaper likely has a slight variation of this chart, letters, symbols, and numbers are usually counted as shown in Figure 7–14. Note how "fat" letters or symbols count more than "thin" letters or symbols because they occupy more space.

Cap M and W	2 counts
Cap I	½ count
Other caps	1½ counts
Lower case m and w	1½ counts

Fig. 7–14. Headline unit counts.

Lower case f l i t	½ count
Other lower case letters	1 count
Symbols ($#%)	1 count
Punctuation	½ count
Quote marks	½ count
Numeral 1	½ count
Other numerals	1 count
Space between words	½ count

Fig. 7–14 *(cont.)*.

Copy editors soon become proficient at counting headlines. It is an exact science. If a headline is one count too long, for example, it must be rewritten. Otherwise, it would extend into an adjacent column of type. Conversely, if a headline is several counts too short, it leaves an unwanted excess of white space. Below is an example of a one-line headline which has a total count of 38:

When counting multiline headlines, each line must be totaled separately (the count is not continuous from one line to the next).

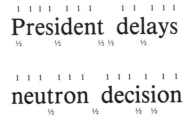

The top line of this two-line headline counts 14½; the second line counts 14.

Headline counting and processing procedures naturally vary. On non-electronic copy-processing newspapers, headlines are normally written or typed on pieces of scratch paper. Many editors find that typing the headline is faster. Though the *M* occupies the same space on a typewriter space bar as does an *i* or *t* (in contrast to "fat" and "thin" spaces in headlines), editors can quickly tell if their initially composed headlines will be close to the proper count. For example, if a headline is to count 28 and it stretches from 10 to 35 on the typewriter's space bar, the writer can assume that the count is approximately 20–30. However, if it stretches from 10 to 50, the writer can tell that he is well over the limit without taking time to count it.

Responsibility for securing the proper count rests squarely with the copy editor. Some experienced writers count headlines precisely in their minds; others use a method similar to the above illustration to secure the specific count. Whatever the method, accuracy is imperative. Time is lost each time the composing room has to send a headline back to the newsroom to be rewritten because it is too long or too short. Headlines are sometimes altered in the composing room when there is not time for them to be sent back to the copy desk. This often results in less-than-adequate headlines.

Editors at many electronic newspapers, however, no longer have to count headlines—their video display terminals do it for them. Working with Hendrix VDTs, copy editors at the *Omaha* (Neb.) *World-Herald,* like journalists at hundreds of other newspapers, compose headlines and set them in type via computers. Here, for example, is how *World-Herald* editors are assigned stories and how the computer counts them.

As discussed in chapters 2 and 5, editors are often assigned a queue that generally conforms to three letters of their names. Thus, editor Henion has HEN as his queue. The editor activates his queue by typing HEN and pressing the SIGN ON button. The machine responds, telling him that he is, indeed, signed on and that he is ready to copy edit, write headlines, or compose stories.

The editor then presses LONG DIRECTORY, a button that tells the computer banks to give him a list of the stories in his queue. At this point, he finds one story. He moves the cursor to the beginning of the file name and presses OPEN EDIT. This button tells the machine the entire text is required and it is displayed a screenful at a time. The editor then reads a notation at the top of the copy placed there in MEMO MODE by the slot person.

"HEN: Need a 2–24–2 roman with kicker. Keep to 10 inches for page 2 Bulldog." This tells the editor that the slot wants a two-column, two-line headline in 24-point roman type with a kicker for the second page of the first edition. At the top of his story, the editor types:

$<$g24$>$ $<$dd$>$ Bulldog $<$ed$>$ Bulldog

Bulldog page 2

HEN

$<$af36$>$

🔔   8

🔔   1 $<$cw10.6$>$

These are instructions to the computer that this is an international story (g . . .) and that the headline size is a 2–24 with a kicker ($<$g24$>$). The "Bulldog$<$ed$>$Bulldog" is a routing command for the composing room. These are instructions that the story is for page two of the Bulldog (early morning) edition. The top line of instructions will not be printed on the film, but the second line will. The editor also puts his name on the film so that makeup editors will know who to question if there is a problem.

To separate these commands from the headline commands that follow, the editor tells the machine to advance film 36 points ($<$af36$>$), then he enters his first "bell command." The various bell codes are used to program the computers on what size headline or body type to set. When the machine first reads $<$g24$>$ and later finds the 🔔8 command, it automatically sets its "mind" into the 2–24 headline mode.

All the editor has to do is type out a headline with each line separated by a "flush left" or "flush right" ($\leftarrow$ $\rightarrow$) arrow. Following the headline, he places another code—🔔7—which instructs the machine to measure only matter prior to this command. Then, by pressing the COMPOSE button, the machine automatically counts each line of the headline and tells the editor how many characters short or long each line is.

The editor then removes the 🔔7 command or uses another combination of buttons to override the 🔔7. He can now fit the story. The machine tells him exactly how many lines, picas, and inches the story is long and whether or not he made command errors—such as failure to route the story, failure to tell the machine the pica width (in this case, 10.6), or failure to eliminate extraneous symbols within the coding system. If there are errors, the machine will indicate what they are and on what line they occur.

The machine will not, however, deduce errors such as spelling, punctuation, and the like. The errors it notes are merely in the computer command symbols. After composing a headline that fits and after cutting the story to the required length, the editor presses the END button to signify completion. He then presses the SET button or assigns the story to the slotperson for a final check. Machines and makeup personnel do the rest.

Headline Ordering Systems

Once a journalist learns to count headlines or process them on the computer, he is ready to write them. Many newspapers have a chart or schedule to follow. This chart provides reporters and editors with available type faces, sizes, and per-column counts. Though practices vary among newspapers, headline ordering systems generally follow a pattern similar to this: the first number indicates column width, the second number indicates headline point size, and the third number indicates number of lines. Thus, a 2–36–2 means that the headline is to cover two columns, the type size is 36-point, and the headline is to be two lines. For italic type headlines, the numbers are usually preceded by the capital letter X. Thus, X1–18–3 is an order for a one-column, 18-point, three-line italic headline. An order in which the numbers are preceded by the capital letter K indicates that the headline must have a kicker. Thus, a K3–36–1 calls for a three-column, 36-point, one-line headline with a kicker. When a headline is to include a deck, the numbers are preceded by a D. A D1–36–2 would be an order for a one-column, 36-point, two-line headline with a deck. For newspapers which use hammer headlines, the numbers are preceded by an H.

Some newspapers use letters to order specific headlines. Under this alphabetical designation, for example, an A headline might refer to a 1–18–2, a B headline might refer to a 1–24–2 and so on. Note the following chart for a six-column format (14 picas per column) newspaper which uses Bodoni Bold headlines.

If a copy editor is assigned to write a 3–36–1 headline, he would check the chart and find the maximum count is 31. If assigned to to write a 2–24–2 headline, each line would count a maximum of

HEADLINE SCHEDULE COUNTING
14 PICA COLUMNS

Point Type Size	1 col.	2 col.	3 col.	4 col.	5 col.	6 col.
12	30					
18	20	40½				
24	15	30½	46			
36	10	20½	31	41½	52	62½
48	7½	15	22½	30	37½	45
60	6	12½	19	25½	32	38½
72	5	10½	16	21½	27	32½

Fig. 7–15. Headline count chart for a 14-pica, six-column newspaper which uses Bodoni Bold headlines.

30½. As the chart illustrates, the smaller the headline point size, the higher the maximum count per column; the larger the point size, the lower the maximum count per column.

Writing headlines which count accurately is particularly challenging when multiline headlines are assigned. Though copy editors should strive for a perfect count (each line counts exactly the maximum), this is often impossible when operating under deadline pressures. Copy editors should, however, make sure that if an equal count is not possible, the longest line should be no more than two counts in excess of the shortest line. Also, editors should work to get the longest line within two counts of the maximum.

Writing Headlines

Once the copy editor is given instructions to write a particular headline, he faces his greatest challenge: creation of an accurate, grammatically correct headline that will fit the designated space. Editors approach headline writing in different ways—methods which, through experience, they find work best for them. Though the following suggestions are not sacrosanct, many experienced editors find these steps logical and helpful:

• *Quickly skim the entire story to get a "feel" for it.* Then, give it a careful, detailed second reading. Strive to locate the news peg or the primary element or elements of importance. If the story has been conscientiously edited, this is routine; the most important elements should be near the top of the story.

● *Summarize the essence of the story in a sentence.* Don't worry about proper count at this stage. Rather, concentrate on formulating an accurate, appropriate, smoothly flowing sentence which captures the significant thrust of the story. Make the headline conversational. Assume that you have just witnessed the event and, during informal conversation, someone asks you to capsulize it for them. Most editors prefer to get their thoughts on paper—or on the computer screen.

● *Polish the story's essence into a headline that counts.* This can normally be done by rearranging words, eliminating unnecessary adjectives or considering synonyms for words which count "long" or "short."

Standards for Headlines

Like copy editing, headline writing is an art. Any journalist who has been frustrated while struggling to fit the essence of a long, involved story into a short headline space knows this. As copy editors become proficient at their art, they concentrate on and take extreme pride in polishing each headline so it conveys precisely the impression intended. Copy editors strive to meet minimum standards for headlines; after this is accomplished, they can hone the headline until it sparkles. Minimum standards for headlines include:

● *Headlines must be accurate.* This goes almost without saying. Copy editors quickly discover, however, that a misplaced comma or hyperbolic adjective can strip a headline of its intended, accurate meaning.

● *Headlines must count properly.* The best-phrased headline ever written is of little utility at deadline time if it exceeds the allotted space. To spill over one count results in jamming against copy in an adjacent column. A headline one count too long, as emphasized in the section on headline counting, is little better than exceeding the maximum by ten counts. It still must be rewritten.

● *Headlines must be grammatically correct.* Bold headlines are read with more scrutiny than the internal paragraphs of a news story. Though a copy editor is embarrassed when he leaves an ungrammatical passage in the body of a news story, the error is compounded when it leaps out at the reader in 36-point type.

● *Headlines normally should be written in the historical present tense.* Headlines should convey a sense of immediacy. For example, if a story focuses on Congressional approval of the President's welfare reform package on the previous day, the headline should not say, *Congress approved welfare package.* Rather, it should read, *Congress approves welfare package.* Though most headlines will be written in the historical present tense, there are exceptions. If the story concerns an upcoming event, the future tense would be used: *Council to consider plan.* Or, if to phrase the headline in the historical present tense would be awkward, the past tense could be used. For a story which concerns Thomas Jefferson's contributions to press freedom, it would be best to write a headline something like *Jefferson felt strongly about First Amendment.* To say *Jefferson feels strongly about First Amendment* would be clumsy.

● *Headlines should contain a subject-verb sequence.* Headlines that begin with verbs will be discussed below. The most effective headlines are those that contain a subject and a very strong verb. The strength of a headline depends on the vigor of its verb. Use active verbs whenever possible. *Nicklaus captures golf tournament* is superior to *Nicklaus is winner in golf tournament.*

● *Headline tone should match the story.* Clever, sometimes frivolous headlines should not be used over hard news stories like presidential addresses, deaths, Congressional hearings, and the like. Light, informal headlines, however, can often be effectively written for feature stories or humorous articles.

● *Headlines should be punctuated properly.* Copy editors must be just as concerned with proper punctuation in headlines as they are with proper punctuation in sentences in the body of a news story. With one exception—periods do not follow the last word—headlines should be punctuated the same as text sentences. Also, when using quotation marks in a headline, single marks ('), rather than double marks ("), are standard practice at most newspapers.

Headline Pitfalls

While copy editors must always strive to meet minimum standards for headlines, they must also avoid falling victim to these pitfalls:

● *Avoid splitting logical units from one line to the next.* Splitting of verb forms is most often abused:

Grain prices during 1982 to
average more than last year

Splitting logical units also includes, but is not limited to, dividing titles and names from line to line:

> Report to be given Mayor
> Veys at Tuesday meeting

● *Avoid label headlines.* Label headlines contain no action. They do not tell the reader anything about the content of the story; they emphasize only the event. This headline tells the reader nothing about the day's happenings:

> Legislative session

Headlines should tell the reader what happened during the legislative session. For example:

> Legislature considers
> death penalty proposal

● *Avoid verb headlines.* Some newspapers persist in using verb headlines (headlines which do not contain subjects). Most newspapers, however, have strict rules against them. An example of verb headlines (with nonstated subject in parentheses) follows:

> (Grand jury)   Indicts Jones
> in tax scheme

Though verb headlines should be avoided, editors, particularly when working with one-column headlines with short counts, will sometimes feel forced to use them. If verb headlines must be used, editors should make sure the verb agrees with the implied subject. The following headline contains improper understood subject-verb agreement:

> (City Council)   Approve increase
> in city sales tax

● *Avoid unattributed opinions.* The copy editor has no more literary license to editorialize or thrust his interpretations into headlines than does the reporter when writing the story. The following headline contains opinion:

> Patrol's use of informers legally questionable

Who says? The headline writer owes it to the reader to tell him who thinks the patrol's use of informers is legally questionable. The headline could be adjusted in one of three ways. The copy editor could tell the reader whose opinion is being conveyed by putting the person's name at the beginning of the headline. When this is done, the man's name is followed by a colon:

Jones: patrol's use of informers legally questionable

Or, the headline writer could place the person's name at the end of the headline. When this is done, the man's name is preceded by a dash:

Patrol's use of informers legally questionable—Jones

If using the source's name would make the count too long and if no words could be edited from the headline, the copy editor could simply place single quotes around the headline (double quotes are not used in headlines):

'Patrol's use of informers legally questionable'

Though the single quotation marks do not tell the reader who holds this opinion, they do tell the reader that someone other than the headline writer drew this conclusion.

● *Avoid using articles or unnecessary words to pad the headline count.* After the headline writer struggles with a headline that continually counts short, he is tempted to insert articles or words which add nothing to the content. Since headline space is generally tight, the editor should resist padding counts with words which fail to elaborate on the content of the story. For example:

Costello *is* appointed
as ag marketing chief

In a story about an influx of residents from abroad in Beverly Hills, Calif., one newspaper's copy editor developed this headline:

Foreigners *are more and more* making
their homes in Beverly Hills *area*

Use of *are more and more* is totally superfluous, as is *area,* since the story referred specifically to Beverly Hills per se.

Another often-used headline writing device is to identify a person by his state. Unless this is germane to the story, it merely pads the count. Note how the following headline, which appeared over a story about a Portland, Ore., man who was fighting a losing battle with the Internal Revenue Service, contains more flab than content:

> Oregonian is a loser
> all of the way around

The headline really doesn't say much. The reader is unaware of what kind of situation he was losing, and, the fact that he was an Oregonian is not particularly pertinent to readers in Mississippi or Minnesota.

• *Avoid using the conjunction "and."* Instead, a comma should be used. Headline space is valuable. Do not waste it when shorter means of communication can be used:

> Food and fuel supplies
> threatened by snowstorm

• *Avoid uncommon acronyms, initials, or abbreviations.* Some initials such as CIA, FBI, and so on, are well known. Also, they represent efficient shortcuts when headline space is valuable. It is certainly permissible to use them in headlines. But headline writers should not saddle readers with initials which might communicate different meaning to different people. A story in a Utah newspaper, for example, was headlined:

> OSU captures
> league title

Among other things, OSU could mean Oklahoma State University or Ohio State University. OSU could be widely used in Oklahoma newspapers, and most readers would readily know the story focuses on Oklahoma State. But when OSU is used in a Utah or North Dakota newspaper, the reader could be confused.

Editors should also avoid cramming several abbreviations into a headline. If the campus chapter of the American Association of University Professors were to seek collective bargaining rights with the state university board of regents, a campus newspaper copy editor might be tempted to write:

> AAUP of SU hopes
> for bargaining rights

At best, it's awkward.

For the most part, copy editors must use common sense on whether certain abbreviations or initials will be readily comprehended. For example, if the following headline appeared in a Wyoming newspaper, most readers would probably understand it:

NCA: cattle prices during 1981
to surpass earlier projections

The National Cattlemen's Association is well known in some western states, but NCA would do little more than wrinkle some brows in other parts of the country.

Copy editors should never abbreviate words which would not be abbreviated in the story itself. For example, the writer of the following headline encountered difficulty in fitting Nevada into the second line:

Trouble in capital
of Nev. investigated

Under no circumstances should shortcuts like this be taken in headlines.

● *Avoid slang, jargon, and headlinese.* Headline writers should follow the same rules for proper English that they expect reporters to. In a story about Nebraska Rep. Virginia Smith's criticisms of portions of President Carter's budget, one copy editor wrote this headline:

Mrs. Smith *rakes*
president's budget

One wonders what she did with the budget after she raked it. Possibly she took it to the trash barrel and burned it.

Another common shortcut headline writers have been taking for decades is using "nix" for rejecting or disapproving. Copy editors should never take such language liberties.

● *Avoid repeating words.* Copy editors who are working hurriedly often do this without realizing it. The problem is most likely to occur when writing headlines with kickers. The following headlines illustrate this taboo:

Firemen extinguish warehouse fire,
Senators probe Sen. Johnson's involvement

● *Avoid double meanings.* With copy editors often working under extreme deadline pressure, headlines with double meanings are sometimes going to work their way into print. However, copy editors should scrutinize every headline to see that these often embarrassing instances are kept to the minimum.

One newspaper story told about Sen. William Proxmire of Wisconsin who was surveying federal departments and agencies to determine which government cars were being used to chauffeur officials to and from work. The headline said:

> Senator pursues
> chauffeur study

The story said nothing about Sen. Proxmire returning to school to prepare for a vocational change.

Another headline writer must have perceived a Maryland creek to be much more than a smoothly flowing, peaceful body of water:

> 3 Maryland girls found
> stabbed to death by creek

● *Avoid ambiguity.* For a story about cab drivers being denied rate increases, one copy editor wrote:

> City cabs
> denied hike;
> hearing set

It's doubtful that the cabs requested the increase.

After the U.S. Supreme Court ruled that it is constitutional for law enforcement agencies to obtain search warrants to examine papers, documents or other property of reporters, many state legislators introduced bills designed to halt harassment of journalists in newsrooms. One such bill banned issuance of search warrants unless an investigation of a criminal offense had begun and the reporter was suspected of that offense. A paper headlined the story:

> Anti-press search
> bill is submitted

This sounds as if the bill is aimed at stifling, rather than helping, the press.

● *Avoid lack of specificity.* A story which made the national news evolved from Iowa City, Iowa, where a woman was temporarily suspended from her job as a city firefighter for nursing her baby while on duty. It should have been carefully scrutinized by a copy editor to avoid lack of specificity in the headline. This, however, was the result:

> Nursing incident
> causes suspension

The headline is far from clear; one might think of a nursing home or possibly an accident involving a nurse at a hospital. The headline should have focused on breast feeding by an on-duty firefighter.

• *Avoid emphasis on minor news angles buried deep within the story.* As mentioned in an earlier section, headlines should focus on news elements in the lead or the beginning of the story. Though a reader had to go to the ninth paragraph to find a statement made by Creighton University basketball coach Tom Apke that his team "owed" Wichita State a game, this headline was written:

Apke claims Jays
owe Wichita one

Besides frustrating the reader, headlines which zero in on buried story items or statements can sometimes end up being erroneous if a makeup editor is forced to cut the end of the story for space.

• *Avoid "so what" and "say nothing" headlines.* As pointed out in chapter 3, copy editors must work diligently to hone the lead of a news story; it must emphasize the major elements of the article. This rule logically extends to headline writing. "So what" or "say nothing" headlines should be avoided. The copy editor who formulated the following headline was hardly doing his job:

Heat wave linked to temperatures

Few people want to waste the price of a newspaper for that kind of "inside" information.

"Say nothing" headlines are usually the end product of lazy copy desk work. After all, it hardly takes much effort to produce a headline like this:

Suspect captured

• *Avoid libel.* Editors must remember that libel suits can be brought based on items other than news stories. This includes headlines. Particular care must be taken when suspects of crimes are apprehended. The following headlines are inviting libel actions:

Murderer Jones apprehended

Tax evader stands trial

Jones is not a murderer until he is found guilty of murder; the person standing trial for tax evasion is not a tax evader until found guilty.

• *Avoid "cute" headlines.* The line between clever and cute headlines is a fine one. What is appropriate, understandable, and funny to one person might be ridiculously trite to another. Clever headlines effectively handled can make a newspaper sparkle; trite, juvenile headlines can make a newspaper look foolish. Draw your own conclusions on these two examples:

For a story which concerned movements in Wyoming, Colorado, Utah, Oklahoma, Texas, and Nevada to introduce legislation to repeal the speed limit imposed after the Arab oil embargo, a copy editor formulated this headline:

> Old West says draw
> over 55 speed limit

For a sports story which led with the heroics of Willie Mays and Juan Marichal, a copy editor wrote this headline:

> Wonderful Willie,
> juanderful Juan
> lead Giants win

● *Avoid overusing "bill."* During state legislative sessions, hundreds of bills are introduced. A copy editor is challenged to write headlines that don't all sound the same (the sports editor is faced with the same task the morning after high school basketball games: after all, there are only so many ways to say one team beat another in headlines with short counts). Thus, a reader would think "Bill" was a busy fellow on the day these three headlines were placed on the same page:

> Bill would eliminate flood fees

> Bill would limit taxing authority

> Bill would raise retirement age

● *Avoid using both first and last names.* With headline space precious, copy editors should not use first and last names unless the story refers to two or more persons with the same last name. Note that the first name adds nothing to this headline:

> Bernard King leads Tennessee win

By using only the last name, the headline can be more specific:

> King's 27 points pace Vols to win

● *Avoid style inconsistencies between story and headline.* One would think this would not happen, but it does. For example, an Associated

Press story dealt with enforcement of antitrust (one word according to the AP stylebook) laws. Though the word was used correctly in the story, the headline read:

> Lower Court procedures hamper
> enforcement of anti-trust laws

● *Avoid understatement.* Some thing are so obvious, they don't merit headlines:

> Bankrupt association
> termed in poor shape

● *Avoid overstatement.* Since at least one "game of the century" or "game of the decade" is played in college football each season, it is unlikely that one would be played between two high school teams:

> Superior edges Hebron
> in 'battle of century'

● *Carefully check headlines.* This is particularly important for copy editors on electronic copy processing newspapers which have eliminated proofreaders. To wit:

> Council spits on
> shade tree proposal

Actually, the vote was split.

Chapter 8

Photos
and Cutlines

THE SCENARIO IS FAMILIAR. A daily newspaper city editor wants pictures to accompany a city council story. The meeting is important. Dozens of citizens are going to protest a proposed zoning change; it promises to be heated. The editor hurriedly scrawls a photo assignment: get pictures at city council meeting. A photographer, already disgusted that the city editor did not use some enterprise photos he took the day before, grudgingly examines the order. He sticks his head in the newsroom and asks the editor if he wants a picture of anything or anyone in particular. "Can't you read?" the editor asks. "I want you to take a picture at the council meeting to accompany a news story. How do I know what is going to happen at the meeting?" The editor then grumbles to a reporter: "The journalism school that graduated that guy should lose its accreditation." The photographer picks up his camera and mutters something about the editor "not knowing a good picture if it stared him in the face."

Tension is in the air; the council chambers are packed. The photographer has another assignment in a half hour. He feels pressed to get an early picture. He takes a handlful of photos: one picture shows the crowded area where citizens sit; another picture shows two councilmen talking before the meeting begins; a third photo shows the city clerk chomping on a cigar; a fourth photo shows the mayor with his arm around a leader of the citizen group; the fifth photo is out of focus. At any rate, the photographer fulfilled his assignment; he took pictures at the city council meeting. He departs.

The session turns out to be lively. Two men are escorted from the chambers for emotional outbursts. Normally passive councilmen sit with contorted faces as voting time approaches. The mayor, who was smiling happily with the leader of the group before the meeting, loses his composure, stands up, bangs his gavel, and screams that a citizen is out of order. The reporter dutifully records every word. He returns to the office and writes a solid, hard-hitting story. The city editor reads it and likes it. He requests photos. The photographer ambles in, nonchalantly tosses two prints on the editor's desk and smiles; one photo shows the packed chambers, the other photo centers on the cigar-smoking clerk. The editor is furious. By now, the photographer doesn't much care. He followed the editor's instructions; he even asked the editor to be more specific.

Fortunately, this scene likely doesn't occur with the frequency it did a few years ago. Many editors have become picture conscious. No longer is the photographer considered "a reporter with his brains kicked out"—at least he shouldn't be. Instead, editors and photographers are teaming up to give readers an improved editorial product. Stories communicate ideas to readers; pictures, when handled diligently, also communicate messages.

Photojournalist Donald P. Blake wrote that too many editors "have not accepted the photographer as a member of the editorial family." Blake said many editors "think of photographers as 'shutter-trippers' —lacking an appreciation of news value and knowledge of journalism fundamentals." But, as Blake points out in a *Quill* article, this situation is a two-way street: "Too many photographers are certain that editors have no feeling for pictorial principles, no idea of the problems involved in making photographs, and no ability to recognize good pictures when they see them."

Bob Warner, a photography department columnist for *Editor & Publisher,* once quoted an anonymous photographer: "If I make a suggestion on a layout or a picture to an editor he'll say, 'Sounds like a good idea, let's do it.' The next day I bring the picture in, lay it in front of him and he sticks his nose up in the air and says, 'Well, yes, I guess we can use that.' Then he crops it down to nothing, uses it for two or three columns, without a by-line and never a word that it was a good picture."

Newspapers and wire service bureaus are making greater efforts to coordinate news and photos. James A. Geladas, managing editor of the award-winning Dubuque (Iowa) *Telegraph Herald,* encourages formal and informal educational programs which involve photographers, editors, and reporters. His newspaper holds a formal critique session each week. With the coming of age of offset printing and concomitant quality photographic reproduction, newspaper editors must become increasingly conscious of combining words with photos. As William Stephenson, distinguished research professor at the University of Missouri's School of Journalism, said: "News pictures are the daily butter, if not the bread, of newspapers and magazines."

Too often, however, editors will discard a picture before eliminating a story on a tight news hole page. At some newspapers, this is routine procedure—regardless of the quality of the photo. This is not to say that pictures are more important than words and that stories should be eliminated first. Rather, editors should consider the merits of each. Some pictures might be more important than some stories on a given page, just as some stories might be more important than some pictures. Blanket rules about picture elimination, in any event, are not sound editorial policy. *Washington Post* picture editor Sandra Eisert terms the competition for publication in her newspaper "space wars." Pictures and words constantly compete for a limited amount of space. However, the *Post,* where competition for space is indeed intense, usually exhibits an awareness of good photography. Pictures hold down many of the pages each day. Even on tight news days, pictures often get good play. This is not necessarily the case on many metro newspapers.

With space decisions being made constantly at daily newspapers, a well-coordinated procedure to select and match news with photos is imperative. Many larger newspapers have staffers designated as picture editors or photography directors, but many others continue to haphazardly coordinate photos and news.

Photo Editing Procedures

In the early 1960s, *Editor & Publisher* carried an extensive story which focused on a discussion by photographers from seven major dailies. The photographers said they dealt with a variety of editors but primarily with the picture editor (if the newspaper had one), the managing editor, the news editor, and the city editor. In 1968, Don Alan Hall, a daily newspaper picture editor, wrote a master's degree thesis at the University of Indiana which centered on picture editing.

Hall surveyed and analyzed the content of forty-seven newspapers with circulations of more than fifty thousand. In addition, he selected ten newspapers which had reputations for pictorial quality. After questioning officials of the National Press Photographers Association, Hall formulated this "top ten" list: *Milwaukee Journal, Houston Chronicle, Denver Post, Charlotte* (N.C.) *Observer,* Louisville *Courier-Journal, Miami Herald, Topeka Capital, Washington Post, New York Herald-Tribune,* and *Minneapolis Star.* Hall polled managing editors to determine if the papers had designated picture editors and precisely how the picture editing chores were coordinated.

Hall's study focused on newspaper staffers who performed any or all duties necessary in getting pictures published: sizing; cropping; placement; cutline writing; picture page production; planning of specific coverage; scheduling of photographers' time; giving assignments to photographers; supervising the darkroom; and buying cameras and equipment. Less than half the papers in the study had designated picture editors. On those papers without picture editors, Hall found that the city editor and news editor performed most of the duties normally associated with picture editing. Hall did find, however, that picture editors on the "top ten" papers performed a greater percentage of the total photo editing duties than did editors on other newspapers in the sample.

Among other things, Hall wanted to determine if the inclusion of picture editors on a staff has any real effect on the quality of photos the newspaper publishes. Hall found that the mere presence of a designated picture editor did not insure pictorial excellence. Rather, Hall said, pictorial excellence is dependent upon the personal attitudes and technical training and experience of each editor and photographer involved in the process. Hall pointed to "human factors" —like pride—that made his "top ten" pictorial papers outstanding. The study did emphasize, however, the great variation in duties performed by editors in the picture editing process on various papers.

Indeed, a survey of some of the country's top pictorial metro papers in 1979 illustrates that Hall's observations of a decade earlier are still valid. Practices continue to vary from paper to paper. But the picture editors surveyed said that photographers and photo displays have risen in stature on many American dailies.

C. Thomas Hardin, director of photography at the Louisville *Courier-Journal* and *Times,* is involved in the coordination of news and photos at both the morning *Courier-Journal* and afternoon *Times.*

Though Hardin works for both papers, as do the photographers, the *Courier-Journal* has three picture editors and the *Times* has two. All assignments are channeled through the picture editors who are also responsible for selecting photos, sizing them, laying them out, and writing cutlines. In other words, photo editors at the two Louisville papers essentially serve as city editors for photographers. They even sit in on news conferences and planning sessions. Both papers are committed to organized coordination of photos and news.

Hardin emphasized, however, that though the picture editors are responsible for the photo content of the papers, "It's still the managing editor's newspaper." In essence, the managing editor has many sub-editors (specialists in their areas) under him. The photo editor is one of these specialists. This emphasis on coordination of news and pictures aids in packaging the two into a neat communicative element for the reader.

At the *Miami Herald,* another metro paper with a reputation for pictorial excellence, the graphics arts editor is in charge of visuals—photographers, photo editors, and artists. The photo desk, set up in the middle of the newsroom, coordinates photos and news. Photo editors attend news meetings twice a day to stay current and to lend their expertise in the matching of news and photos. Cutlines, however, are not written by picture editors. At the *Herald,* photographers give their information to copy desk editors who then write the cutlines. When differences arise as to treatment of a photo between the copy desk and the photo desk, the managing editor or an assistant managing editor is called upon to resolve the conflict.

The picture desk at the *St. Louis Post-Dispatch* is also involved in the day-to-day coordination of news and photos. Gene Pospeshil, photo editor, said representatives of the picture desk attend news meetings daily. The *Post-Dispatch,* among metro pioneers in color photos and prominently played artwork, strives to match good photos with good stories. Each day, according to Pospeshil, brings a scramble for quality photos. The news side and the photo desk work together in selecting the best photos. As at the *Miami Herald,* picture editors at the *Post-Dispatch* do not write cutlines—that job is left to the copy desk. The philosophy is that the copy desk editors have complete control over the story and they are in a better position to write the cutlines, thus avoiding the risk of repeating information. The photographers identify for copy editors precisely who and what are in the picture, but the "word people" write the cutlines.

At the *Washington Post,* there is no picture desk per se. The picture editor, Sandra Eisert, coordinates assignments, special projects, wire photos, free lance photos, picture agency photos, and photos from other external sources such as government. But reporters go through their editors to assign photos. After the assignment is carried out by the photographer, either the picture editor or a photography department staffer edits the film. An editor or reporter is then given the photo, complete with information so he can write a cutline. The desk editor then coordinates the photo with a news story. The individual in charge of the page the photo is to appear on generally makes the choice of which photo to select, sometimes in consultation with the picture editor. The news editor also usually crops the picture, though again he may consult with the picture editor. At the *Post,* many editors, reporters, and photographers are involved in the complete picture editing process; it is not as centralized as some of the other metro papers.

Picture editing procedures on daily newspapers which circulate fifty thousand and under are generally less complex. It is unusual, in fact, for one person on a small daily to be designated as the photo editor. Most likely, each of the editors—managing, city, news, sports, and society—makes assignments directly to a photographer. Each editor then supplies details—some assignments being more specific than others—to the photographer. These details might include the type of picture desired, some information about the story it is to be matched with, some tips on personalities involved in the picture, and the like. These suggestions might be written on the photo order or they sometimes are discussed orally. The photographer takes the picture, makes the proofs, and, in consultation with the editor, decides on which photo to print. The editor then crops and sizes it and, with information supplied to him by the photographer, writes the cutline. Space on newspapers with smaller circulations is normally not as competitive as on metro dailies. Thus, a good photographer is—or at least should be—often encouraged by editors to produce news enterprise and feature photos in addition to straight news photos which can be given prominent display.

Harold G. Buell, AP's assistant general manager for news photos, has suggested ways to encourage enterprise photo production. Though he was referring to wire service bureaus, his suggestions are applicable to newspapers: (1) Set up an "idea pool." Everyone should be involved—editors, photographers, darkroom personnel, reporters, and composing room personnel. (2) Assign a specific number of photographer hours to be used exclusively for production of enterprise projects. This will result in better quality photos and it will also improve morale in the photography department. (3) Talk over assignments with the photographer. Discuss picture possibilities in detail. It is important, however, to encourage the photographer to expand on both your and his ideas; in other words, he should use his ingenuity and imagination.

Donald Tremain, a still photographer with the Nebraska Educational Television Network and a former weekly and daily newspaper photographer, emphasized the relationship between editor and photographer: "A picture editor should realize he is in a very sensitive position. He is the link between the work a photographer turns out and the aesthetic and ego building rewards a photographer receives when that work is displayed to the public in the form of a published newspaper photo. Any photographer worth his paycheck is concerned about how and where his work is published just as any reporter is concerned about the same thing."

Indeed, the editor should communicate with a photographer before and after photographic assignments. If a picture editor wants a particular photographic approach to a story, he should (unlike the city editor in the scenario at the beginning of this chapter) tell the photographer about some possibilities. After the assignment has been shot, the editor should involve the photographer in the choice of pictures and possible cropping.

Ultimately, the final decision must be made by the picture editor. If the choice is at odds with the wishes of the photographer—and this is inevitable on occasion—chances are the two will still be friends if the photographer feels he at least had some voice in the decision. In other words, rapport between editor and photographer is important from the time the assignment is made until the photo is published. If an editor takes the attitude that the photographer is a second-class citizen, bickering and resentment between photographers and the news side will likely develop, and, in turn, the photo staff will turn in poor, unimaginative, lazy work because "that idiot editor wouldn't use a good picture if I took the effort to take one."

Editors should cultivate strong bonds between the news side and the photography department. An effective coordination system can be built only after mutual respect is established. Editors should strive to find out as much as possible about the photographers—their interests, work habits, and personalities. Thus, an editor is in a better position to know which photographers function best when taking certain kinds of pictures. For example, a sports editor will likely get his best pictures from a photographer who has a keen interest in and understanding of sports. If the need arises for a sports photo assignment, it would be only logical to assign a photographer who has an interest in that area.

Editors should also barnstorm for ideas throughout the newspaper, picking up photo possibilities from others. But, good photo ideas might not turn out to be effective photos unless the editor establishes a strong relationship between the newsroom and photography department. An editor who fails to build this relationship will often turn his photo staff's work into mediocrity. In the final analysis, the friction that can develop between verbally oriented copy editors and visually oriented photographers and art directors should not pose major problems if both respect and understand the abilities and philosophies of the other. Prof. William Korbus of the University of Texas at Austin said: "The primary point for editors to remember is always the same —they should select elements which communicate the message best. It might be words, photos or a mix of both. *Communication,* at an optimum level, is the goal."

Photo Selection

Like the news editor who must determine which stories will be published, the picture editor or the editor who coordinates photos with news is a gatekeeper. He determines *whether* the picture should be used, *which* picture should be used, *where* the picture should be used (front page, inside page, sports page), and *how* the picture should be used (with a story, standing alone as "wild art," as a two-column photo, as a three-column photo, etc.). Though pictures carry considerable impact, their selection is far from scientific. Malcolm S. MacLean Jr., and Anne Li-An Kao wrote in *Journalism Quarterly*: "Despite the thousands of readership and audience studies, editors and photographers still have to fly pretty much by the seat of their pants in their decisions on pictorial communication." Though picture selection may not be scientific, communication must be an overriding factor. As Korbus said, "Communication, not art for the sake of art, must be the goal." He wrote that editors should look for photojournalism when selecting photographs: "A photo that tells a story, that reinforces or supplements the verbal with the visual will help achieve the communication goal."

So perceptive and significant were the words of Stanley E. Kalish and Clifton C. Edom in the preface to their 1951 book, *Picture Editing,* that they have been quoted many times:

> The key to successful picture editing is the feeling for pictures. This cannot be overemphasized. A person who is going to edit pictures, must sense pictures, must interpret every experience in the light of pictures it suggests. Thus far there has been too little of this feeling for pictures. In many a newspaper office picture editing is nothing more than a spare-time job for a newsman. Often the captions are written by anyone who is available, although caption writing is as specialized as is headline writing. Publications (and the whole publishing industry) sadly need people who have a knowledge of picture editing.

Geladas tells his editors, photographers, and reporters in Dubuque that "photographs in the *Telegraph Herald* should be treated with respect as worthy and important communications elements. Words and pictures, of course, can enhance one another. But many times a picture can communicate as much or more than any number of words."

A "feeling" for photos is important. The problem, however, comes in acquiring this feeling. Though editors might think they have a feel for their community and the types of photos their readers want, this might not necessarily be the case. Photo editors should, like the news editor making story judgments, be familiar with the community and with demographic information about its citizens.

In addition to a knowledge of the paper's readers, editors who work with photos should consider several other elements before making publication decisions. Though making photo publication decisions in checklist fashion can be futile, it is important that an editor consider certain factors. Factors to consider include:

● *The photo should inform.* If the event is significant, editors will probably use even a photo that is low in technical quality. For example, if the president of the United States is signing an important document during a ceremony abroad and the early photos are not of excellent quality, most papers will publish them if deadline time is at hand. Or, if the local mayor is signing a document which will affect thousands of city residents, though the photo is rather ordinary, it still communicates an important message.

● *The photo should communicate.* Photos should not be used simply for the sake of using them. They should communicate a message to the reader. If a pictorial essay is being published on the hard times of skid row inhabitants, then close-ups of faces, empty wine bottles, and humans huddled in crowded doorways to keep warm communicate a message. The photo must have sufficient content; it should tell what the story is about. Newspapers, however, often run color photos strictly because of the color, rather than the content. If the shot isn't good in black and white, then it won't be in color. Many newspapers, though, use "cute" color photos—youngsters with Easter eggs, people with funny costumes, seasonal shots, and the like. However, Prof. George Tuck of the University of Nebraska-Lincoln stressed that while color photos of this nature might "draw good audience reaction, it's not good photojournalism. Color can be shot in a fast-breaking news situation. Candid color *is* possible."

● *The photo should have news value.* A photo of two friends standing on a street corner shaking hands—assuming there are no other important variables—has little news value. But a similar photo of a city councilman standing on the same street corner shaking hands with an individual he has been publicly at odds with might be considered newsworthy.

There are also other questions a photo editor might ask himself before deciding to publish a picture:

● *Does the photo have impact?* If a photo is borderline and doesn't grab the editor—and presumably the reader—right away, it likely never will. The photo is the signpost when used with a story. Or, if the photo is being used for display, standing alone without a story, it should pull the reader's attention. Editors should look for photos which contain emotion and reality, as opposed to set-up shots.

● *Is the photo historically significant?* Some rather ordinary photos in composition or impact, however, might have historical significance. A photo of a bricklayer placing the final brick in place on a private residence is hardly historically significant. But that same bricklayer placing the final brick on a multimillion dollar civic center is historically significant.

● *Can readers identify with the photo?* Even though striking school teachers in a city thousands of miles away might not seem relevant to local readers, if local school teachers are contemplating similar action, this type of photo might be identifiable to many readers who ordinarily would be little concerned with it.

● *Will the photo reproduce well?* Naturally, a certain percentage of pictorial quality is lost during the production process. Thus a photo of marginal quality to begin with will reproduce even more shabbily. Though, as mentioned earlier, photos of overriding importance will likely be published regardless of technical quality, this should not be the case with most photos. Editor Geladas tells his editors that, "Committing a bad photo to print is compounding the sin." Technically sound picturesque or feature photos, though they carry no hard news value or significance, can be among the best-received and effective photos a newspaper can publish.

In the final analysis, editors should strive to make their pages as attractive and informative as possible. Whether the communicative elements are hard news photos, stories, or feature photos, all should be selected to meet a specific communication goal; they should not be art for the sake of art.

Cropping Photos

Once photos have been selected for publication, they must be cropped. Cropping should not be done haphazardly; it is done, after all, to create greater reader interest in the photo, and there is a growing trend toward larger and more dramatic photos. Picture quality is often emphasized; it makes a paper look much more professional. Traditional thought on picture editing for newspapers has centered around cropping tightly—that is, eliminating all but the most essential parts of the photos. This general rule is still applicable in most situations. But tight cropping can be overdone. Selecting essential elements of a photo is highly subjective, and these essential elements can be overlooked by an editor bent on cropping to the bare bones.

Twenty years ago, when a lot of rules for cropping were being established, the standard equipment of many photographers was the 4″ x 5″ Speed Graphic camera. It was used primarily with a normal focal-length lens. Because of the size of the negative and partly because most photographers shot a little looser, most photos needed some cropping. Also, it was very practical technically since the editor or photographer had such a large negative to work with. Today, however, most photographers use 35mm cameras with an assortment of lenses. The negatives are much smaller. Thus, most photographers try to use as much of the negative area as feasible to keep the image quality as good as possible. Photographers are aided in this effort by different lenses (particularly telephotos) which enable them to get as close to a subject as they wish to fill the frame. In other words, today's photographers usually do quite a bit of "in-camera" cropping before a picture editor gets the photo—more so, anyway, than photographers twenty or more years ago were able to.

Photographer Tremain likens cropping concepts to the novelist who is allowed by his editors to write two or three pages of descriptive narrative about a character—the clothes he wears, the pipe he smokes, the odor of the pipe smoke, the chair he is sitting in, the pictures hanging on the far wall, and the smell coming from dirty clothes on the unmade bed next to him. The novelist is praised for vivid descriptions. On the other hand, a photographer can put most of the same information in a photograph, only to be met by some picture editors who cannot accept the photo unless everything but the man's face is cropped out.

A trite, awful phrase emerged in the late 1960s and 1970s which went something like this: "You know man, I've really got to have my own *space,* you know what I mean?" Though the person for whom the message is intended likely has only a vague idea about the intangible space being referred to, this space is more tangibly detected in photographic subjects who also are entitled to their space. The space a photographic subject has gives the viewer a frame of reference from which he can judge the main elements in a photo. Severe cropping can sometimes hurt a particular subject or communicative photographic element by removing the natural look or space. An example is a photo of a man with his head turned slightly—looking off to one direction. Though the first inclination of the editor might be to crop the head tightly and perfectly symetrically, it is a bit illogical that a person would be staring off at nothing. A person doesn't do this; he looks off into a particular space. Thus, by leaving in part of this space, cropping can achieve a more natural look and make the communicative element of the photo complete.

Among other things, cropping controls the size of the reproduced photo, and it controls the focal point of the photo. Necessary cropping tools for an editor include a grease pencil to mark in the white borders around the photo, L-shaped frames, and a pica pole. Though cropping guidelines are not etched in granite, the editor should carefully consider *why* he wants to crop a photo a particular way. The editor is, after all, attempting to improve the photo—not lighten its impact. Editors must take into consideration the way the picture is to be played. If it is to run as a one-column head shot, it is likely being used to communicate identification. Thus, it can be cropped rather loosely. If, however, the photo is designed to communicate the personality of the person—his wry grin or twinkling eyes—the photo must be cropped tighter for detail. The first step, then, in cropping a photo is to determine specifically what the picture should communicate to the reader. Once the editor decides this, he is ready to crop. Considerations here include:

● *Emphasize the heart of the photo.* In intensifying the important part of the photo, an editor might narrow the focal point or he might broaden it, bringing in fringe materials if they intensify the heart of the primary communicative element of the photo.

● *Eliminate distracting elements.* The editor should crop in essential points of the message the photo is trying to communicate and crop out distracting elements such as door knobs, poles, areas of dark space, foreground floors, or even printing mistakes such as scratched negatives. In other words, the editor can achieve the maximum pictorial impact by removing elements superfluous to the primary communicative element of the photo. The simpler the photographic image, the more impact it has. Less clutter makes it easier for readers' eyes to focus on the heart of the photo. However, the editor must watch for story-telling elements in the negative. More than one element may help tell the story. If more than one element is important, keep them in the cropping.

● *Don't crowd the image.* As does the character of the late 1960s and 1970s quoted above, the subject or heart of the photo deserves its rightful space.

● *Look for odd shapes.* Clever or unusual cropping, according to an Associated Press factbook, can "lift a picture out of the ordinary, if there is anything extraordinary in it." Not all pictures have to be reproduced in squares or rectangles. By cropping out a corner of distracting material in a rectangular photo, for example, the cutline could be inserted in the white space, thus creating a bold, unique look.

Sizing Photos

After an editor selects a photo for publication and crops it, he must size the picture, always keeping in mind the images in the photograph and ultimately how the photo will appear in the paper. Some photographs will look best if enlarged, others will look better if reduced. Handling a photo on the copy desk or picture desk is much like editing copy—it normally can be improved. Photo impact can be height-

Fig. 8–1. Cropping can alter the message a photograph communicates. For example, in the first photograph the intended message is that two die-hard football fans watch the closing seconds of a lopsided game after most of the thousands at Memorial Stadium on the University of Nebraska-Lincoln campus have exited. In the second cropped photograph, however, the intended message is that two football fans are concentrating intently on the action. (Photo courtesy of Professor George Tuck, University of Nebraska-Lincoln.)

ened by judicious cropping and intelligent sizing. Contemporary newspapers with their six-column formats and horizontal design (newspaper page design will be discussed in chapter 9) are tailor-made for bold, innovative photo displays. Though most earlier era newspapers routinely categorized photos as one-columns or two-columns, today's newspapers feature a steady diet of photos reproduced to widths of three columns and more. Of course the depth of photos grows correspondingly deeper. Fewer newspapers use postage stamp size photos today.

Common sense is a major ingredient in sizing photos. If the photo is of a tall water tower, for example, it would likely reproduce best as a deep, two-column, or possibly even a one-column. On the other hand, if the photo is of a city's skyline, a horizontal photo reproduced to a width of three to six columns would likely be most appropriate.

Once the editor selects, crops, and decides on a column width for a particular photo, he is ready to determine its reproduction size. Though this can be done mathematically, using a proportion wheel is the fastest and most efficient method. Proper use of the proportion wheel, though possibly confusing to the novice, soon becomes automatic. The proportion wheel is a kind of circular slide rule; when used properly, it tells the editor the finished dimensions of a reproduced photo.

Photos reproduced for publication are always in precise proportion to the cropped photos from which they are made. When the width of a photo is increased or decreased, the depth changes proportionately. Likewise, when the depth of a photo is increased or decreased, the width is altered proportionately. The important thing to remember when using the proportion wheel is that the inner wheel is the size of the originally cropped photo. The depth of the reproduced picture is generally the unknown number. To determine the reproduction size of a photo, the editor takes these steps:

1. He crops the photo.
2. He uses a pica pole to measure the width and depth of the cropped photo.
3. He decides the column width to which he wants to reproduce the photo in the paper.

Assume that he finds the cropped photo has a width of 37 picas and a depth of 42 picas. He feels this will make a good three-column photo. Three columns in a six-column newspaper whose columns are 14 picas wide would be 44 picas (14 plus 14 plus 14 plus 1 pica between the first and second columns, plus 1 pica between the second and third columns).

The editor sketches this equation:

	original crop		reproduction size
width	37	$\longleftrightarrow$	44
depth	$\overline{42}$	$\longleftrightarrow$	$\overline{X}$

By finding "X," the editor will know to what depth the photo will reproduce. To find X, the editor aligns the original crop width (37 picas) on the inside wheel with the reproduction width (44 picas) on the outside wheel. Then, without moving the wheel, he locates the original depth (42 picas) on the inside wheel. He determines what the 42 aligns with on the outside reproduction wheel. In this case, the 42 aligns with 50. Thus, X is 50 picas; the photo will reproduce to a width of 44 picas and a depth of 50 picas. By looking at the window on the inside of the proportion wheel, the editor notes that he has enlarged the photo to a size 119 percent of the original.

After the editor completes his computation, he marks the necessary figures on the back of the photo. Many newspapers have a sticker to attach which calls for essential information such as:

1. percent of the original;
2. finished size in picas;
3. slug line for the picture;
4. publication date;
5. page on which the photo is to be published.

Working with Wire Photos

Daily newspaper editors are not limited, in most instances, to selecting only staff-produced photos. They often rely extensively on either the Associated Press or United Press International for state, national, and international coverage. Some papers subscribe to both services. Both AP and UPI presently deliver dry prints to their members and subscribers. Each service uses a different means of photo production, though both are transmitted over telephone lines of a quality comparable to that used for private long-distance phone calls. Such lines are, of course, much more expensive than are the lower-grade lines used for movement of news copy. The reason is that any noise on the phone lines can affect the quality of the photos being transmitted. Thus, noise-free lines are essential. Such very low noise levels have little effect on transmission of text material.

The UPI photo system employs an electrostatic process, much like that used in a copying machine. The AP system employs a very low-power laser beam. In both cases, a transmitting device uses a light beam to convert the various tones in a given glossy photograph or drawing to sound tones. Those tones then move on the telephone line to a receiver which translates the tones back into light which is then printed on to photo paper in the receiving unit. The quality of today's wire service photos is far better than what was obtainable a few decades ago when photo transmissions via radio or telephone inaugurated the now far-flung photo networks of AP and UPI.

In a report prepared for the Associated Press Managing Editors Photo and Graphics Committee in 1979, Jenkin Jones, Jr., of the *Tulsa Tribune* wrote that "AP's worldwide photo network might be likened to an interconnecting series of spider webs, with New York the big daddy in the middle, able to feel the most distant tremor along the line." Jones points out, however, that New York does not make all the photo decisions. The domestic network, for example, spreads across the country. Regional controls include New York, Washington, Atlanta, Chicago, Dallas, Los Angeles, and Seattle. In addition, there are more than twenty-five state legs which handle either a single state or several states. The AP foreign desk has contacts in 110 countries, ranging from member arrangements to work with stringers and government agencies.

Jones stressed the importance of communication when working with wirephotos: "Good description is vital to smooth working of the Laserphoto net. Generally New York and its regional controls have to take a picture only on verbal descriptions. This requires realistic evaluation of a picture's merits at the sending point so a good picture gets proper exposure and a weak one doesn't clutter the wire." AP is able to move six pictures an hour, twenty-two and one-half hours a day except Sunday mornings. Ninety minutes each day are devoted to maintenance. It takes eight minutes to run a standard eight-inch by ten-inch picture on Laserphoto. There is an approximate two-minute break between photos.

In most cases, photos from the wire services can be handled in much the same manner as a glossy photo provided by a staff photographer on a newspaper. Wire service photos can be cropped, reduced, or enlarged without a great loss of quality. A photo from a state legislature committee hearing, for example, might have six persons in it, two of them from a newspaper's city of publication. The newspaper might be interested only in the two local persons for publications purposes. The wire service photo can be cropped and that portion showing the local residents can be enlarged.

AP's Buell is quick to emphasize that his organization can provide members with an abundance of services for relatively small fees. A paper can request pictures from the millions of negatives in AP's photo morgue or it can request photo coverage of local politicians at national or regional conventions.. The possibilities are almost unlimited. Thus, coordination between daily newspaper editors and the wire services when matching photos with stories can be just as important as coordination between editors and photographers within a newspaper.

Thanks to advisories transmitted by the wire services, newspaper editors can plan at the time they handle a story whether they will use art with it. If an editor knows that a photo will accompany a story, he can accordingly leave space on the page for the photo. On stories about individuals, editors frequently use only head shots, even if they must be severely cropped from an overall view provided by a wire service photo. This, too, can be planned in advance thanks to wire service advisories. Most daily newspaper editors also routinely file away wire service photos which they think they might have reason to use in the future.

As is the case with story coverage, editors have the option of calling on their state AP or UPI bureaus to arrange for specific photo coverage of events both in or outside of the state. The AP, for example, has approximately eighty staff photographers domestically and the same number abroad. They are supported by stringers, editors, darkroom technicians, and the like. It is apparent, however, that the AP depends heavily on its members.

Many individual newspapers have wire service transmitters for movement of photos either on the general news service photo wire or for movement by long-distance phone call, referred to as LD, to a specific point. This greatly increases the flexibility and usefulness of the news service network by increasing the accessibility of the network and enabling newspapers to receive special photos of interest only to them, but not of general network interest.

Editors can also cement the all-important relationship with their staff photographers by transmitting for state or possibly national use their best work. In addition to contributing to the general wire report, it can serve as a matter of pride for the newspaper and the photographer.

Writing Cutlines

Cutlines describe and explain a picture to the reader. Sometimes called captions, underlines, or legends, cutlines should help the editor and photographer communicate the intended meaning of the photo. Too often, cutlines are given little thought and slap-dash treatment by editors. Cutline writing, however, is not a task to be taken lightly. One researcher found, for example, that cutlines can alter the interpretation of pictures, particularly when the pictures themselves are ambiguous. Thus, a picture of two persons hugging would likely be interpreted as a "happy" picture if the cutline read, "At the station: reunion." On the other hand, if the cutline read, "At the station: parting," it would be interpreted as a "sad" picture. Jean Kerrick, in her study published in *Journalism Quarterly,* found that for the most part, "the influence of a caption can be anticipated by the writer." In a later study, Kerrick concluded that if both the picture and cutline are judged to be "happy," the combination will be judged "happier." In other words, when pictures and cutlines are similar in original meaning, added together, the elements "produce a more extreme judgment" by the reader. If, however, the picture and cutline are not similar in meaning (one happy, one sad), the "element meanings compete for dominance." This could confuse the reader and seriously impair the chances of the editor getting the reader to respond to the photo in the intended manner—unless, of course, he intended to frustrate the reader, and this isn't likely. Indeed, cutlines should be structured to convey the intended meaning of the photograph. The tone of the picture and the cutline should be consistent.

Cutline writing is far from routine. Describing each photo in a minimum of words challenges the most experienced editor. A synthesis of a variety of sources, including newspaper stylebooks, Associated Press Managing Editors Continuing Studies Committee recommendations, interviews with photo editors, and suggestions contained in various articles, results in these cutline writing guidelines—

● *The editor should have the picture in front of him when he writes the cutline.* Beware of including people in the cutline who have been cropped out. Likewise, make sure all the people pictured are identified.

● *Cutlines should be readable.* Make the cutline easy to read, with sentences that are short, descriptive, and to the point. Avoid cumbersome lead-in clauses. Don't say, "Preparing for a final history examination is history major Thomas Johnson as he labors hard over his notebook." Instead, merely say, "Thomas Johnson, a history major, studies for a final examination."

• *Cutlines should identify fully and clearly.* Though identification procedures will vary from newspaper to newspaper, people are generally shown by correct title and position. Be sure that the negative does not get reversed, thus causing a discrepancy in identification. Check spellings of names and occupations in a city directory or other available source.

• *Cutlines should tell where the picture was taken.* Though this is a fundamental rule, busy deskmen often overlook location. This can frustrate the reader.

• *Cutlines should tell when the picture was taken.* Be honest with the reader if the photo is not current. If, without warning, a community gets an early snow, an editor might choose to run a file photo from a snow the year before—particularly if deadline time is at hand. This is fine so long as the cutline explains it is a file photo.

• *Avoid using "is pictured" or "is shown."* Terminology such as this is an insult to the intelligence of the reader who is capable of realizing it is a photo. Also, avoid using "pictured above" or "shown above." If the cutline is beneath the photo, obviously the scene being described is above it.

• *Avoid clash of tense.* Use the present tense for action, but don't mix tenses in the same sentence. Do not for example, write, "Joe Blow *hits* a 10-foot jump shot in *last week's* home game." Blow should not be hitting a jump shot in the present tense in last week's past tense game—at least not in the same sentence. A clash of tenses can be avoided by writing, "Joe Blow hit a 10-foot jump shot in last week's home game." Or, better still, the cutline could contain two sentences. "Joe Blow hits a 10-foot jump shot. The shot came in last week's home game."

• *Be accurate.* Double check all information. It is particularly important, for example, to update information in cutlines for photos which accompany developing stories. Death tolls in airline crashes, for instance, are constantly revised. Don't be caught in the embarrassing position of having the story give one figure and the cutline give another.

• *Don't repeat information in the cutline that is in the story.* If a photo is coordinated with a story, tell only essential information about the action in the photo. Cutlines for photos which accompany stories will be noticeably shorter than cutlines for photos which stand alone.

● *When identifying people, make it "from left," not "from left to right."* And, if John Jones and Sally Smith are pictured, it is not necessary to say, "John Jones, left." If one of the persons is clearly a male, further identification is not necessary.

● *Explain any background material or unusual objects in the picture.* If these objects cannot be cropped out or are included to communicate a particular message, don't puzzle the reader with their presence, explain it.

● *Avoid describing self-evident action.* If the individual is smiling broadly, it will be obvious to the reader. Or, if the man is sitting behind a desk or a boy is riding a bicycle, don't hit the reader over the head with this information. On the other hand, if the action is not self-evident, it should be explained. If a senator is shown glancing through a government report, the subject of the report should be included in the cutline.

● *Avoid libel.* Libel suits can be brought as the result of cutlines as well as stories or headlines. Thus, it is important to double check identifications, particularly if the photo centers on suspects in criminal activities. The writer must also be careful to avoid referring to the individual as an "alleged murderer" or whatever. Words like "alleged" and "accused" describe the act—not the man.

● *Cutlines should fit the tone of the photo.* Just as copy editors should not write frivolous, clever headlines over hard news stories, cutlines should match the photo in tone. If it is a feature photo, the cutline can be light and airy. If, however, the photo deals with a tragedy, like a traffic fatality, the cutline should give only the facts in a straightforward manner.

● *Cutlines should emphasize the action in the photo.* They should not center upon background information. For example, if a soldier who had been a prisoner of war is shown getting off an airplane, the cutline should emphasize the immediate action. "John Jones, prisoner of war for three years, arrives at Los Angeles International Airport." After the immediate action is portrayed, the writer can give background information. The cutline should not, however, lead with the background: "John Jones was a prisoner of war for three years. After diplomatic negotiations involving several key government officials, he was released today. Jones arrives at Los Angeles International Airport."

• *Avoid overuse of adjectives or editorial observations.* Copy editors can be as descriptive as possible, but they should avoid invading an area where the reader can exercise his own judgment. Let the reader judge whether the girl in the, photo is glamorous, quizzical, depressed, or elated.

After cutlines are written, the source of the photo generally is noted. Though the practice varies, most newspapers carry agate credit lines under each photo, with the general exception of head shots. New staffers should check the stylebooks of their newspapers. At the *Miami Herald,* for example, there is an agate credit line distinction made between photos by full-time *Herald* staff photographers and photos by bureau personnel, part-time photographers, or free lancers. For full-time photographers, the *Herald* uses: —Herald Staff Photo by John Smith. For non-full-time staff photographers, the *Herald* uses —Herald Photo by John Smith. For Wirephotos, the *Herald* uses: —Associated Press Laserphoto; or —United Press International Telephoto. The *Washington Post* uses a similar, but slightly different method. For example, the *Post* handles all photos taken by reporters, editors, full-time photographers, news aides, and copy aides like this: By John Smith—Washington Post. Stringer and special photos made at The *Post*'s request are credited like this: By John Smith for The Washington Post. AP or UPI photos carry an agate credit line: Associated Press or United Press International.

No matter what the credit line procedure, editors must always stay within the suggestions for good cutline writing. Many times this is complicated by the fact that the editor is dependent upon information supplied to him by another source, generally a photographer. As a result, Louisville *Courier-Journal* and *Times* director of photography Hardin instills in his photographers a sense of responsibility to get correct and complete information for the editor who writes the cutlines. Again, a solid working relationship or rapport between editors and photographers can be beneficial. Hardin instructs his photographers to always get complete information because they can never be sure how much the editor will want to use. If, for example, the photographer takes a routine springtime photo of a man playing with his dog in a city park, the photographer gets not only the name of the man, but also the name of the dog, the kind of dog, the name of the park, why the man and dog are in the park, whether they visit the park often, and so on. In other words, photographers should be mandated to get complete and accurate information. The editor is then in a better position to judge what is essential information.

Writing cutlines for Wirephotos is a simpler process. Complete information is generally provided. If questions still remain, the editor can call his state bureau. Information for a wire service photo includes a dateline, date, brief two-to-four-word capsule (overline) of what the photo is, and then a one-paragraph piece of information detailing facts about the picture, such as what it shows and who the subjects within the picture are. Similar information appears on various charts, graphs, or cartoon artwork provided on wire service networks.

Each wire service photo transmission has a number, much like the number contained on wire service stories. (Wire service filing procedures are discussed in chapter 11.) However, photo numbers are not likely to be consecutive, unless by chance a given location transmits two or more photos in succession on the photo network. The AP numbering system, for example, consists of two or three letters, followed by a number, as the first bit of written information on the cutline. The letters and numeral are the photo's call letters. The letters stand for the AP bureau, and the numeral stands for the number of the photo transmitted from a particular bureau that particular day. Two-letter designations indicate the photo was transmitted from a bureau location. Three-letter designations followed by a number indicate that the photo was transmitted from a non-bureau location, usually from a member transmitter or from a remote location where the AP may have set up a temporary transmitter for a specific news event. An example would be NPT2, which would signify the second photo of the day transmitted from the *North Platte* (Neb.) *Telegraph*.

The AP Laserphoto cutline in Figure 8–2 tells the editor it is the first photo of the day moved from Trenton, N.J., (TN1). The name and state of the city where the picture was made is next (TRENTON, N.J.), followed by the date (MARCH 14). EINSTEIN'S DAUGHTER CELEBRATES is the overline. Information about the picture follows. After explanatory information about the action in the photo comes the credit line (AP LASERPHOTO). Next, SEE AP WIRESTORY tells the editor a story accompanies the photo. The last bit of parenthetical information (jsk41300stf-kanthal) tells the editor the initials of the individual who wrote the cutline (jsk); the day and time the cutline was written on a twenty-four-hour clock (in this case the 4 is for Wednesday, the fourth day of the week, and the 1300 means it was one o'clock in the afternoon); and the final set of letters (stf-kanthal) provides the source of the picture (staff) and the photographer's name or initials (kanthal). For library reference, 1979 is the year of the transmission.

```
(TN1)TRENTON, N.J., MARCH 14--EINSTEIN'S DAUGHTER CELEBRATES--Margot
Einstein, the 79-year-old daughter of famous physicist Albert
Einstein smiles in Trenton, N.J. Wednesday on the 100th birthday of
her father.  Miss Einstein recalled her father as a warm and gentle
person.(AP LASERPHOTO)(SEE AP WIRESTORY)(jsk41300stf-kanthal)1979
```

Fig. 8–2. Associated Press Laserphoto cutline. (Courtesy of
The Associated Press.)

When writing cutlines for wire photos, editors must still be careful to stay within the guidelines. Clash of tense and other mistakes can occur within wire service cutlines. Editors should be particularly conscious of including *where* the picture was taken. Though the Trenton example includes the site of the photo, oftentimes this information is not repeated in the cutline since wire service photos generally have datelines. Few newspapers use datelines on photos; thus, editors must be certain that this essential information is included in the cutline.

As is the case with credit lines, newspaper style on cutline formats varies widely. In fact, there are nearly as many cutline formats as there are daily newspapers. A sampling is presented in Fig. 8–3.

Working with Picture Pages

Picture pages have traditionally been a part of American daily newspapers. In fact, they continue to be a regular feature for many publications. Picture pages take various forms—the entire page might be devoted to pictures; copy and pictures might be mixed; the page might be composed of a hodgepodge of photo leftovers on various unrelated subjects; or, as is today's trend, the page might feature photos which communicate a particular message. The page might center on an individual, an event, or a general theme. No matter what the subject, today's best picture pages convey a message in a way more effective than words. For example, a newspaper might decide to depict small-town living in Upland, Nebraska (population 200). An editor could assign a reporter to interview its residents, or he could conclude the best way to capture the spirit of the village

Antique car inspected

Mr. and Mrs. William Morgan of Athens gave this 1929 Ford Model "A" roadster a thorough inspection Friday. The old car is one of more than 250 autos up for auction at the Fourth Annual Detroit-Lansing Collector Car Auction at Long's Convention Center today. The bidding starts at 9 a.m.

1 Dies, 6 Hurt Firemen and fellow construction workers try to help workmen hurt Friday on a highway project in Beaumont, Texas. One man was killed and six were injured when they fell 30 feet when a make-shift ladder beside a bridge apparently collapsed. The workers were building wooden concrete molds during work to widen the bridge from two to four lanes. They fell onto an unused portion of Interstate 10 beneath the bridge.

Watch this!

Jamie Morse, 4, demonstrates his under-the-leg Frisbee toss at Water Works Park here recently. He is the son of James and Marjorie Morse of Ankeny. Temperatures climbed into the 70s in Des Moines Monday.

Fig. 8–3. Newspaper cutlines take various forms: "Antique car" (courtesy of *The State Journal,* Lansing, Mich.); "1 dies" (courtesy of the *Oklahoma City Oklahoman & Times);* "Watch this!" (courtesy of the *Des Moines* (Iowa) *Register*).

would not be through extensive interviews and a series of stories, but rather through photos. What comprises small town living in Upland? Church socials, town team baseball, girls' softball, farmers bringing their crops to the elevator, community pride in the accomplishments of school children, alumni banquets, community dances, horseback riding, and informal conversations and card games at the local cafe or tavern are possibilities. Most likely, a series of photos would convey these scenes—would communicate what small town living entails —better than words would.

In addition to effective communication, picture pages can be morale builders for newspaper staffers. Picture pages involve both photographers and editors. The pages give photographers a forum to display their work. Also, well-conceived pages provide a showcase and pull readers to them. Several ingredients go into attractive, effective picture pages. First of all, an editor and photographer should have an ample selection of photos to choose from. Six or seven photos should be chosen from a sampling that could be four to six times that number. Once the staffers determine the photos which best communicate the intended message, the page can be designed.

Suggestions for good pages include:

1. Select a dominant photo. This will be the focal point of the page. Possibly it could be placed in the upper left corner.

2. Arrange the remaining photos in an order which best tells the story. Like a carefully written research paper, a picture page should have the communicative equivalent of an introduction, a body, a summary, and a conclusion. It is wise to experiment with the order and placement of photos. Move them around until the best combination is found.

3. Experiment with horizontal and vertical design for each picture. Be certain to develop variety in photo sizes and shapes. Some photos will be horizontal and shallow; others will be vertical and deep; still others might be innovatively cropped into odd, unique shapes.

4. Limit the number of photos to six or preferably fewer. In fact, some editors follow a common practice of eliminating one additional photo after they feel they have the right number.

5. Make sure there is ample white space, but be careful not to trap the white space between photos. Strive to give the page a light, airy, white appearance.

6. Keep cutlines brief, communicate only essential details. Don't repeat information that is given under another photo.

7. If a headline is called for, place it where it aids in the communication process. Also, an editor can use typefaces not normally used for headlines.

Obviously, one cannot design an effective picture page by the numbers, but these are factors that editors should consider. Each photo should be an important link in the intended communication; it should not repeat similar information, just as cutlines should not duplicate facts. The ultimate goal is to develop a communicative element that is organized so that the total page exudes a sense of unity and harmony.

Photos and the Law

Editors who work with and supervise photographers and their works are touched by the law in several areas. Though the role of the editor when legal issues arise is discussed in more detail in chapter 12, attention is given here to the rights to gather photos and how libel and privacy concerns affect the photographer and picture editor. Editors should also keep in mind that when legal actions arise over photos, the defenses discussed in chapter 12 are available just as they are for suits evolving from the printed word.

The photographer is generally free to perform his duties in public places such as at athletic events, in city streets, and so on. In 1972, a federal district court in Minnesota said that photographers should be allowed to film public proceedings—in this case the arrest by law enforcement officials of suspected burglars—so long as they did not interfere with police duties. In some public places like courtrooms, however, access by photographers is limited.

Though photographers can normally carry out their assignments in public places, there is a limit. This was vividly illustrated in a case involving free-lance photographer Ronald Galella and Jacqueline Kennedy Onassis. In 1973, the Second U.S. Circuit Court of Appeals rejected Galella's claim that the First Amendment serves as a wall of immunity protecting newsmen from any liability for their conduct while gathering news. The *Galella* case is a classic. Galella sued three Secret Service agents for false arrest, malicious prosecution, and interference with his trade. The agents, however, were responsible for insuring the safety of Mrs. Onassis. Mrs. Onassis, in turn, filed a counterclaim, seeking to enjoin Galella from harassing her or her children. The court noted that Galella fancied himself as a *paparazzo*—a kind of annoying insect. Galella said he liked to make himself visible to the public to aid in advertising his works. Actor Marlon Brando once reacted a bit more strongly to the photographer's tactics than did Mrs. Onassis. He reportedly broke Galella's jaw during an altercation. At any rate, Galella did repeatedly thrust himself into the lives of Mrs. Onassis and her children. He once jumped into young John Kennedy's path when the youth was riding his bicycle; he interrupted Mrs. Onassis's daughter Caroline at tennis; and he invaded the children's private school. Once he came "uncomfortably close in a power boat" while Mrs. Onassis was swimming. He admittedly bribed apartment house, restaurant, and nightclub doormen to keep him advised of movements of the family—public and private.

The appeals court upheld the grant of summary judgment and dismissal of Galella's claim against the Secret Service agents and supported the lower court's findings that the photographer was guilty of harassment, intentional infliction of emotional distress, assault and battery, commercial exploitation of Mrs. Onassis' personality, and invasion of privacy. The appeals court modified the injunction against Galella. The photographer was, however, prohibited any approach within twenty-five feet of Mrs. Onassis; prohibited from any blocking of her movement in public places and thoroughfares; prohibited any act foreseeably or reasonably calculated to place her life and safety in jeopardy; and prohibited any conduct which would reasonably be foreseen to harass, alarm, or frighten her. In addition, Galella was enjoined from entering the children's schools or play areas; from engaging in action which would place their safety in jeopardy; from harassing, alarming or frightening the children; and from approaching within thirty feet of them.

Clearly, then, photographers have a right to perform their tasks in public places—subject, of course, to the law and responsible regard for common sense and decency. Once pictures are taken, however, editors must handle them carefully. Libel and privacy suits can evolve from photos and cutlines, just as from publication of a story. Cutlines are a primary source of libel dangers. The AP warns that "misidentifications, misrepresentations of the situations in which pictures were taken, or misrepresentations of what the pictures actually show, can cause trouble."

Intrusion into private domains can often prove legally dangerous for the photographer, unless he obtains permission. This is why photographers should sometimes ask subjects to sign release forms. To insure validity, these forms should be carefully worded and checked by the newspaper's attorneys. Also, some institutions such as state hospitals, mental retardation centers, and the like have release forms on file which have been signed by the patients or their parents, allowing photos to be published under certain conditions. These release forms, too, should be cleared with a newspaper's attorney if there is any doubt of their legality.

In essence, then, photographers and editors must exercise sound judgments when considering methods to take photos and when determining what photos will be published. Release forms can provide a certain protection to newspaper staffers if the releases are carefully written and checked by responsible attorneys—but the releases should not be abused. Newspaper editors and photographers should not purposely attempt to invade the subject's privacy or to make the subject look foolish. When this happens, legal action could result.

Chapter 9

Newspaper Page Design

P AGE DESIGN IS an important function at any newspaper. Readers are more likely to be drawn to an easy-to-read, comfortable page than to a cluttered collage of pictures, stories, and headlines. Attractive pages do not instantly materialize; they take planning. Skilled editors must carefully blend available stories, art work, and headlines into a total page concept.

Good design is not a luxury to a newspaper—it is a necessity. A muddled, confusing page will frustrate the reader. The process of deciding where to position stories and art is often referred to as laying out or making up. An editor, utilizing a dummy sheet, puts a page together story by story and picture by picture until all space is filled. Design is the final form or structure of the page; it is the finished product. Thus, editors should constantly envision the completed page when laying it out element by element. Well-conceived design helps readers—it simply makes newspapers easier to read.

James A. Geladas, managing editor of the Dubuque (Iowa) *Telegraph Herald,* an award-winning daily, instructs his editors to consider six key words when designing a page—simplicity, balance, dominance, variety, unity, and harmony. Geladas emphasizes the importance of well-designed pages:

> Good typography enhances copy and pictures, forging the mix of words, images and graphics into a cohesive, coherent, purposeful

whole. Typography adds a dimension of meaning and interpretation that aids understanding. No longer is typography the sprinkles on the cupcake—mere decoration, or the path of least resistance—but it's an important catalyst that makes our product meaningful. By glancing at a page, the reader should be able to tell instantly what picture goes with what article or what articles are related. Confusing typography wastes the reader's time and frustrates him, giving him a good reason to throw down the newspaper.

Geladas describes typography as "a tone of voice which shouts when it should and whispers when it should, and has the capability of all the inflections and nuances of the spoken word."

Attractive, yet meaningful, page design is receiving more attention than ever before. No longer is it something that editors let the composing room personnel do with as they want. The graphics stylebook of the *Cincinnati Enquirer* emphasizes that newspaper design is important because "the way the stories are arranged and the devices used to bring them together tell readers almost as much about what kind of paper they are reading as the content of the stories."

Design should be consistent; though no two pages of the same paper look exactly the same from day-to-day, the design philosophy —personality, if you will—of the newspaper should be apparent. It is, after all, the design or appearance of a newspaper that allows readers to recognize it on a newsrack filled with other publications. The *Cincinnati Enquirer* editors firmly believe that good design makes a newspaper easier to read; it entices readers into the paper and keeps them there. Well-designed pages draw readers naturally and easily from one story to another, allowing them to discover quickly what interests them.

Indeed, the primary aim of good design is to help the reader, to make it convenient for him to absorb the newspaper's contents. Merv Hendricks, managing editor of the award-winning *Wabash* (Indiana) *Plain Dealer,* likens good design to a road map—it unobtrusively guides the reader without the reader knowing he is receiving the message. Robert H. Spiegel, editor of the *Wisconsin State-Journal,* also adheres to the philosophy that newspaper design should help readers. He feels pages should be clean, uncomplicated, and without gimmicks. "Don't make readers choose this story or that," he says. "Make it easy for them to read both. Above all, keep it simple."

Simple, clean design is the thread that ties together the philosophies of award-winning newspapers. Phil Marty, managing editor of the

Cherokee (Iowa) *Daily Times,* claims that, "It doesn't have to be fancy to be good. Sometimes it's fun to play around with boxes and rules and fancy type, but as a general rule, I keep it simple and stay away from the 'circusy' stuff."

James R. Brown, managing editor of the *Sandusky* (Ohio) *Register,* puts the emphasis on design in perspective: "Our visually oriented world demands something to look at. If we don't give it to them, they will yawn and let our product slip through their fingers to the floor and eventually the bottom of the parakeet cage."

One of the country's foremost typography experts, Professor Edmund C. Arnold, feels that attractive design and good typography get the reader through the first three paragraphs of a story—but it is up to the writer and editor to get the reader through the remainder of the story. Indeed, attractive design greatly enhances good writing; it tempts the subscriber to read a story. But, not even the best-designed newspapers will be read if news content is sorely lacking. The key is to combine good news content with attractive design. They do not have to be mutually exclusive. Today's award-winning newspapers in design competition bristle with excitement. Their dynamic, clean appearances figuratively beg to be read.

Suggestions for Effective Design

Attractive page design can be facilitated by incorporating some of the following suggestions:

● *Keep it simple.* Attractive pages are easy to read. Their clean, wide-open appearance is in contrast to newspapers that crowd a dozen or more elements (art work and stories) onto a single page, that persist in using small, poorly cropped photographs and that use obtrusive ornamental devices such as gaudy stars and extra bold borders.

● *Make it readable.* Headline styles and sizes and body type should be selected with readability in mind. Type that is difficult to read is not conducive to clean design. Crowded stories and tightly spaced body type create masses of grayness that often discourage readers from burrowing into the page to see what is there. The bland grayness is simply too much for the tired reader to overcome.

● *Keep the design functional.* Every design element, whether it be a special headline, a border, a tightly cropped picture, or a map, should have a specific function or purpose; elements should not be used simply for the sake of ornamentation. All design elements should aid the reader.

● *Use six-column formats.* Most prize-winning newspapers in design or typography competition have six-column formats with column widths ranging between 13.5 and 14.5 picas. Some papers have only five-column formats with the columns correspondingly wider. Six-column newspapers, with no column rules and ample white space between columns, have an air of readability—an openness—that most eight-column or nine-column newspapers do not possess.

● *Eliminate column rules.* Though most newspapers fifteen or twenty years ago had column rules, today's award-winning publications have eliminated them, for the most part. The late William L. White's *Emporia* (Kan.) *Gazette* was one of the first to eliminate column rules throughout the paper. Some newspapers had already experimented by eliminating column rules on the women's and sports pages to achieve more readability. But it was White who decided to eliminate them throughout the paper. He reasoned: "If it was more readable [for certain sections of the paper] why not on page one as well? Didn't the publisher also want these pages read?"

● *Use boxes and borders.* Borders are used to attract attention—to set certain elements such as pictures or stories off from the rest of the page. Also, borders can be used around a series of articles or pictures to tie them together in a neat package for the reader. Borders should not, however, be used simply for the sake of using them; the boxed material should be worthy, and the border should enhance the appearance of the page. The standard box uses a two-point rule and has square corners; some corners, however, are rounded. Good makeup should allow two picas of white space between the copy and the border—copy should not be jammed against the border. Also, one must be careful not to use too many borders on the same page—it is disastrous if they run into each other. One is usually sufficient. Likewise, bordered stories should not be placed adjacent to advertisements that have been boxed. Borders are considered art work; competing art work (two bordered elements) is distracting, not aesthetic.

● *Use wide-measure type.* The grayness of a page can be broken up by using wide-measure type. For example, if a newspaper's normal column width is 14 picas, a story could be set 26 picas. The story should not be set the full 28 picas; by setting it two picas less, the white space enhances its appearance and breaks up the standard format. Or, a story could be set 20 picas to fill a three-column hole. Again, as was the case with boxed stories, the makeup editor should be careful not to overuse wide measure stories. Sparingly used, wide

Peace Corps chief loses her job

WASHINGTON (AP) — Former Peace Corps director Carolyn R. Payton feuded with her boss for months over what type Americans the volunteer agency should be sending abroad.

She even made an indirect appeal to President Carter, who appointed her, to help her stay on the job.

But she's out today and her boss, ACTION director Sam Brown, also appointed by Carter, is still in.

As late as Thursday, Ms. Payton was reacting to reports of her impending departure by saying: "I have not resigned, nor do I wish to resign." Her top aide said Ms. Payton assumed that if Carter were dissatisfied with her he would ask her to resign.

One day later, she wrote the president: "I deeply regret that I am required to offer you my resignation . . . effective immediately."

Ms. Payton, who headed the Peace Corps for 13 months, said she had not succeeded in her job, "in part because of conditions which had arisen before you or I took office and in part because there have been deep differences between the ACTION administration and the Peace Corps."

One of the higher-ranking blacks in the Carter administration, Ms. Payton, 53, said her irreconcilable differences with Brown was an "issue of substance about the Peace Corps and not one of my sex, color or age."

In a statement accepting her resignation Friday evening, Carter said: "I have come to the conclusion that there are unresolvable differences" between Ms. Payton and Brown. Carter said the action in no way reflected on Ms. Payton's "competence, integrity or sincerity" and thanked her "for the good service she has rendered."

Brown said simply, "I appreciate the contributions that Dr. Payton has made to the Peace Corps."

Sources in the Peace Corps said Brown went to the White House Wednesday and asked President Carter for permission to dismiss Ms. Payton, a presidential appointee. The sources, who declined to be identified, said she had been under pressure from Brown to quit for some time.

Ms. Payton is a psychologist and former director of counseling services at Howard University here.

Elimination of utilities tax urged

LINCOLN (AP) — Business doesn't have to pay sales tax on utilities in Nebraska but homeowners do and the result is a "terribly unfair" tax that works a hardship on young families, the poor and the elderly, Sen. Bernice Labedz of Omaha told the Revenue Committee Tuesday.

Mrs. Labedz urged committee support of her LB144, which would give homeowners the same exemptions given now to industrial, commercial and agricultural operations. It exempts residential consumers from the sales tax on electricity and natural gas and other energy sources and exempts the sales and purchases of water and sewer services from the sales tax.

If enacted, the additional exemptions would cost the state $13.8 million in sales

tax. Omaha would lose $2.1 million and Lincoln would lose $550,000.

The measure has the "complete and unqualified support" of the Omaha Public Power District, said OPPD Board member John Munnelly.

"The only argument against LB144 is that the state and several cities will lose revenue," Mrs. Labedz said. "However, that revenue can be replaced in many ways, while there is only one way to correct the injustice of Nebraska's present utilities sales tax policy."

Sen. Neil Simon of Omaha, co-sponsor of the bill with Labedz and Omaha Sen. Carol Pirsch, called the levy "the most unfair tax we have in Nebraska today."

Nineteen states provide some relief from the tax and 17 don't tax residential

consumers of gas and electricity. Four of those tax business only, Mrs. Labedz said. Only 12 other states tax residents and not businesses, as does Nebraska.

Committee chairman Cal Carsten of Avoca asked Mrs. Labedz why she hadn't brought up the issue before. She responded that last year she presented a bill providing an additional $10 million in homestead exemptions, and she didn't think she could have repealed the sales tax on utilities at the same time.

Only Kansas and Indiana, like Nebraska, tax residential water use while not taxing water use for manufacturing or irrigation.

She said Omaha Mayor Al Veys told her the city could tolerate elimination of the

sales tax on food or on utilities, but not both. Carsten said, "I can't believe what I'm hearing," because the city wants an extension of its one-half percent sales tax.

Mrs. Labedz said the extension would allow elimination of the utilities tax.

When the 1967 Legislature approved the tax, she said, it had no way of knowing inflation would send utility costs soaring, and thus the tax would create an increasing burden to the poor, the elderly and others.

She, Simon and Mrs. Pirsch joined Munnelly, OPPD board member Mary Alice Race and Ruth Blankenship of the Commission on Aging, in arguing that it is simply unfair to allow all commercial and industrial interests to escape the tax, while placing it on homeowners.

Fig. 9–1. Borders can set one story off from another, serving a functional and an aesthetic purpose. (Courtesy of the *Hastings* (Neb.) *Daily Tribune*.)

measure columns call attention to the story; thus, the article should be worthy of the emphasis.

● *Use white space.* White space enlivens a page when properly used; it reduces clutter and adds appeal. On the other hand, Dubuque *Telegraph Herald* managing editor Geladas warns that "Improperly used white space can ruin the page's cohesion, making the layout fall apart. The rule is: Keep the white space to the outside of the typographical elements; don't trap it." One easy, yet functional, way to achieve white space is to lay out three columns of regular width type in a space designed for four columns. Or, one could lay out five columns of regular width columns in a space designed for six columns. This is sometimes referred to as "one-up" makeup.

● *Use blurbs.* Blurbs have high readership. They break up the story and page. But don't waste the reader's time with "so-what" unimportant extracts from the main story. Blurbs should be at least 14 points and should contrast with the headline type. If the headline is italic,

Record crops forecast
by agriculture board

WASHINGTON (AP) — U.S. farmers and what Howard Hjort used to refer to as "the weather gods" are doing it again.

The Agriculture Department's Crop Reporting Board toted up the results so far of this year's growing season:

— A record crop of 7,108,938,000 bushels of corn, 27 million more than last year's once-unthinkable 7.08 billion. A mere 6.66 billion was forecast a month ago. This year's crops average out to a record 102.1 bushels per acre.

— A record crop of 2.13 billion bushels of soybeans, 16 percent more than were harvested last season.

— A record crop of 136.7 million hundredweight of rice. That's 2 percent more than 1978, when the board said, 133.8 million were harvested instead of the 137.8 million previously reported.

— Record wheat yields of 34.3 bushels an acre for all types and 36.9 bushels for winter wheat, making the all-wheat harvest of an expected 2.13 billion bushels the second-largest ever. An improved winter wheat harvest of 1.6 billion bushels is nearly over.

— A record peanut crop of 4.06 billion pounds despite relatively lower supports.

— And, perhaps most important for some, a record grape crop of 4.83 million tons. Raisins should be easier to find in supermarkets now, with crops 15 percent larger. The vines of wine grapes are producing a record 1.8 million tons in California.

Later, Hjort, chief USDA economist and policy analyst, faced reporters with this deadpan comment, "I believe we will clearly have a lot of corn available."

He said that because record exports also are in the offing, the huge supplies may have little effect on farm prices and income and food prices.

Hjort did say that the chances for continued federal attempts at controlling feedgrain acreage have now risen from zero. They have been lifted for the 1979 crop of wheat.

Last year, he would repeatedly cite "the weather gods" as the ultimate farm-policymaker. He didn't mention them this time — or Secretary Bob Bergland's frequent warnings that the odds are against this fifth consecutive bumper grain crop.

In a separate report USDA held to its estimate that the Soviet Union's total 1979 grain harvest would be 185 million metric tons, down 22 percent from last year's record 237.2 million.

The board's first estimate of production of grain sorghum, was 779 million bushels, up 4 percent from 1978, while its initial forecast of the cotton crop indicated 13.7 million bales, up 26 percent.

Trying to gauge the farm economy as a whole the board put its "all-crop" index at a record 37 percent higher than the 1967 benchmark of 100. The new figure is 6 points above last year.

Record foodgrain and oilseed crops, plus cotton's sharp advance, are responsible, the board said.

In a third report, USDA said world grain production now is seen at 1.51 billion metric tons, a drop of 4 percent but still the second-largest ever.

Pork to be purchased
for lunches in schools

WASHINGTON (AP) — Hog farmers, who have seen their market prices plummet this year, may get at least a psychological boost by an Agriculture Department decision to buy pork for this fall's school lunch program.

More poultry also will be bought than in previous years in an effort to trim costs of buying more expensive beef, mostly in the form of hamburger, for the school lunch program.

Assistant Secretary Carol Tucker Foreman said Thursday the purchases of canned pork will be the first by USDA in significant quantity in at least five years. Records show the last substantial pork purchases were in 1974-75.

Last April, the Council on Wage and Price Stability told Agriculture, the Defense Department and the Veterans Administration to reduce beef purchases as a way of fighting inflation and to buy more less-expensive pork and poultry.

Ms Foreman told a reporter that the pork buying for schools is primarily a result of the White House order.

"We are seeking ways to avoid reducing (total) meat purchases and still stay within our budget, and we will be reducing beef," she said.

Noting that meat prices, including those paid by USDA for school donations, have climbed sharply the last couple of years,

Ms. Foreman said pork is a relative bargain right now.

Cattle prices have dipped this summer from their peaks of last spring, but hog prices at the farm have declined even more sharply.

The department also is buying ground beef for schools, beginning with purchases announced on Aug. 16. Those will continue until enough is bought under the reduced program for the 1979-80 school year.

Last year, ground beef purchases totaled 80.6 million pounds at an average wholesale cost to USDA of about $1.16 a pound. Previously, in 1977-78, ground beef for schools totaled 93.9 million pounds at an average of 72 cents a pound.

So far in the current program, about 4 million pounds have been purchased at an average cost of $1.19 a pound, with some as high as $1.26 a pound in the most recent weekly orders.

The meat is offered by processors under bids, and USDA has rejected many of the offerings because of prices being too high. In the latest bids, for example, a top of $1.42 a pound was rejected.

About 26 million children regularly eat in cafeterias in the 94,000 schools that participate in the program. The donated commodities from USDA are in addition to federal and state money that is allocated to help schools operate their meal programs.

Fig. 9–2. The top story, set two columns wide, breaks up standard one-column widths. (Courtesy of the *Hastings* (Neb.) *Daily Tribune*.)

FTC charges defect kept a secret

WASHINGTON (AP) — Ford Motor Company manufactured up to 1.8 million cars from 1974 to 1978 with a costly engine defect, then kept the problem from consumers even after learning of it, the Federal Trade Commission staff charges.

The allegation is in a document filed without public announcement this week in a case the FTC previously launched against Ford.

The staff charge that improper lubrication of the camshaft can cause premature wear to it and to the rocker arm assembly makes no allegation that the potential problem is a safety defect.

However, it said the estimated cost of repairs, if paid for by the car owner, would be $226.

The staff said the premature wear, which could lead to more serious engine problems, occurs in many of the 1.8 million Ford Motor Co. vehicles with four-cylinder 2.3-liter engines manufactured in the five model years. This is one of Ford's most popular engines, used in such cars as the Pinto, Mustang, Capri and Bobcat.

"Vehicles have been failing as early as the first 163 miles of service" because of the camshaft-rocker arm problem, said the document, filed by lawyers for the FTC's consumer protection bureau. "The defect substantially affects the durability, reliability or performance of affected vehicles," it said.

The document urges the five-member commission to authorize a federal suit to seek an immediate injunction forcing the company to notify owners of cars that may have the alleged defect.

George Trainor, spokesman for Ford's parts and service division, said in a telephone interview, "Our position is that the whole subject of what we refer to as the company's 'good will program' is now a matter of litigation with the FTC and it would be inappropriate for us to discuss any facet at the moment."

The FTC staff alleged that Ford knew of the problem at least by 1976. It does not say what, if anything, Ford did to correct the problem after it learned of it or how many engines were manufactured after the problem became known to the company.

After realizing the problem, the company did tell Ford dealers to repair affected cars at no charge, but many dealers still did not perform the work because they spent more in doing the repairs than they could recover from the manufacturer, the staff said.

Normally, a new-car warranty extends for 12,000 miles or 12 months, but the manufacturer told dealers to do repairs on cars with the problem up to 36,000 miles or 36 months, the staff said.

Egypt offering treaty concessions

JERUSALEM (AP) — Egypt is offering two concessions in exchange for Israeli acceptance of a timetable for Palestinian self-rule in the Gaza Strip and the West Bank of the Jordan River, the Jerusalem Post's Cairo correspondent reported today.

The report said Egypt is prepared to extend by three months the deadline for Israel's preliminary withdrawal from the Sinai and also is willing to join Israel in formulating a peace treaty provision that would "insure against any collapse of the treaty in case the autonomy plan for the West Bank proves objectively impossible to realize."

The paper said its information came from a "well-placed source who has access to President Anwar Sadat" and who was speaking "on the highest authority."

Israeli officials said the proposals had not been received by the government.

"Once such an idea will be put forward through official channels, it will be discussed," one official said.

Israel has vetoed Egypt's demand that the peace treaty include a timetable for Palestinian self-rule. It contends such a linkage would allow Egypt to back out of the treaty if the timetable is not fulfilled.

The Israeli Cabinet, in its regular Sunday meeting, reaffirmed its position that there is no need to send its negotiators back to Washington yet. Cabinet spokesman Arieh Naor said the government is waiting to hear Egypt's position on the U.S. draft peace treaty. The draft, accepted by Israel last week, does not include a specific timetable for implementing Palestinian self-rule.

Sadat said Sunday that he believes a peace treaty will be signed "sooner or later."

"There are problems and it will take time but that does not mean I am pessimistic, not at all," Sadat told reporters in Cairo. "Sooner or later we shall be signing an agreement. This is a fact."

Arafat has made similar statements in the past, but not since the Camp David accords were concluded two months ago.

Fig. 9–3. The bottom story, set 20 picas wide, fills a space equal to three 14-pica columns. (Courtesy of the *Hastings* (Neb.) *Daily Tribune*.)

the blurb type should be roman; if the headline is roman, the blurb should be italic. Blurbs should have white space around them. Hairline rules are often placed above and below the blurb to set it off from the rest of the story.

● *Use subheads.* Subheads can be used to break up a long-running story. They might be placed every six or seven paragraphs. Some newspapers set subheads in bold face, others set them in bold face caps, while still others set them in 16-point or 18-point italic. There should be at least three points above the subhead and two points below it. Most newspapers have an established style. The point is, they should be functional—subheads help break up gray matter, thus adding to the design, and they make it easier for a reader to move through a lengthy article.

New trial is ordered for Simants

LINCOLN (AP) — Condemned mass murderer Erwin Charles Simants must be given a new trial because of improper conduct by a county sheriff, the Nebraska Supreme Court ruled Tuesday.

Simants was convicted of the Oct. 18, 1975, slayings of six members of the Henrie Kellie family of Sutherland. He was convicted of killing three adults and three children.

The high court based its decision on a showing that Lincoln County Sheriff Gordon Gilster improperly visited the motel in which the members of the trial jury and alternates were sequestered.

The state did not deny that Gilster visited with jurors at the motel, but contended there was no evidence that Gilster's actions prejudiced the jury against Simants.

"The fraternization of Sheriff Gilster with the members of the jury during the course of the trial presents problems of constitutional dimensions," wrote Judge Hale McCown. "The sheriff was an important lay witness on the issue of the sanity of the defendant, which was the only real issue in the murder trial."

"Where an error of constitutional dimensions has occurred, the state has the burden of proving beyond a reasonable doubt that such error was harmless," the high court said.

Lincoln County Judge Hugh Stuart also visited the motel briefly to check on the jurors' accommodations. The high court didn't criticize Stuart's visits.

The Supreme Court, noting Gilster testified twice in Simants' trial, outlined the contacts he made with jurors.

"Sheriff Gilster had no valid reason or excuse for communicating or fraternizing with the jury," McCown wrote. "An inference may be drawn that the sheriff was attempting to enhance his credibility and reliability as a witness in the eyes of the jury. There can be no doubt whatever that the trial court was correct in finding that the sheriff's contacts with the jury on the three occasions disclosed by the evidence were unwarranted, as well as erroneous."

However, the Lincoln County District Court had rejected Simants' motion for a new trial, based on his writ of error which brought Gilster's activity to the high court's attention. The Supreme Court

overturned that decision and vacated the convictions and sentences imposed on Simants, sending the case back to Lincoln County for another trial.

"Whatever its motivation, the sheriff's conduct was unwarranted, erroneous and presumptively prejudicial," McCown said. "Under such circumstances the state has the burden of showing beyond a reasonable doubt that such conduct was harmless."

"A fair trial before a fair and impartial jury is a basic requirement of constitutional due process," McCown said. "To condone the conduct of Sheriff Gilster in this case would violate the fundamental integrity of all that is embraced in the constitutional concept of a fair trial by a fair and impartial jury."

"The stability and integrity of the American system of justice demands that those principles be maintained inviolate," McCown concluded.

Simants had pleaded innocent by reason of insanity, and Gilster testified in part on that issue. The state argued that, given the testimony of numerous other witnesses, Gilster's testimony was merely cumulative.

However, the Supreme Court said Simants' sanity was the only real issue in the murder trial, and expert testimony was conflicting on that point.

The jury had to weigh evidence, the high court said, and "in deciding the issue, the opinion testimony of a lay witness in whom the jury may have had special confidence because of unwarranted contacts such as are shown by the evidence may have been the critical factor in determining the one key issue which was determinative of the defendant's guilt or innocence."

Judge Leslie Boslaugh dissented from a portion of the opinion which held that, under the evidence in the Simants case, prejudice or lack of prejudice can be determined only by inference and speculation.

Boslaugh said that part of the majority opinion seemed contrary to the rule regarding prejudice which the majority adopted in the case.

"When an improper communication with a juror or jurors is shown to have taken place in a criminal case," the high

court held, "a rebuttable presumption of prejudice arises and the burden is on the state to prove that the communication was not prejudicial."

"Unauthorized communications between juriors and third persons or witnesses during the course of jury deliberations are absolutely forbidden and invalidate the verdict unless their harmlessness is made to appear," the Supreme Court further held.

The Supreme Court also noted that, before his motion was rejected by the lower court, the lower bench had questioned jurors concerning whether Gilster's remarks prejudiced their decisions.

The high court noted that the law allows a juror to testify as to whether extraneous prejudicial information was improperly brought to the jury's attention, but it also held that "no evidence may be received as to the effect of any statement upon a juror's mind, its influence one way or another, or the mental processes of a juror in connection therewith."

The major area of conflict in the testimony of Gilster and the jurors involved the conversations they had.

Gilster testified the conversations were general and that he didn't recall speaking of his experiences as sheriff while the jurors recalled that he did, McCown noted. The jurors' recollections were that he talked mostly about his experiences as sheriff.

Some jurors recalled that the sheriff related to them an incident in which the sheriff was a witness in a county court. The sheriff told them that, when an attorney objected to his testimony, the county judge overruled the objection and made the comment that the sheriff was the only one who knew what he was talking about.

All courts agree that contact such as that between Gilster and the jurors is improper, the Supreme Court said, but not all courts agree on the appropriate rules to be applied.

"We believe the better view to be that, when an improper communication with a juror or jurors is shown to have taken place in a criminal case, a rebuttable presumption of prejudice arises and the burden is on the state to prove that the communications are not prejudicial," the high court held.

Fig. 9–4. White space can be achieved by setting a story "one-up"—i.e. by placing three columns of standard width type where four would normally fit. (Courtesy of the *Hastings* (Neb.) *Daily Tribune*.)

● *Use pleasingly shaped stories.* Stories in horizontal rectangular shapes are easier to read than irregular, jagged-shaped stories, particularly "inverted L's." Readers are often hesitant to wade through long, vertical columns of type. Always attempt to work in modules.

● *Use digests.* News digests, which often appear on front pages, give the reader a summary of the most important stories, some of which are late-breaking.

In addition, the can provide white space and art work to enliven the page. Digests are often set in wide measure type, are boxed, and sometimes contain small photographs.

● *Use special headlines.* Special headlines, such as kickers, hammers,

By NEIL AMDUR
N.Y. Times News Service

COLORADO SPRINGS — The use of drugs — stimulants, steroids and growth deterrents — in international sports has reached "epidemic" dimensions, increasing competitive pressures on world-class amateur athletes while the issue itself further polarizes East and West.

In an attempt to educate and alert American competitors, the sports medicine task force of the United States Olympic Committee, meeting here last week, recommended that drug testing procedures be implemented at all national championships. At the moment no comprehensive doping control program is administered in this country.

"It's an epidemic," Dr. Clayton Thomas, a member of the task force, said last week at the USOC's national training center.

Dr. Daniel Hanley: "The problem is worse than it's ever been."

"The problem is worse than it's ever been," added Dr. Daniel Hanley, another task force member, who has served as a team physician for United States Olympic squads as well as on the International Olympic Committee's medical commission.

Dr. Tony Daly, an orthopedic surgeon from Inglewood, Calif., has treated amateur and professional athletes. "Athletes are trapped," Daly said. "Based on peer pressure and folklore, they feel that in order to improve they have to experiment."

Several recent events illustrate the problem:

— The disqualification last month of five track and field athletes for anabolic steroid abuses at the European championships was a specific area of the task force's discussion. After their tests had proved positive, Nadechda Tkacenko of the Soviet Union was ordered to return her gold medal in the women's pentathlon, and Yevgeny Mironov, a teammatte, lost a silver medal in the men's shot-put.

Fig. 9–5. Blurbs make long-running stories easier to read. They also create white space. (Courtesy of the *Hastings* (Neb.) *Daily Tribune.* © 1978–79 by the New York Times Company. Reprinted by permission.)

Cultist toll now nears 900

GEORGETOWN, Guyana (AP) — The death toll from the Jonestown mass murder-suicide is about 900, some 500 more than originally estimated, U.S. officials said today. American troops wearing surgical masks and rubber gloves continued to remove the decayed bodies from the jungle settlement.

The count jumped from 408 to about 775 Friday when soldiers found the corpses of children and small adults lying three deep under other victims of the ritualistic death rite performed by members of the California-based Peoples Temple cult last Saturday.

In Washington today, State Department press officer Jeff Dieterich said department sources in Guyana reported nearly 900 bodies had been found. At Dover Air Force Base, Del., where the bodies are being sent, department lawyer Michael White also reported the revised count.

CHARGED WITH MURDER

In Georgetown, meanwhile, Charles Edward Beikman, 43, of Indianapolis, Ind., was charged today with the murders of four members of the Peoples Temple at the sect's Georgetown headquarters.

Court records identified the victims as Sharon Amos, Martin Amos, Christa Amos and Liane Harris, found with their throats cut at the headquarters last Saturday night. They had earlier been identified as suicide victims.

The stocky, blond-haired Beikman, 43, a sect member for 20 years, made no statement. He will appear again in court Dec. 4.

First-degree murder in Guyana is punishable by hanging, although there has been no hanging here since independence from Britain in 1966 and there is a strong lobby for abolition of the death penalty. Wednesday, Larry Layton, 32, of San Francisco, was charged with the murders of Rep. Leo J. Ryan, D-Calif., and four others at the Jonestown airstrip.

Two other men are being held as apparent suspects but have not been arraigned.

PLANE SCHEDULED TO ARRIVE

Six Air Force C-141 cargo planes had ferried 421 bodies back from the failed jungle utopia by Friday night, and another plane was scheduled to arrive at mid-day today with up to 80 more bodies.

Military officials estimated it might take two to three weeks to complete the airlift, identification and processing of the badly decomposed bodies.

Morticians were waiting for 18 FBI fingerprint experts to finish the identification process before starting work to embalm the bodies.

Although U.S. officials in Guyana said they had tentatively identified 174 of the cult members, the only body positively identified here was that of the Rev. Jim Jones, the man who directed the deaths of the Peoples Temple members.

The task of returning the bodies was doubled Friday when officials learned that the death count at the Jonestown commune was at least 775, not 409 as previously announced.

WRAPPED IN BAGS

Most of the bodies here were wrapped in black plastic bags and stored in five rented, refrigerated vans. About 141 were stacked in aluminum cases in a base storage shed.

Inside the base mortuary, the FBI men were checking fingerprints at the rate of five to six bodies an hour, and they had taken prints from 104 bodies by early Friday evening.

One military officer, who asked not to be identified, said "the bodies had maggots all over them," and limbs had fallen off some, adding, "I've been in two wars and it's the worst I've ever seen."

Fig. 9–6. Subheads are placed in long-running stories to break up typographical grayness. (Courtesy of the *Hastings (Neb.) Daily Tribune.*)

and side-saddles, can be effective design elements, as well as telling the reader what the story is about. (Examples of and a discussion of these special headlines are in chapter 7.) Kickers create white space and give additional information to the reader. Graphics purists caution against the use of kickers at the tops of pages because they detract from the functional aspects of creating white space; white space is already abundant at the tops of pages. Hammers, in addition to calling the reader's attention to a story through the use of a strong summary word or phrase ("Fire," "Strike," "Help"), can be typographically pleasing to the eye and can effectively break up otherwise gray blocks of type. Side-saddle headlines are particularly useful on inside pages when advertisements climb nearly to the top of the page.

● *Use large, effectively cropped photos.* Award winning newspapers often emphasize dominant photos. Remember, when a photo is dominant, keep it on the top portion of the page. A reader is drawn to the photo and his eye will then continue downward, scanning other

Cities warned of cuts

ST. LOUIS (AP) — President Carter appealed to city officials from the 50 states today to join the battle against inflation, warning that next year's federal budget will contain "little money for new initiatives" in urban areas and elsewhere.

The president also was scheduled to fly to Salt Lake City later to receive a family unity presentation from the Mormon Church before returning to the White House tonight.

In his text for an appearance at the annual meeting of the National League of Cities, Carter argued that "the future of our cities is at stake" in the inflation fight.

To emphasize his point, he said inflation by next year will have eaten away one-third of the purchasing power of the $6.2 billion in general revenue sharing money that has been sent to cities by the federal government since 1972.

"Cities badly need these dollars," the president said, "and the federal government cannot replace such major losses to inflation."

While declaring that the fiscal 1980 federal budget he will send Congress in January will "be very tight," Carter said, "I promise that the cities will bear no more and no less than a fair share of budget restraint."

Dollar gains in foreign trading

LONDON (AP) — The dollar rose in quiet trading on foreign exchanges today as gold prices fell back, reflecting the dollar's healthier showing.

The dollar closed in Tokyo at 196 yen, up more than two yen from Friday's closing rate of 193.975.

Early dollar rates in major European financial centers were:

Frankfurt — 1.9342 marks, up from 1.9260 at the close of trading Friday.

Zurich — 1.7440 Swiss francs, up from 1.7315.

Paris — 4.4350 French francs, up from 4.4150.

The pound was unchanged in London at $1.9830.

Gold sold in London for $200 an ounce, down from $201.75 late Friday, while the early price in Zurich was $199.375, down from $202.875.

Fig. 9–7. Editors should avoid laying out stories in L-shapes ("Cities warned of cuts"). If possible, stories should be modular in form.

stories on the page. If the picture is placed at the bottom of the page, the reader, once he focuses on the photo, might not return to the stories and elements at the top of the page. When two photos are used, one should be vertical and the other horizontal. Avoid two pictures of similar shape on the same page.

• *Use the total page.* Newspapers of earlier eras featured the best stories and pictures at tops of pages. The bottom half was a gray mass of type that looked like it had been indiscriminately pushed down because there was nothing better to do with it. Today's total page con-

National

Demand for engineers rises

Evanston, Ill.—The demand for engineers with bachelor's degrees is up 27 percent since last year, a national job market survey indicates. The demand for graduates of liberal arts and other non-technical degrees, though, is down 3 percent, the survey shows. **Page 2A.**

Arkansas, N.C. to vote

Gov. David Pryor and two congressmen will be the major candidates tomorrow when Democratic voters choose a candidate for the Senate seat once held by John McClellan. In North Carolina, meanwhile, Democrats will chose between two candidates seeking to unseat Republican Sen. Jesse Helms. **Page 2A.**

Nixon-book sales pick up

Atlanta—Richard Nixon's autobiography has sold between 150,000 to 175,000 copies, the book's publishers report. The president of Grosset and Dunlap says "RN: The Memoirs of Richard Nixon," is doing much better than earlier publicity indicated. **Page 5B.**

FBI scheming on King disclosed

Washington—The FBI apparently worked with a black leader in its campaign to discredit Dr. Martin Luther King Jr., FBI documents indicate. The tentative scheming was disclosed in a memo from the "official and confidential" files of J. Edgar Hoover. **Page 2A.**

All is not well at casino

Atlantic City—The response to New Jersey's first casino has been excellent, but all is not 7s and 11s in the seashore resort. With the gamblers came litter in the aisles, battles over slot machines and long, slow lines down the Boardwalk from the casino. **Page 8A.**

Student kills brother, himself

Lakewood, Calif.—A student who became despondent after he had been rejected by a medical school shot himself to death after killing his 10-year-old brother. The brothers' father, Edward Ishkanian, suffered a heart attack after he found the bodies. **Page 7A.**

NATO summit to open

Washington—The NATO summit meeting will open tomorrow, and a notebook thick with "secret" papers details the long-range hopes of military leaders. The papers describe how members could get "more bang for the buck" to combat the Warsaw Pact forces. **Page 8A.**

Fig. 9–8. News digests, which summarize important stories, can be an effective typographical device. (Courtesy of the *Minneapolis Star*.)

162

cept calls for equal attention for all portions of the page. Editors should avoid making a page top-heavy or bottom-heavy. The entire page should have overall appeal.

● *Package related stories.* Editors are making increased efforts to package the news for reader convenience. For example, if a national wire story about rising grocery prices is carried on page one, a sidebar story about local reactions to rising costs could be adjacent to it. Possibly a border could tie the two stories together.

● *Use appropriate art work, such as maps and charts.* A recent report, prepared by the Associated Press Managing Editors Graphics and Photo Committee, concluded that "intelligent use of maps and graphics in newspapers today is no longer a luxury. It is a must if your newspaper expects to remain competitive or wants to remain in the twentieth century with everybody else." Maps not only brighten a page—they also inform the reader.

● *Use logos and standing headlines.* These elements not only guide the reader to features that he is interested in, but they also break up large blocks of type and gray matter.

Design Shortcomings

Editors should make a concerted effort to avoid certain practices when designing pages:

● *Circus makeup.* Pages that are littered with a number of bold, screaming headlines, multiple-boxed stories, an overabundance of poorly used white space, and occasional color headlines admittedly do not lull the reader to sleep but neither are the pages conducive to a simple, orderly presentation of the day's news. Few newspapers have persisted in this sensational method of design.

● *Overcrowded pages.* The trend toward contemporary, streamlined design has led most prize-winning newspapers to reduce the number of elements on a single page, particularly on the front page. Newspapers of earlier eras often crowded from a dozen to twenty elements on the front page. A few newspapers, including some metropolitan dailies, continue to feature the multi-element front page. These, however, are seldom cited for typographical or design excellence. Contemporary front pages feature from five to ten elements. Reduction in the elements on a single page creates brighter, more readable, and more attractive design.

● *Postage stamp photographs.* Small, poorly cropped photographs add little to a page. A well-conceived front page demands at least two

Armaments

Carter, Gromyko make 'some headway' in talks

WASHINGTON (UPI) — Soviet Foreign Minister Andrei Gromyko said Saturday he and President Carter made "some headway" in their four hours of discussions at the White House on limiting strategic weaponry.

"Neither side is losing optimism," Gromyko told reporters outside the Oval Office. "We are making some headway on some parts of some questions."

With Secretary of State Cyrus Vance nodding assent at his side, Gromyko said the talks were much "like a tree, branching out in different ways."

He said the fact progress was made on part of one question does not mean the whole question was solved.

"The important thing," Gromyko said, "is to create and not destroy."

Neither Vance nor Gromyko would discuss details of the talks which began at 8 a.m. and ran two hours beyond schedule, ending during the noon hour.

U.S. officials say two issues remain to be settled before a second Strategic Arms Limitation Treaty can be produced. Talks have been going on since 1972.

Despite recent signs of tensions in other areas of the super power rela-

tionship, the arms talks have continued to make steady progress, apparently insulated from the other strains and disputes over Africa and human rights.

Vance and Gromyko met in New York Thursday to deal with the remaining issues left on the SALT agenda: Limits on development of new families of missiles, and controls over the Soviet Backfire bomber.

American officials believe the remaining issues can be settled, but the Backfire issue is so delicate — in both political and military terms — that the U.S. administration now favors leaving the question to be settled at a summit meeting late this summer between Carter and Soviet President Leonid Brezhnev.

The American side hopes the numbers and location of the Soviet Backfire fleet can be settled in a series of letters, which would be made part of the Salt II package that will be submitted to the Senate for ratification.

The Soviets, according to U.S. officials, offered to guarantee that production of the planes would be limited but, in light of the Soviet disregard of the Helsinki human rights agreement in prosecuting members of a Soviet monitoring group, the administration does not believe that solution could be sold to the Senate.

Canada asks removal of U.S. nuclear missiles

UNITED NATIONS (UPI) — Canadian Prime Minister Pierre Trudeau says the United States has been asked to remove its nuclear-tipped air-to-air missiles from Canadian soil, making his country the first "to have chosen to divest itself of nuclear weapons."

Trudeau delivered a 40-minute address Friday to the U.N. General Assembly Special Session on Disarmament.

"We have withdrawn from any nuclear role by Canada's armed forces in Europe and are now in the process of replacing with conventionally armed aircraft the nuclear-capable planes still assigned to our forces in North America," he said.

"We were thus not only the first country in the world with the capacity to produce nuclear weapons that chose not to do so. We are also the first nuclear armed country to have chosen to divest itself of nuclear weapons."

Canada ended its nuclear role in Europe in the 1960s but two years ago decided to ask the United States

to remove the "Genie" nuclear air-to-air missiles from North American Air Defense Command (NORAD) bases in Canada, a Canadian disarmament expert said.

William Epstein, a specialist on disarmament and a member of Trudeau's delegation, said the United States has been asked to remove the Genie missiles as soon as Canada replaces its F-101 Voodoo interceptors with more modern — but conventionally armed — aircraft.

The new aircraft are not expected to be in place until at least 1981, so the missiles will remain on Canadian soil until then, Epstein said.

Also, U.S. nuclear planes of NORAD will continue to fly in Canadian airspace.

Trudeau said President Carter "has shown the way in recent weeks with his farsighted postponement" of a decision to produce the neutron bomb and he called on the Soviet Union to make a reciprocal gesture "to make it possible to extend that postponement indefinitely."

Fig. 9–9. Makeup editors should always watch for related stories which can be packaged. These two stories dealing with armaments were packaged and bordered. (Courtesy of the Dubuque (Iowa) *Telegraph-Herald.* Also reprinted by permission of United Press International.)

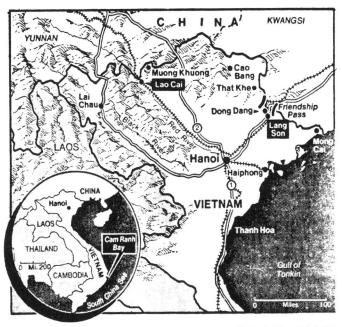

The New York Times / Feb. 25, 1979

Fighting was reported continuing near Lao Cai and Lang Son. The United States was reported fearful that Soviet Union might use China-Vietnam conflict as a pretext for establishing a naval base at Cam Ranh Bay (inset).

The New York Times / Feb. 25, 1979

Fighting was reported at Qataba, Mukheiras and Beihan.

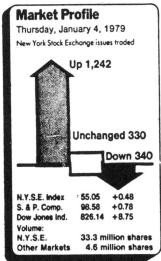

Market Profile

Thursday, January 4, 1979

New York Stock Exchange issues traded

Up 1,242

Unchanged 330

Down 340

N.Y.S.E. Index	55.05	+0.48
S. & P. Comp.	98.58	+0.78
Dow Jones Ind.	826.14	+8.75
Volume:		
N.Y.S.E.	33.3 million shares	
Other Markets	4.6 million shares	

The New York Times / Jan. 5, 1979

Fig. 9–10. These maps provide a frame of reference for the stories which they accompany. (© 1978–79 by the New York Times Company. Reprinted by permission.)

TV and radio highlights today

Fig. 9–11. Logos and standing headlines help guide readers and make pages more attractive. (Reprinted with permission from the *Minneapolis Tribune*.)

strong pieces of art; usually one large photograph is dominant. Dubuque *Telegraph Herald* managing editor Geladas suggests that editors should size most pictures a column bigger than their first inclination.

● *Tombstone headlines.* Headlines of the same type face and size that appear side by side should be avoided. At first glance, it appears that instead of two separate headlines, there is one continuous headline which does not make sense. Predominantly horizontal newspapers can more effectively avoid tombstone headlines than can multi-element vertical newspapers.

● *"Bump" headlines.* Headlines that land side by side but which are of different type sizes should also be avoided. Bump headlines, however, are not so confusing as tombstones. Also, the impact of the "bump" can be lessened by setting one of the headlines in italic type or by placing a border around one of the heads and stories.

Administration claims support of steel industry

WASHINGTON (AP) — The Carter administration is claiming support for its anti-inflation program from the steel industry, which often resists presidential efforts to hold down steel prices.

It would be a big victory for President Carter if the steel industry does agree to follow the voluntary wage-price standards since steel price increases usually are passed on to auto makers and other industries which in turn raise their prices for consumer goods.

Treasury Undersecretary Anthony M. Solomon said that virtually all of the steel companies he had talked with promised to go along with the anti-inflation plan.

He declined to list the companies he talked to, but said: "The key steel executives in the country have indicated to me they will comply with the president's program."

In other economic developments,

Damage delays construction of big hydro plant

GRAND COULEE, Wash. (AP) — Some $500,000 in damage to three giant electrical generators has indefinitely delayed completion of the Grand Coulee Dam hydroelectric project, planned as the largest power plant of its type in the world.

The FBI has joined Okanogan County authorities in investigating the damage, which plant officials say could only have been done by someone who was familiar with the huge electric plant.

Robert Mueller, superintendent of the area housing the damaged generators, said the gouging of the coil bars in the generators could have been done with a small crowbar or chisel.

"He has access," said Mueller. "It has to be an inside job."

Okanogan County Sheriff Jerry Beck said police have no suspects.

An FBI spokesman said the crime involved would likely be destruction of government property because one of the 700,000-kilowatt turbine generators had been completed and turned over to the federal government. The generator had been shut down for maintenance when the damage was done, officials said.

The other two damaged generators were still under construction.

Fig. 9–12. Tombstones (two headlines of the same type size and type face which are placed side by side) should be avoided.

• *Crowded copy.* Copy should not butt against headlines. Editors should make sure that there is slightly more white space above the headline than below it to alleviate confusion over which story should be matched with which headline.

• *Monotonous headlines.* The trend toward horizontal, contemporary design has led to the monotony of similarly shaped stories and identically sized headlines being stacked upon each other. This monotony, however, can be avoided. If, for example, four front page stories are to be given four-column, 36-point headlines, an editor

Two Bluffs stores ink union contract

COUNCIL BLUFFS, Iowa (AP) — Two Council Bluffs grocery stores have signed contracts with a meat cutters union.

Neil Shaver, owner of Shaver's Food Mart, said a contract was signed Wednesday with the Amalgamated Meat Cutters. Shaver declined to discuss details of the contract.

Agreement on a union contract ended a strike at Rog & Scotty's Super Value stores. Representatives of the store and the local could not be reached for comment.

Sugar bill is killed

WASHINGTON (AP) — The House killed Sunday a compromise bill that would have added 1.5 cents to the retail price of a five-pound bag of sugar this winter.

The 194-177 vote against the bill, endorsed by the administration and passed earlier by the Senate, means that consumer prices for sugar could drop by as much as 50 percent next July when current support prices expire.

Another 6.4 cents would have been added to the retail price by 1983 — a 6.1 percent increase over five years' time.

The House defeated the bill in the last hours of its session, shortly after the Senate rebuffed a move to defeat it there for giving producers too little.

The House vote also killed two attached Senate-passed measures that President Carter had sought — to allow him to sell back to a House-Senate conference committee. "We have a bill that's been dictated by the White House . . . I don't know anyone who likes it," Dole told the Senate.

Dole said sugarbeet farmers and corn farmers who compete with sugarcane growers and those in the sweetener market all denounced the measure.

The Senate approved the compromise on a voice vote after rejecting Dole's bid to send it back to committee by 36 to 20.

Fig. 9–13. Bumps (two headlines with different type sizes which are placed side by side) should be avoided when possible.

could make one headline a one-line roman, the second headline could have a kicker, the third headline could contain two lines and the fourth headline could be one-line italic. One of the responsibilities of editors is to make judgments on story importance; it is unlikely that four front page stories would be of equal importance. Therefore, putting the same headline on each story could prove confusing to the reader.

• *Uninterrupted gutters.* In past years, it was a cardinal sin for editors to allow a gutter to extend the length of a page. However, it is not as displeasing to the eye with contemporary design as it was with vertically designed newspapers. Just the same, a gutter that divides a six-column newspaper in half should be strictly avoided, though a gutter that creates a two-column/four-column split can be tolerated.

• *Headlines that don't stretch across stories.* Unless a story has a side-saddle headline, its body type should stretch across the same number of columns as the headline. For example, a story with a three-column headline should have three columns of type under it. Though the practice used to be more pervasive, some newspapers still persist in wrapping columns of type beyond the scope of the story's headline. This should always be avoided.

• *Jump headlines.* Research indicates that readership decreases when stories are "jumped" (continued) to another page. With the trend toward fewer but longer front page stories, some newspapers regularly

Analysts are puzzled over Peking posters

TOKYO (AP) — Political analysts are puzzling over the latest writing on the walls of Peking, a flurry of wall posters that appear to be hinting of a power struggle between China's two key leaders.

The latest poster, which went up Friday night, called for revocation of the 1976 Communist Party decisions that purged Teng Hsiao-ping and named Hua Kuo-feng premier and Communist Party chairman to succeed the late Mao Tse-tung.

The poster called the decisions "wrong" and said they "must be officially retracted."

Teng's star has been rising in a week-old barrage of wallwritings, which often presage shifts in official government policy.

In a report from the Chinese capital, Japan's Kyodo news service said the latest poster criticized the decisions of April 7, 1976, as "a product of feudalistic fascism."

Earlier this week, a similar poster calling for revocation of the decision to oust Teng appeared in Peking. It did not mention Hua.

This Thanksgiving special for family

BATTLE CREEK (AP) — The Charles Hrabanek family had a special reason to be thankful this Thanksgiving — their daughter, Ann, is alive after a near fatal bout with aplastic anemia.

The 19-year-old recently was released from medical care at the Fred Hutchinson Cancer Research Center in Seattle after 100 days of treatment.

Life for the 1977 Battle Creek High School graduate was running its normal course early last summer. She was employed at the Madison County Agricultural Stabilization and Conservation Service Office in town and was on a softball team.

She dismissed early warning signs of aplastic anemia — excessive bruising and tiredness — and continued her active schedule. Then, in mid-July, she developed a throat infection which did not respond to penicillin treatment.

Her fever climbed to 105 degrees and she was hospitalized in Norfolk, then was transferred to Omaha where the aplastic anemia was diagnosed.

The disease is characterized by the inability of the bone marrow to produce blood cells to maintain life. The cause, in Ann's case, is undetermined.

Only a brother or sister could be a suitable donor, the girl explained, and tests were run on her nine brothers and sisters. Dave, 16, proved to be the closest match and the donor.

Ann, her parents and brother and two doctors for in-flight care were flown in a private jet, donated by Mutual of Omaha, to the Seattle center recommended to the family because of its success rate.

There, doctors performed the transplants from Dave's hip to Ann's body. Dave also was able to provide his sister with the white cells needed to fight off infection and platelets needed for blood clotting.

Patients must stay under the center's care for a minimum of 100 days, Ann said.

"I came home on the 100th day. I was so glad to be home. I was so glad to see them all. I really missed them," she said of her family.

"We were all living for the day she'd come home," said Mrs. Hrabanek.

"I feel real good," Ann said of her condition.

She is "taking it easy" and watches her diet and rest and takes vitamins and a prescription drug daily. Once a week, she travels to Omaha for blood tests and next year she is to return to Seattle for a checkup.

The Battle Creek Fire Department has established the Ann Hrabanek Trust Fund at the Battle Creek State Bank to collect donations to help defray the hospital and medical expenses, estimated at about $100,000 by the family.

Fig. 9–14. The impact of bump headlines can be lessened when a border is placed around one story and headline and when the story is set wide measure.

jump stories. Though it is best, at least in the interests of readership, to avoid this practice, when stories must be continued, measures should be taken to make it as convenient as possible for the reader. The headline emphasis on the jump page should be similar to the main headline, and the headline should not be buried on the jump page.

Designing Front Pages

The front page is the showcase of a newspaper. More care has traditionally gone into its design than any other page. Equally impor-

Carter praises Congress

WASHINGTON (AP) — The 95th Congress passes into history praised as "courageous and constructive" by a president who battled with it about many issues and is uncertain whether to sign the tax cut that was its crowning effort.

"Whether they have made enough progress to merit our signing of the bill will depend on our analysis," President Carter's chief domestic adviser, Stuart Eizenstat, told reporters shortly before the House and Senate adjourned late Sunday.

But in a telephone conversation with House Democratic Whip John Brademas of Indiana, Carter said from his presidential retreat at Camp David, Md., that the 95th was "one of the most courageous and constructive congresses in the history of the country."

Other assessments were not all as rosy. Interviewed on NBC's "Meet the Press," Sen. George McGovern, D-S.D., said the 95th did "less for the average working person in this country" than any Congress he had seen.

House Speaker Thomas P. O'Neill Jr., however, said Congress had voted the biggest tax cut in history and "still kept its long-standing commitment to meet the social needs of the nation."

Senate Democratic Leader Robert C. Byrd of West Virginia said, "This has not been a rubber stamp Congress, yet it has not been a balky, unyielding Congress." He said he thought Carter's record in the Congress was "very good."

And Sen. Howard Baker of Tennessee, the Republican leader, said GOP members of Congress had "changed the whole direction of the federal government" by pushing for tax relief and less government intervention in business.

The last major action of the 34-hour, 17-minute weekend session that ended Congress' two-year run was passage of compromise legislation cutting taxes on individuals and corporations by $18.7 billion.

Among other votes in the closing hours, the lawmakers:

—Completed action on an energy program gradually lifting federal price controls from natural gas and giving tax credits for home insulation and solar energy. The program also calls for taxes on gasoline-wasting cars.

—Passed a revamped Endangered Species Act, giving the federal government more leeway to decide whether projects such as dams should be halted because they threaten wildlife.

—Approved a watered-down version of the Humphrey-Hawkins "full employment" bill spelling out goals for cutting inflation and boosting employment. The bill creates no new programs for meeting the goals.

—Eased restrictions on taxpayer-financed abortions voted earlier by the House as part of a $56 billion spending bill for the Departments of Labor and Health, Education and Welfare.

—Sent to Carter a bill restricting loans and overdrafts by banks to their officers and major stockholders — legislation prompted by disclosures about the financial affairs of former Budget Director Bert Lance.

—Passed an administration-backed bill giving airlines greater authority to compete by cutting fares and embarking on new routes without getting the approval of the Civil Aeronautics Board.

Fig. 9–15. Editors should avoid wrapping columns of type beyond the scope of the headline.

tant, however, is the selection of stories and quality of writing. Bright, effectively designed pages, as mentioned earlier, will not make a subscriber read a story; it might lure him to start reading, but it cannot make him finish. Thus, makeup editors should strive not only for attractive front pages, but for pages that contain an array of some of the most important and best-written news stories of the day.

News judgment is immensely important. Timely, significant stories should not be relegated to inside pages solely for the sake of front page design, but neither should editors take the easy way out and put a dozen or more stories on the front page simply because "somebody will be interested in them." Editors should seek a lively balance of stories and art work on page one; it is important that a feature story or feature picture lighten the overall effects of a basically hard-news front page.

Once the elements (stories, pictures, and art work) are selected, editors should concentrate on attractive design. Stories should be laid out in pleasing shapes; most of the elements on a horizontal page are rectangular. The best-designed pages have a limited number of elements (never more than ten). Since contemporary newspapers use fewer elements on front pages, news digests have become standard fare; while only a handful of stories are given full-blown treatment, other newsworthy events are capsulized, with references made to inside pages where the stories are presented in detail.

Today's best-designed newspapers are basically horizontal. They feature one strong element—usually a large picture—on the front page. Many newspapers use processed color photos. Pages are modular at least to the extent that they avoid lengthy one-column stories under one-column headlines. Though today's most attractive newspapers have a basic horizontal appearance, they have at least one strong vertical element (picture, digest, or story) on the front page.

The easiest way to create a basically horizontal page is to use multicolumn headlines. Lead multicolumn headlines should be 36-point, 48-point, 60-point, and occasionally 72-point or 84-point. They are usually one-line, never more than two. Headlines in 24-point type should never be stretched across more than two columns; they are not heavy enough. When using one-column headlines, they should never be more than three lines deep; when single column heads contain too many lines, they often command as much space as the stories.

Most award-winning newspapers keep their headlines flush left; centered headlines and step headlines are nonfunctional. To create a horizontal appearance that makes for easier reading, editors should avoid running a story more than four inches deep under multicolumn headlines.

Though many newspapers persist in running their flag (nameplate) across the top of the front page, there is no general rule that says it has to run in this position each day. Many newspapers move the flag around and vary its size from day to day. However, flags should not be so obtrusive that they dominate the page.

These front-page design recommendations are obviously general; editors should also incorporate many of the suggestions for effective design discussed earlier. Much care should be taken when designing the front page; it is, after all, the focal point of the newspaper.

Fig. 9–16. The Louisville *Courier-Journal* is a leader in contemporary newspaper page design. Note the bottom left corner which is anchored with bordered elements and white space. (Courtesy of the Louisville *Courier-Journal*.)

Fig. 9–17. The digest column extending the length of the first column gives the Dubuque (Iowa) *Telegraph Herald* a unique look. The *Telegraph Herald,* which often uses color photographs on page one, features an ample amount of white space. (Courtesy of the Dubuque *Telegraph Herald.*)

Fig. 9–18. The *Los Angeles Times* features a vertical, clean appearance. The wide measure type in the middle of the page provides variety. (© 1978, *Los Angeles Times.* Reprinted by permission.)

Fig. 9–19. Page one banner headlines are common in the *Chicago Tribune*. The *Tribune* makes effective use of white space and art work. (Courtesy of the *Chicago Tribune*.)

Fig. 9–20. Despite the trend toward horizontal design, the *New York Times* retains its unique identity with vertical makeup and multideck headlines. (© 1978–79 by The New York Times Company. Reprinted by permission.)

Fig. 9–21. Many of the country's daily newspapers with relatively small circulations are extremely well designed. The *News-Enterprise,* Elizabethtown, Ky., is an award-winning newspaper which features a horizontal appearance, ample white space and strong photographs. (Courtesy of the *News-Enterprise.*)

Fig. 9–22. A bordered story with a side-saddle headline and white space which emphasizes the lead story lend an attractive readability to the Orlando (Fla.) *Sentinel Star.* (Courtesy of the *Sentinel Star.*

Fig. 9-23. Large, horizontal photographs and a simple, clean design make the *Chronicle-Tribune* of Marion, Ind., an award winner. (Courtesy of the *Chronicle-Tribune*.)

Designing Inside Pages

Designing inside news pages is often more difficult than designing front pages, because stories, pictures, and art must be built around advertisements. Thus, editors must work even harder to entice readership. Attractive modules can be formulated on pages loaded with advertisements. Packaging the news is important. Editors can group related stories on inside pages; more and more newspapers are doing so. For example, several lengthy international news stories could be condensed and edited into short, punchy capsules. By grouping these stories under a standing headline, such as "Around the World," readers are immediately drawn to them. A border around the compilation aids readership and is functional. The border ties the related stories together under a standing headline, and it helps make the page more attractive.

"People in the news" items which are transmitted daily by the wire services are ideal for prominent inside page treatment. These crisp items enjoy high readership. Also, the wire services normally move photos of the people. Head shots within the people columns, like borders around the stories, are functional—they not only illustrate the story but also brighten the page. Borders obviously help package related news stories and call attention to them; they are particularly valuable on inside pages. Bordered stories on these sometimes gray pages help to break up masses of type, particularly when the pages are so tight (heavy percentage of advertisements) that photographs cannot be used.

Editors should also strive to use pictures or appropriate maps whenever possible; these, too, brighten inside pages and increase readership. In addition, puzzles, cartoons, weather reports, weather maps, and syndicated advice columns are usually found on inside pages. Editors can use them to provide contrast.

Though some newspapers take great care in designing their front pages, inside pages are often neglected. Too often, composing room personnel indiscriminately arrange "left-overs" on inside pages, particularly when they have early deadlines. Editors should remember, however, that although the news content of these pages is not so significant as on page one, the pages should still be attractive and lively.

Designing Sports Pages

Sports pages are tailor-made for bright, brisk design. Sports editors need not feel inhibited by the stoic overtones of historical political

Soviets rap neutron bomb

Carter reported ready to discuss nuclear test ban

Robards' Jim Lee Owen performs here tonight

An album cut, 'Hank' Owen is home again

By JUDY JENKINS
Staff Writer

'Owen becomes Williams ... it's eerie'

Most offices, businesses to lock up for holiday

Gleaner Staff Report

police beat

gleaner

newscope

the world

Workers' sit-in rattles Leaning Tower

the nation

Labor law proposal aids small business

Eastern casino opening draws thousands

Nine-year-old plays the stock market

Fig. 9–24. The bordered feature story, photograph and white space provide the focal point for this inside page in the Henderson (Ky.) *Gleaner.* The "newscope" provides an effective, functional forum for wire service stories and helps balance the page. (Courtesy of the *Gleaner.*)

181

Carter aide raps Russians

Tough Soviet stand urged

Zbigniew Brzezinski

NATO warned of Soviet buildup

Chinese exodus brings Vietnam call for talks

Day once less a holiday

Lack of veteran aid cited

Federal court ruling leads to booming firework sales

Bill Stogos displays his fireworks

Violence in Zaire rooted in mines

VOL. 124   No. 22

THE STATE JOURNAL

SUPER SPECIAL GRABBERS

GTX 10W50 74¢ qt.

20W50 69¢ qt.

Grand Prix 59¢

MOTORCYCLE OIL
for 2 & 4 Cycle Engines

GIANT SAVINGS AT GIANT DISCOUNT

Sell your car with a low-cost Classified ad.

GERANIUMS $1 25

Fig. 9–25. Wide measure type, bordered related stories and a general horizontal appearance make this inside page from the *State Journal,* Lansing, Mich., attractive and readable. (Courtesy of the *State Journal.*)

182

events or world crises. Sports elements literally beg for innovative treatment. In no other section of the paper is there such a consistent flow of dramatic photos: pole vaulters stretching and straining eighteen feet in the air; distance runners struggling through the final yards of an exhausting race; sinewy basketball players driving the lane through a forest of arms, legs, and torsos; 255-pound linebackers crushing back-peddling quarterbacks; gymnasts gracefully performing their poetic routines; and sleek hurdlers gliding over barriers. In addition, game stories, league roundups, analysis pieces, feature stories, ratings, predictions, columns, and statistics compete for space on sports pages.

The editor who designs sports pages has a unique challenge; he must fit a variety of writing styles, photos, and statistics into a neat, readable package. But he also has an advantage over an editor who designs news pages. On most days, sports editors can plan well in advance the contents of a given page; late-breaking, unexpected news is the exception rather than the rule. News and makeup judgments are often made well in advance of actual events.

Well-designed sports pages are bright—as crisp as a line drive. Outstanding sports pages are often built around large, dramatic, well-cropped photographs. In fact, action photos should be the staple of well-designed sports pages. Wide-measure type is often used on personal columns. Standing heads over results, roundups, ratings, statistical leaders, and carefully edited sports shorts also add brightness to the pages. Borders can draw attention to feature stories or tie together a story and related photo. White space can create a bright, lively atmosphere.

Designing Editorial Pages

In earlier years, newspaper editorial pages were as staid and lifeless as some of the topics discussed. Day after day, they looked the same —gray and bland. Their appearance was unstimulating to many readers—the pages simply looked boring. Opinion pages—the intellectual mainstream of the paper—should be identifiable; they should be differentiated from the rest of the newspaper—but they need not be drab. Stimulating ideas should not be relegated to gray masses of type that provide little enticement to the reader. Editorial page design can be lighter and airier—generally more readable—without sacrificing its unique identity within the newspaper.

The Washington Star

Sports

• Comics

SECTION C

THURSDAY, JUNE 1, 1978

If the Bullets Should Win It All...

PRESIDENT CARTER
State Dinner . . .

MAYOR WASHINGTON
Keys to the City . . .

SPEAKER O'NEILL
Joint Session . . .

Dick Heller

Be forewarned, Washington. This is what will happen if the Bullets win:

• • • •

The team flies back into pandemonium at Dulles Airport. The traffic jam stretches all the way back to and completely around the Beltway.

The first man off the plane is Phil Walker, who receives an uproarious welcome from the seven people in a crowd of 60,000 who recognize him.

Then comes Joe Pace, who tells the first breathless TV interviewer to reach him that, no, nothing like this ever happened to him at Coppin State.

Elvin Hayes attempts to get through the crowd without being mobbed by riding sidesaddle on Kevin Grevey's wheelchair.

Coach Dick Motta has no problems affecting a disguise. He puts on a necktie.

• • • •

President Carter, in his press conference the next day, congratulates the Bullets for having "a much better year than I did." Then he flashes his famous grin and adds, "But they have to defend their title next year. I don't until 1980."

Afterwards, Press Secretary Jody Powell announces that the White House will hold a state dinner for the Bullets. Presidential assistant Hamilton Jordan leaks the news that the President may allow hard liquor to be served along with the usual wines. "But no Amaretto," Jordan says quickly, spitting out the words.

• • • •

The dinner is a huge success. Entertainers include Johnny Cash, Frank Sinatra and Beverly Sills, who does a duet with Wes Unseld. Brent Musberger is master of ceremonies. He is interrupted periodically by Rick Barry, a featured comedian.

President and Mrs. Carter propose a toast to owner Abe Pollin and the Bullets. "To paraphrase John Kennedy," the President says, "I think this is the most extradordinary collection of talent that has ever been gathered together at the White House, with the possible exception of when Wilt Chamberlain dined alone."

At the head table, NBA Commissioner Larry O'Brien smiles at the memory. When it is his turn to speak, O'Brien acknowledges the presence of the President and then says, "It's good to finally have a real winner in Washington."

Every important person this side of Jerry Brown is at the dinner. The Philadelphia 76ers, who made it all possible, have a table of their own but nobody will pass the vegetables. Halfway through the meal, a waiter hands Lloyd Free a hard roll. He tosses it at a punch bowl 40 feet away and misses.

Referee Earl Strom is there, too. He grows very excited when Johnny Cash begins to sing "I Walk the Line."

The climax of the evening comes when the President calls Elvin Hayes to the podium and hugs him. "Elvin is the kind of man every American can look up to," the President says. "I'm glad that the Bullets won. Of course, I'm also sad that Seattle lost."

Carter's smile grows broader. "I am proud to announce that a portrait of Elvin Hayes will be hung in the White House tomorrow. It will replace the one of former President Ford, although he is a decent and good man."

The next day, hundreds of thousands line Pennsylvania Avenue for the parade to the Capitol. Mayor Walter Washington stands on the steps of the District Building to present Motta with the keys to the city, but he is too slow. Motta's limousine already has passed.

Halfway down the Avenue, Motta suddenly jumps out of his car and begins to walk. Hayes is next, then Bobby Dandridge and Tom Henderson. As they pass the Department of Justice, Charlie Johnson replaces Henderson and the spectators go wild. A small boy throws a basketball, and it rolls around in the street for a moment until Mitch Kupchak dives on it.

Many old-timers recall a similar parade in 1949 when the Washington Senators won nine straight games on the way to finishing last. Now, just as they were 29 years earlier, homemade signs are visible.

See HELLER, C-4

Andrew Beyer

Who Says Boxing Doesn't Pay Off?

Mr. S. spends most of his waking hours analyzing and betting on sports events. Because of the breadth of his knowledge, he can ferret out great gambling opportunities in such unlikely things as Colgate football games, Arizona basketball games and even occasional tennis tournaments.

He devotes hard work to every day's sporting schedule, but in his day-to-day activities this spring, Mr. S. has been thinking steadily about a future wager. His excitement has been building week by week until now, with only eight more days to wait, he can barely contain his enthusiasm.

Mr. S. is waiting for the nationally televised World Boxing Council heavyweight title fight between champion Ken Norton and challenger Larry Holmes on June 9. He says that Holmes, the underdog, is an absolute cinch to win.

"When I saw Holmes fight at the Capital Centre a couple of years ago, I thought he'd be the next champ," Mr. S. said. "They've brought him along slow, and he hasn't gotten all beat up. Everybody says he hasn't beaten anybody, but I thought he looked great in his last fight against Earnie Shavers. Holmes must have beaten him in all 15 rounds."

ALTHOUGH MR. S. thinks that Holmes is generally underrated, that is only a peripheral part of his analysis. He thinks that Norton is the perfect foil for Holmes' style and every time he envisions the nature of the fight, he sees the same result: Norton keeps coming at Holmes aggressively and Holmes keeps holding him off, jabbing, counterpunching, wearing him down until he finishes him off.

"The key to the fight," Mr. S. said, "will be Holmes' left jab. Norton is always the aggressor in his fights, but the jab will keep him at bay. Holmes' jab may not be as accurate as Muhammad Ali's, but it has as much power. When Holmes jabs, you should hear a good, sharp thud.

"Now, you might say Norton did well against Ali, who has a great jab. And if he could bypass Ali's jab, why can't he do the same with Norton? Well, to throw a jab effectively you have to have movement of foot, but Ali had it for only about 30 seconds a round. You can't stand around flat-

See BEYER, C-5

How to Reserve A Championship

By Steve Hershey
Washington Star Staff Writer

SEATTLE — Second-stringer, bench-warmer, back-up man — all are descriptions with derogatory connotations. No one enjoys being referred to as a fill-in for someone else.

On the Bullets, however, it should be an honor to belong to the reserve corps. This team has a stronger bench than the Supreme Court. If it wins the National Basketball Association championship, the subs should receive an equal share of the credit.

Charlie Johnson, Larry Wright, Mitch Kupchak and Greg Ballard all played vital roles in the Bullets' stirring comeback for a dramatic 120-116 overtime victory Tuesday night that tied this best-of-seven series at 2-2.

"In mid-season, before all our injuries, I said we had the best bench in the league," Coach Dick Motta said while winding down at poolside here yesterday. "One thing those injuries did was give our reserves more playing time. I think that's been to our advantage in the playoffs."

IN THE San Antonio Eastern semifinal series, when the Bullets surged to a 4-2 victory after losing the first game, Johnson came off the bench to score 80 points in the last four and fill the void left by a frustrated Kevin Grevey.

As the Bullets shocked heavily favored Philadelphia, 4-2, in the Eastern finals, Wright made 55 percent of his shots, scored 80 points in the last five games and did an excellent defensive job against Lloyd Free to give his team the boost it needed.

In the Seattle series, Kupchak has snapped out of his slump and provided the spark that enabled the Bullets to overcome a 15-point deficit in 14½ minutes Tuesday night.

Ballard has the toughest task of all. The rookie from Oregon is used only in special pressurized instances, but he has come through every time with the poise of a veteran.

"I'm not afraid to use Greg in any situation," Motta said. "He was a clutch player in college, he's very

See BULLETS, C-4

Teamwork Turning Into Desperation

By John Schulz
Washington Star Staff Writer

SEATTLE — For two teams that supposedly epitomize team basketball, the Bullets and Seattle SuperSonics look more like desperate contestants in a game of H-O-R-S-E.

If this is team basketball, these teams have a funny way of showing it. When Seattle gets behind, it turns to the king of the street-shooters, "Downtown" Freddy Brown.

When the Bullets are in a pinch, the ball goes to Bobby Dandridge or Elvin Hayes, if the latter is available and open to get that one vital pass.

So far, except in the fourth quarter of Game 1 when Brown scored 16 of his 30 points, shots from Downtown have been errant. Brown opened the overtime in Game 4 by missing two typically long-distance shots, setting up the Bullets' first two baskets by Charlie Johnson on plays that simply involved three-quarter court passes. Naturally, everybody marveled at the "teamwork."

NOW THE Sonics have turned to Dennis Johnson, who is about the best team player they have. Even so, he shows strong tendencies at times to drive the middle of the lane and simply allow his superior jumping ability to take over.

"Basketball is a very funny game," Dennis Johnson said. "We really wanted to blow out the Bullets when we led by 15 in the third period. We ran for three quarters and then stopped. We started taking the first shot. There won't be any blowouts by either of these teams."

That is because both play decent pro defense. Seattle utilizes center Marvin Webster like the back man in a 1-3-1 zone defense, although mentioning that four-letter word to the Sonics is like talking to a brick wall.

"What's a zone?" Paul Silas asked innocently. "That's something they use in college, isn't it?"

WHATEVER THE Sonics are using, the Bullets' big men have been able to handle it for the most part. Because their guards have been erratic, the Bullets' shooting this series (42.8 percent) isn't as high as

See SONICS, C-4

The Bullets' bench deserves much of the credit for the team's surprising surge to the brink of an NBA championship. Key performers in the playoffs have been subs Charlie Johnson (left), Mitch Kupchak (top), Larry Wright (center) and Greg Ballard.

Did Flanagan Set the Stage For a Streak by the Orioles?

By William Taaffe
Washington Star Staff Writer

NEW YORK — It was either Lord Acton or Casey Stengel who said that pitching depth corrupts and absolute depth corrupts absolutely. Whoever it was must have been talking about the Baltimore Orioles and New York Yankees, circa 1978.

The Orioles seemed to have the right amount of pitching — just enough to keep everybody happy. The Yankees seemed to have too much pitching — just the kind of surplus to keep every hurler in George Steinbrenner's traveling road show glowering at the manager, Billy Martin.

Left-hander Mike Flanagan, one of only four regular starters on the Orioles' staff, proved that less can indeed be more last night when he beat the Yankees, 3-2, on a tidy three-hitter. Ed Figueroa, the losing pitcher, proved the opposite just the other day.

ANGRY THAT he had not been starting every fourth day, Figueroa demanded to be traded. "I'm tired of all this crap," he moaned. "I want to be traded somewhere where they need me. Soon (Andy) Messersmith and (Don) Gullett will be back and they'll have eight starters. That's too many pitchers."

Martin's response to this bleating was predictable: He whined a bit himself. "I'm sick and tired of all this 'trade-me' (bleep). Any player who says trade-me is a copout."

Acrimony aside, though, Figueroa has a point. The Yankees are so laden with famous arms (the parade begins with Ron Guidry and ends with Ken Holtzman, who's pitched 17 innings this year) that most of New

See ORIOLES, C-5

The Orioles' Mike Flanagan retired the last 16 men in a row while pitching a three-hitter against the Yankees last night.

Labre Signs a New Contract, 11 Others Leave Caps' Payroll

By Russ White
Washington Star Staff Writer

Captain Yvon Labre, the most popular player with the hockey Capitals for the past four years, has agreed to a new two-year contract (plus option year). Defenseman Labre, who earned $55,000 a year on his old contract, was raised close to the $70,000 plateau.

Labre's signing yesterday came within hours of the June 1 free agent listing by each National Hockey League franchise.

There are at least 11 Caps on the free agent list today, including veteran forwards Ace Bailey and Billy Collins.

This means that the Caps will make no further effort to sign either Bailey or Collins until they have inspected the free agent lists of the other NHL teams and participated in the June 15 amateur draft.

Other players who leave Abe Pollin's payroll today are defensemen Jean Lemieux, Larry Bolonchuk, Murray Anderson and Bill Mikkelson, and forwards Paul Nicholson, Brian Kinsella, Tony White, Alex Forsyth and Gordie Brooks. Two more players are on a special listing because of injuries — Pete Scamurra and Don MacLean.

LABRE, AT his summer home in Brace Bridge, Ont., said he was delighted to be back with the Caps. Knee surgery and a one-month rehabilitation with the Hershey Bears in the American League kept Labre, 28, away from his defensive duties at Capital Centre. When Labre returned, the Caps made significant late season strides.

In 22 games, Labre had eight assists with 41 penalty minutes, but his plus-minus rating was even and the Caps were able to close the season with respectability.

"Yvon Labre has seen the good and the bad of Capitals' hockey and has contributed greatly to the good days," General Manager Max McNab said last night.

Although relations between the club and Labre's agent, Charles Abrams, appeared to be strained a

See CAPS, C-4

Fig. 9–26. Photographs, white space and page balance make for an attractive, easy-to-read, informative sports page. (Courtesy of the *Washington Star*.)

Sports

Holmes rallies late to win WBC title from Norton

Related story on page 11

Area trio picked in NBA draft

Related story on page 11

By JOHN McGRATH
of the Tribune's staff

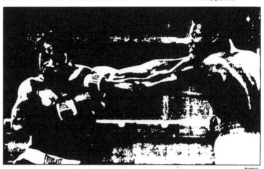

Straight arms   New World Boxing Council heavyweight champion Larry Holmes connects with a left hand to Ken Norton's jaw in the WBC championship bout last night in Las Vegas, Nev. Norton, who was awarded the WBC crown after it was stripped from Leon Spinks, lost on a split decision. It was Norton's first defense of the title. Holmes is expected to face the winner of the Muhammad Ali-Spinks rematch.

Kings hit mother lode with Ford

Related story on page 11

KANSAS CITY, Mo. (AP) — The Kansas City Kings...

Affirmed win would make Triple Crown history

By GERALD STRINE
(c) 1978, The Washington Post

ELMONT, N.Y. — Never in the history of the Triple Crown have there been back-to-back winners.

Cornell signs with Royals

Jeff Cornell, a right-hander Mizzou's pitcher who had completed his junior season yesterday signed with the Kansas City Royals. Kansas City drafted him in the ninth round Wednesday in the major league baseball draft.

Cornell, who is in Hawaii with a summer baseball league team which eventually will play in Alaska, originally planned on delaying whether or not to use his remaining year of eligibility at Missouri for as long as a week.

But the Kansas City offer may have been too hard for Cornell to turn down. He is a Kansas City native and averred Royals fan.

Cornell probably will play next year in Florida once the Royals' rookie affiliate is at Sarasota.

Cornell was 4-2 last season with a regular season earned run average of 2.98.

Fig. 9–27. The combination of a tightly-cropped action photograph and essentially horizontal page format results in an airy, open sports page. (Courtesy of the *Columbia* (Mo.) *Daily Tribune*.)

185

Fig. 9–28. Effective use of action photographs, logos and white space entices readers to this sports page. (Courtesy of the *Grand Rapids* (Mich.) *Press*.)

Professor Arnold, in a *Masthead* article, emphasized that journalists "must make the physical act of reading as painless as possible, releasing as many gray cells as possible for the purely cerebral function." Arnold advocates a five-column or six-column opinion page format, with 1-point leading. He sees merit in changing the appearance of the page daily, making certain to anchor all corners with display elements.

Much can be done with the design of an editorial page. The ingredients are varied—editorials, syndicated columns, cartoons, occasional photographs, letters to the editor, and free lance contributions. David R. Legge wrote in *The Editorial Page,* third volume in the *Washington Post*/Houghton Mifflin casebook series, that "column for column inch, the editorial and opposite-editorial pages are among the most sought-after in the daily newspaper."

The *Post* tries to make the most of the variety. Legge said: "It is almost axiomatic in layout that if a page is difficult to draw on a dummy sheet, it will be difficult to read when made up. Readability— on the editorial pages or on any pages—is the first test of good design. Can the reader tell which story goes with which art?"

Some newspapers continue to design their editorial pages the same way each day. William F. Woo, editorial page editor of the *St. Louis Post-Dispatch,* aims for a simple, dignified, consistent look. The elements on the page never shift: the letters, editorial, cartoons, etc., appear in the same place every day. Readers, it is reasoned, become accustomed to a certain format and feel comfortable with it.

Other newspapers vary editorial page design every day. Robert T. Bernard, opinion page editor of the Louisville *Courier-Journal,* said that his newspaper seeks a different look with each edition. Among other practices, the *Courier-Journal* sometimes shifts the cartoon to the upper left corner (where lead editorials traditionally have been placed) or sometimes runs a boxed editorial across the top of the page. Bernard makes a concerted attempt to liven the page. Other newspapers, such as the *Anniston* (Alabama) *Star,* compromise by keeping the lead editorial in the upper left corner of the page each day, while varying the rest of the layout. The remaining elements are placed "as freely as material and imagination suggest," said executive editor Cody Hall.

Whether a newspaper's editorial page is designed the same way each day or not, a number of devices can help make the page more readable. Art work is a big plus for opinion page design. Of course, newspapers such as the *Washington Post* have the luxury of choosing from several cartoonists. Legge lists the following criteria:

1. Is the art well drawn?
2. Is the drawing compatible with the article?
3. Is the drawing consistent with the "tone" of the page?
4. Is the drawing intelligible? (Most of us have puzzled over the meaning of editorial page art at one time or another.)
5. Will the drawing reproduce? Smaller newspapers also generally have some choice of art work; the decision should not be made haphazardly.

Standing heads for letters to the editor and certain syndicated columnists, a special "opinion page" logo, use of wide measure type, use of blurbs for emphasis, and type face and size variety are among contemporary practices to enliven the editorial page. In addition, packaging can be effectively utilized on the editorial page. Quite often, particularly during times of pervasive public concern about certain national issues, syndicated columnists will write about the same topics. Editors can group these columns and tie them together with a 2-point border—thus providing an organized, convenient marketplace of ideas for the reader. Extra white space, usually above headlines, creates a lighter appearance, as does the use of head shots of columnists. Indeed, contents of the opinion page are often heavy—but well-designed, bright, airy pages can make the material seem less formidable to the reader.

Dummying Pages

Well-designed pages are carefully calculated. The editor who designs pages must be innovative, but philosophically consistent. A newspaper's design philosophy is essentially an extension of its personality. As discussed earlier, newspaper pages can be cluttered and busy looking, or they can be clear and attractive. Though pages differ from day to day, primary design concepts of individual newspapers should not change. For example, the philosophy of some newspapers is to place ten or fewer elements on a page each day, including a dominant picture. If an editor jams seventeen or eighteen elements, including a small, poorly cropped picture, on a page one day, the drastic change in appearance will be noticeable to readers—and it could frustrate them.

Since makeup editors on most dailies do not paste up pages them-

Fig. 9–29. Cartoons, columnists' head photographs, standing headlines, and a clean, airy appearance make this editorial page inviting to read. (Courtesy of the *Gleaner,* Henderson, Ky.)

CONCORD  MONITOR
Monday, June 5, 1978

Thomson's baseless accusations

How to save on a 15-cent stamp

Investigation confirms abuses

Computer in wrong car

Letters

Planes sale hit

Schools mold minds

Issue taken on musical review

Suncook hoodlums

Nominees screened

Carter shuns vets

Fig. 9–30. Ample white space, basically modular design, art work and a bordered letters column make this an easy-to-read editorial page. (Courtesy of the *Concord* (N.H.) *Monitor*.)

selves, they must "dummy" the pages, incorporating all of the design concepts discussed earlier in this chapter. A dummy sheet is a blueprint; just as a carpenter would not begin to build a house without a blueprint, composing room personnel should not be expected to design a newspaper page without specific instructions from the newsroom. Thus, if the dummy is carefully planned, the newsroom is in control of the appearance of its pages.

When dummying a page, the makeup editor should:

• Make sure the dummy is clear and understandable. Clarity is extremely important. Be sure to draw in special effects, like borders. Clearly label them. If it looks confusing, discuss it with the person pasting up the page. Also, label odd-measure columns of type—e.g., 20 picas or 26 picas. It takes but a few seconds more to make an easy-to-follow dummy. A hurriedly scrawled dummy, though initially faster, will often result in confusion and more total time expended.

• Make sure the pictures are accurately sized and the specific pica size is clearly indicated on the dummy. Label pictures with a letter or slug. If two pictures on the same page have similar pica sizes, they could get transposed. Pages are built around art work, so this is of utmost importance.

• Make sure that all stories and pictures scheduled for the page are accounted for on the dummy. Forgetting to dummy a fifteen-inch story or a three-column picture is disastrous.

• Make sure space has been allocated for routine front page elements—the flag, temperatures, and index.

• Make sure the design is functional, e.g., that there are no ornamental devices merely for the sake of ornamentation.

An editor should not be afraid to experiment when designing a page. Seldom is his first effort fruitful. Also, late-breaking stories and pictures often alter already designed pages. Thus, the makeup editor must be flexible.

Note the close relationship between the front page dummy and the final published product of the award-winning *Manhattan* (Kansas) *Mercury*:

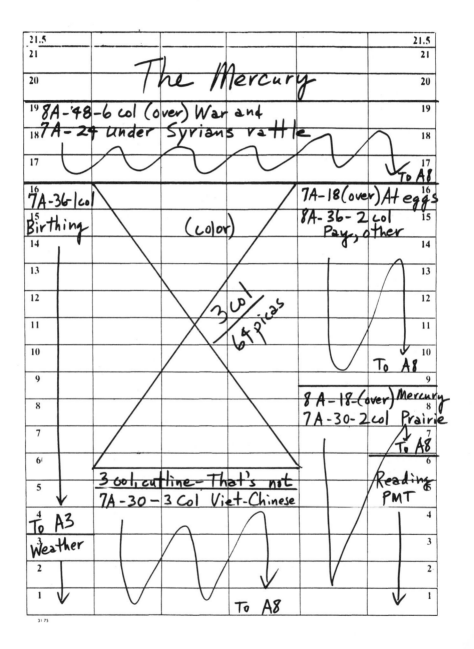

Fig. 9–31. This front page dummy for the *Manhattan* (Kan.)
.*Mercury* gives composing room personnel who paste up the
page a precise road map for story and picture placement. (Courtesy of the *Manhattan* (Kan.) *Mercury*.)

Fig. 9–32. By following directions on the dummy sheet, paste-up personnel can create an attractive, easy-to-read front page. (Courtesy of the *Manhattan* (Kan.) *Mercury*.)

Chapter 10

The Wire Services

MOST DAILY AMERICAN newspaper editors strive to offer a balance of local, state, regional, national, and international news. Editors are constantly challenged to select a news blend appropriate for their readers. Small daily newspapers which circulate primarily in nearby counties emphasize local news. Still, they provide a smattering of nonlocal information. Daily newspapers which circulate statewide emphasize local and regional news, but they also furnish a substantial variety of national and international news.

Selecting and publishing news which will appeal to readers' diverse interests is imperative. Only the nation's most widely circulated newspapers have reporters based in Washington, D.C., and in bureaus in foreign nations. How is it possible, then, for dailies with small and medium circulations—papers with news staffs with limited manpower and finances—to supply their readers with stories from such distant points as Moscow; London; Tehran; Yankton, South Dakota; Stillwater, Oklahoma; and New York?

There is only one economically feasible way—the wire services.

The vast majority of the nation's dailies could not provide extensive nonlocal news coverage were it not for the wire services. Wire services are valuable and indispensable to editors who work diligently to provide readers with a wide-ranging news menu. Thus, it is important that editors understand the contemporary functions of the services which are so necessary to the success of their news missions.

Worldwide today, AP, UPI, Reuters of Great Britain, and Agence France-Press of France form what might be called the "Big Four" wire services. Other nations have domestic wire services but not with the breadth of world coverage provided by the Big Four. In many nations, the news services are owned and operated by the government or, in some cases in the Eastern Bloc nations, by the Communist Party. The Soviet news agency, Tass, is an example.

While only AP and UPI serve United States newspapers and broadcasters with a full range of coverage from every state and around the world, other supplemental wire services have been launched, mainly by individual newspapers. These supplemental wire services, however, make no effort to provide comprehensive national and world coverage. Instead, they zero in on major stories, in-depth reports on subjects of specific concern, news analysis pieces, and feature reports.

There are many such services in the United States today; metropolitan newspapers generally receive news from several of them as well as from the Associated Press, United Press International, or both. Smaller dailies and some broadcast stations receive service from one, or sometimes both, of the basic news services while occasionally subscribing to one or two supplemental services.

Basic News Services

While both the Associated Press and United Press International provide newspapers and broadcasters with basically similar news reports, they vary widely in structure and philosophy. Those newspapers and broadcast stations receiving news from the AP are referred to as "members," reflecting the nature of the AP as a not-for-profit cooperative. On the other hand, those receiving news from UPI are referred to as "clients" or "subscribers," reflecting their relationship to the profit-motive corporate structure of UPI.

Any broadcast station or daily newspaper may receive news today from either or both wire services, as it chooses. There are no restrictions on membership by competitive dailies or stations in a single community or coverage area. Under the terms of its by-laws, members of the Associated Press are considered news-gathering agents for the cooperative and all of its members. The AP is, therefore, protected on happenings in North Platte, Nebraska, for example, by the *North*

Platte Telegraph or any of the broadcast stations holding membership in that community.

Any spot news coverage by an AP member in its own coverage area automatically becomes the property of the AP for its distribution to whatever area it chooses. Each member is required by the by-laws to provide its news to the AP for consideration and distribution.

In most cities where AP bureaus are located, they are housed in daily newspaper buildings and are provided copies of all editions of the newspaper. In many cases, carbons of stories produced by newspaper staff members are provided to the AP bureau and, in some cases today, "electronic carbons" are automatically sent from the newspaper's computer to the AP's computer for processing by AP staff members. Conversely, UPI has no such provision for its clients to provide news to the service. UPI generally pays "stringers," usually a local newspaper or broadcast station newsman, to telephone news to the nearest UPI bureau.

In addition to news stories, both AP and UPI provide their members and clients with a wide range of other services. These include photos moved by wire for newspapers and television stations, color photo slides for television stations, color separations by wire and mail for newspapers, network voice service for radio stations, special features and columns, educational filmstrips, and the like.

Both news services sell material to magazines in the United States and abroad. Both also provide specialized wires for cable television systems and for business firms. The Associated Press also provides photographic services for business, magazines, and others through its World Wide Photos subsidiary. In addition to services within the United States, both the AP and UPI provide news and photo services to subscribers in foreign nations. The AP, for example, provides foreign news reports translated into dozens of languages and distributed either directly by the AP or, as in Italy, for instance, by the Agenzia Giornalistica Italia (AGI). The Soviet Union's Tass is among foreign agencies that receive and redistribute AP news.

Supplemental Services

The content of each daily newspaper varies from that of every other daily primarily through the choice of news from the wire services, the differing local coverage, and the newspaper's philosophical attitudes about what it should be publishing. With but two basic national news services, the AP and UPI, opportunity is limited for a given daily to be substantially different from its competitors in its presentation of national and international news. Both AP and UPI provide tightly-written spot news copy, a selected menu of feature material, and a variety of state, regional, national, and international features.

Nearly every daily newspaper in the United States receives basically this same menu of AP and UPI offerings, thus reducing the opportunities for a newspaper to provide a greatly different selection from that offered by the daily across town or down the highway. Supplemental news services give newspapers a vastly larger choice of copy. There are dozens of supplemental services available, and they offer a multitude of different columns, formats, and ideas for consideration by the nation's daily newspaper editors.

Some supplemental services specialize in coverage of certain types of news, such as Commodity News Services, Inc., which concentrates on agricultural market news. Others supply service only to a select group of clients, such as Gannett News Service, whose clients are all daily newspapers owned by the Gannett chain—the nation's largest group of newspapers under one ownership.

A few services operate their own news wires, providing news by leased wire and printers to their subscribers. Others rely primarily on the mails to deliver material, often in slick proof form for shooting and for offset reproduction without typesetting, to their subscribers.

With the advent of a twelve hundred words per minute computer to deliver news copy by the Associated Press and United Press International in the 1970s, many supplemental services contracted with AP and UPI to provide a transmission vehicle which would deliver their specialized reports to their clients.

A look at the material offered by the *Chicago Tribune-New York Daily News* syndicate reveals the breadth of supplemental news service offerings. This syndicate offers daily newspapers columns dealing with pet care, happenings in Washington, the arts, medicine, bridge, country music, Lou Harris surveys, television, the economy, home repairs, and personal advice through Abigail Van Buren's Dear Abby column.

Similarly varied offerings are available from, among others, the Field Newspaper Syndicate, King Feature Syndicate, *Los Angeles Times* Syndicate, Newspaper Enterprise Association, North American

Newspaper Alliance, Register and Tribune Syndicate Inc., and United Feature Syndicate.

Other supplemental services, such as the *New York Times* News Service, concentrate on in-depth and spot news coverage from around the globe. This coverage often duplicates the subject matter of material available from UPI and AP, but is written from differing viewpoints and often is considerably longer and more analytical than stories from AP and UPI.

Competition of Wire Services

Get it first. Get it right. Those are the most elementary rules by which newsmen operate when employed by the Associated Press and United Press International. From the statehouses to the White House, from Alabama to Wyoming, and from Moscow to Rio de Janeiro, wire service staff members are in head-to-head competition on every significant news story and photo opportunity and on most other stories as well.

Veterans of each wire service can spend hours telling anyone who will listen about their major beats on stories they consider to be highly significant. They usually spend little time, however, telling about those times when the other service got the story first. While both services strive to get the bulletins and urgent stories on the wire first, both also realize that it is equally important to get the information accurately the first time so that time is not lost rechecking information and so that editors and news directors do not have to make corrections after a story has once been published or broadcast.

When one wire service breaks a story the other doesn't have, there's a quick scramble for a "matcher." On its message wires connecting various bureaus, UPI frequently refers to the AP as "the rock," a reference to AP's main offices at 50 Rockefeller Plaza in New York City. On the AP message wires, UPI is often referred to as "brand X" or simply, "the opposition."

Employees of both wire services realize that the copy that first reaches a newspaper which subscribes to both services is more likely to be published than that reaching the newspaper second. But, the employees also are keenly aware that if the other service's copy is better written or more thorough it still may be selected for publication when it arrives later—providing it arrives within deadline time.

Deadline time is every minute in the wire services. Somewhere, it seems, there's always a broadcast station ready for its newscast or willing to break into other programming with a truly significant news bulletin. Somewhere, there is always a newspaper with an edition on deadline.

The need for speedy movement of copy is deeply ingrained in the wire service newsman's spirit. Every wire service employee knows he's likely to get a pat on the back for beating the other service on the big story. He also knows he's likely to be told about it if his copy is late, poorly written, or incomplete and the play goes to the other service.

The competition goes beyond the reporting of news and the providing of photo coverage. In fact, those aspects of the competition heighten the wire services' larger competition—that of competition for members or subscribers and the revenue they provide. The vast majority of the nation's daily newspapers and broadcast stations receive service from only one of the two basic wire services. The decision on which service to receive news from generally is made on one or both of two factors—price and coverage.

Thus both services want to be able to convince newspapers and broadcasters that their news reports are faster, better written, and more comprehensive. Both also want to be able to justify whatever cost difference there may be by pointing to the superiority of the news report.

The Associated Press operates with an annual budget well in excess of $100 million. The bulk of the money comes from membership payments for the news and photo reports. While less than the AP's, the United Press International budget also is substantial and is financed by income from subscribers. Thus, competition between the two services remains intense from the corporate offices to the smallest bureaus.

Cooperation with Wire Services

The Associated Press and United Press International fulfill two essential roles. Both use their far-flung news staffs to cover major stories around the world, and both serve as a channel through which newspapers and broadcast stations can exchange news of regional or more limited interest with each other.

In the structure of the AP as a membership cooperative, the conduit role is a basic part of the service's philosophy. For UPI, the channeling of news is done in large part through payment of stringers on various newspapers or broadcast stations to provide news of their areas for relay to other interested clients or subscribers.

Newspapers and broadcasters throughout the nation should respond to the need to help the wire services to quickly gather facts and photos for major spot news stories. But the avenues of cooperation do not stop with spot news. Sharing of feature stories, combined efforts to gather the various stories needed to make up a major enterprise report on a given topic, quick phone calls to wire service bureaus with reports on less significant stories or tips on other stories —all these things and more are part of the cooperation exhibited between those providing and those receiving wire service reports.

It's not, of course, a one-way street with the wire services receiving and the members giving all. When a daily newspaper editor needs a story on the appearance of a community official before a legislative committee, he simply asks the AP bureau to provide it. If a Denver man is killed in a truck crash in Louisiana, Colorado newspaper editors would ask the AP bureau in Denver to provide the story.

When an editor needs more information on a particular aspect of a story already moved on the wire, he need only call the state bureau of his wire service and explain his needs. If the information is readily available, a response can be made at once. If the information has to be sought, the wire service editor can go after it and then provide it as a lead or insert to the story already on the wire. Or, if the information sought is pertinent only to the requesting newspaper editor, the response can be telephoned for that editor's use. Also when a newspaper experiences difficulty with its wire service printer or its own computers, an editor can call on the wire services to rerun pertinent stories for the newspaper. Inasmuch as the wire services depend largely on members, in the case of the AP, or stringers, in the case of the UPI, to provide the bulk of their regional reports, cooperation is essential.

Chapter 11

Processing
Wire Copy

BEFORE ONE CAN SIT at an editor's desk and process copy pour-
ing in continuously from the wire services, he must have a basic
understanding of what he will be receiving and how to recognize it,
judge its importance, and determine where it fits in the scheme of the
newspaper.

Each day newspapers receive hundreds of wire stories filed from
bureaus around the state, nation, and world. Sorting this voluminous
collection of words, facts, and figures is not, however, as formidable
as it first appears. The wire services have developed coding systems
which, once mastered, enable an editor to efficiently channel stories
to their proper destinations.

Naturally, most newspapers discard far more wire copy than they
use. Dozens of stories are condensed, localized, or summarized. Thus,
it is particularly important that editors process copy as quickly as
possible; deadlines are ever-present. The wire services, through systematic routing, advisories, budgets, priority codes, etc., help the
hurried editor keep pace with the perpetual flow of news. Computerization, in this electronic news editing age, also has streamlined the
process.

Because of early deadlines on most newspapers, decisions must be
made quickly in planning coverage of the day's news events. The wire
editor of an afternoon newspaper enters the office—often half awake

—around dawn. How does he determine the day's top stories, even though some of the far-away news events won't materialize for hours? The editor soon learns that a wire service "budget" is his best friend.

Each morning he will receive on his national wire a listing of the top twelve or so stories around the nation and the world. Here, for example, are portions of the national budget from the two major wire services for the same day. First, the AP budget:

PM-News Digest,

AP NEWS DIGEST
Tuesday PMS

Here are the PMS budgets. The General Desk supervisor is. . . .

THE COLLISION:

Skies Were Clear And Pilots Sighted Each Other

SAN DIEGO—Investigators want to know why two planes—a Boeing 727 passenger trijet and a tiny Cessna—collided in clear skies over San Diego when both pilots had radioed they had the other plane in sight. The flaming crash, the worst disaster in U.S. aviation history, killed 147. Slug PM-Crash, Developing. Laserphotos G01-5.   650.

With sidebars as they develop.

Lack of Warning Equipment Hit

WASHINGTON—The federal government hasn't moved fast enough toward developing warning equipment that might prevent collisions like the one which killed at least 147 persons over San Diego Monday, says the president of the Air Line Pilots Association. Slug PM-ALPA-Collisions.

New Material, lead prospects uncertain.   400.

INFLATION:

Carter Promises Stronger Fight

WASHINGTON—President Carter is promising a sharper attack on rising prices as his advisers seek reinforcement for their prediction that inflation can be held to 8 percent this year. Slug PM-Inflation Rdp. New material, will be led with 9 a.m. EDT release of August Consumer Price Index.   470.

Laserphoto WX2.

And, from the UPI budget:

PM-Sked 9-26

Good morning. The UPI report for Tuesday afternoon newspapers will include:

———

THE WORST CRASH

It was a 100-degree noon and the sky over San Diego was clear. Suddenly, it was raining—raining bodies, fire and wreckage.

It could have been a scene from several Hollywood disaster movies. A small Cessna, its pilot practicing instrument landings, clipped a Pacific Southwest Airlines Boeing 727 at 3,000 feet.

But it was real—too real. As people on the ground watched in horror, the crippled jetliner began to burn, explode and fall out of the sky. Bodies rained down on yards, trees and sidewalks. Two smashed through a car's windshield and killed a woman and her baby. The blazing fuselage plummeted into a quiet residential area like a blockbuster bomb, leveling homes and incinerating occupants beyond identification. At least 150 people were killed, making it the worst air disaster ever in America's skies.

Looters scurried into the burning wreckage to rob the dead and five were arrested. Morgue attendants are still trying to count and name the dead and aviation officials are still trying to answer the question: Why?

We will have an 800-word main lead (Plane) by Stewart Slavin, which will be updated as developments warrant. The main story, a scene-setter, is designed for use in those newspapers that reported the crash in Monday afternoon editions.

For those newspapers with early editions that missed the Monday stories, we will offer an alternate hard-news lead.

Pictures. Color and 9-by-12 have moved.

Related stories include (Terror) on ground reaction, and others on the controversy at the (Airport) and a background piece on the airline (PSA).

WASHINGTON

(Prices) WASHINGTON—The nation's wearisome fight against inflation may finally be showing some positive results. The August consumer price index is due at 9 a.m. EDT. By James Hildreth. 400. Will be led.

Similar digests are transmitted by AP and UPI for their state reports and their sports reports and, on financial wires, for their business reports. Many of the supplemental news services also provide budgets on their wires to help guide the wire editor.

Once the wire editor has skimmed the budget, he is ready to process the news. Again, the wire services, through systematic organization, help simplify the editor's task. Every item coming in on a wire service printer or into a newspaper's computer from the wire services begins with a transmission number. That number contains important information in the letter that precedes the numeral if the newspaper is receiving a high-speed wire (1,200 words per minute) or more than one slow-speed (66 words per minute) wire. If the newspaper is receiving but a single slow-speed wire, the initial letter will be the same on every item and the numerals will always be in sequence.

For example, on a small daily with a single slow-speed Associated Press wire, the first item at the opening of the PMS (afternoon newspapers) cycle may be j001. The stories following will carry sequential numbers such as j002, j003, and on through the total filed on that day's PMS cycle. The *j* is arbitrary; it will vary from state to state and service to service. It is simply a designation placed on the lineup of stories by the wire service computer. On slow-speed wires, each item would carry the single letter along with three numerals.

Here are three one-paragraph examples of the first few items on the PMS wire on a given day:

j001
  r w
PM-Budget Roll Call,100
    WASHINGTON (AP)—The 47-7 roll call vote by which the Senate gave final approval Saturday to a budget for the federal government for the upcoming fiscal year which begins next month included the following vote:
  j002
    r n
PM-Doctors,280
    LINCOLN, Neb. (AP)—The president of the Nebraska Medical Association said Saturday he expects the association will stand firm in its opposition to the creation of a professional standards review organization in the state.
  j003
    r a
PM-Bargaining, Bjt,490
    NEW YORK (AP)—Haggling over prices may seem more suited to a Mideast bazaar than to a Midwest boutique, but give-and-take bargaining can save you just as much money at home as it can abroad.

The system varies slightly for newspapers with three slow-speed wires—a basic state and national report, a sports wire, and a financial wire. The basic state report would include both state and regional news, along with national and international news. It would carry a single letter designation on all copy and each story would be sequentially numbered, just as in the above example, say from j001 through j152 for PMS. For AMS (morning newspapers), the same wire might begin with j500 and run through from there.

The sports reports, which also would be numbered sequentially, might begin with the letter *s* on each item and the financial wire might begin with the letter *f* and also would be numbered in sequence.

On high-speed wires, every item will carry a four-numeral designation, preceded by a single letter. There is no single sequential numbering system on the high-speed wire. Stories beginning with *s* or *f* or *a*, etc., will be intermixed on the wire. All of the stories beginning with the same letter designation will, however, move in numerical sequence.

The single high-speed wire coming into a newspaper might, for example, carry the following stories in the following order:

*a*5001
*a*5002
*s*3000
*f*0001
*a*5003
*f*0002
*s*3001

As on the slow-speed wire, these letters are arbitrary, and once fixed at a location they will not vary. Designators *a* or *b* are always for spot news or advances. Designator *f* is always for financial news, and designator *s* is always for sports copy. It's possible, however, for other letters to designate sports copy, such as *h,* which is used by the Associated Press for the abbreviated sports report provided on the limited DataStream circuit which provides the high-speed report for smaller newspapers.

Letters vary for different state reports. A newspaper, for example, might receive wires from Illinois, Iowa, Nebraska, and Minnesota. Stories from Illinois may carry an *i* designator, from Iowa a *k* designator, from Nebraska a *j* designator and from Minnesota a *d* designator. These designators will vary from place to place and from wire service to wire service. In some technical contexts, the designator letter is termed a "service level designator."

In most cases no combination of letters and figures is used as a transmission number more than once in twenty-four hours. The primary exceptions are the national digests, which are repeated on high-speed wires after the transmission numbers for budget stories have been added, and sports copy on days when more than 1,000 stories are filed nationwide on a high-speed wire.

Transmission numbers are assigned to stories by wire service computers.

Category Codes

Category codes are intended to help newspapers with computer systems sort copy into various queues, or lists, putting all of the stories involving sports, for example, together for the sports editor to process. The sports queue might contain sports copy not only from the national sports wire, but from the state wires read by the newspaper, as well.

The category codes allow a computer at a newspaper to do the job an editor might do in sorting hard copy (copy from a printer) into piles. Editors on newspapers still receiving printer copy can, of course, use the category codes to manually sort copy. Category codes are placed on stories by wire service editors, not by computers. The principal category codes, and their use, according to the Associated Press stylebook:

a and *b*—Domestic general news items, excluding those from Washington. The *a* and *b* codes are used interchangeably.

e—Entertainment items, such as Hollywood columns, television and movie reviews and the like.

f—Copy designed primarily for use on newspaper business or financial pages.

i—International items, including copy from the United Nations and all foreign datelines.

l—Lifestyle items, such as CB radio columns and reports on unusual hobbies or activities of persons.

n—Copy of state or regional interest carrying datelines from points in the United States. If the dateline is foreign, the item would carry an *i* category code. If the dateline is Washington, the item would carry a *w* category code. If the regional item is intended for use on financial pages, the item would carry an *f* category code.

q—This category code is used only for the bare score, or period score, of a single sports event. The code permits a newspaper computer to build incoming scores into a complete list, or to disregard individual scores and await a full list of scores.

s—Sports stories and agate material carry this category code.

v—Advisories involving any stories or photos moved on wire service circuits carry a *v* category code. *V* code items are generally in the form of notes to editors, late news advisories, notations of what has been transmitted, etc.

w—This category code identifies all stories moving under a Washington dateline. If developments cause the dateline to change from Washington, subsequent copy on that story should carry an *a* or *b* category code.

Priority Codes

The urgency of a story dictates which priority code a wire service editor will place on the story. At newspapers, this code can be used to determine the order in which stories should come to the attention of an editor.

The principal priority codes, in order of urgency, according to the Associated Press stylebook:

f—Flash. The highest priority. Seldom used, except for bulletin kills and matters of transcendent importance.

b—Bulletins, first adds to bulletins, kill notes.

u—Urgent, high-priority copy, including all corrections. This code is used on all items carrying an URGENT slug and may be used on copy not carrying an URGENT slug but which must move quickly.

r—Regular priority, covering digest stories, late-breaking stories, special fixture items.

d—Deferred priority. Used for spot copy that can be delayed if more urgent material needs to be moved.

h—The lowest spot news priority. When this priority code is used on high-speed wires, it normally indicates that a story bearing it will not move on the A wire, which carries the most important stories only.

s—For Sunday advances intended for use more than twelve hours after transmission.

y—This code is used for internal copy routing among Associated Press bureaus. It is rarely seen by a newspaper and generally indicates a rerun.

x—This code is used by AP bureaus to move copy to AP's New York sports and financial departments only. It is not seen by newspaper editors.

Transmission numbers, category codes and priority codes can be seen on an editor's screen or on hard printer copy as indicated below:

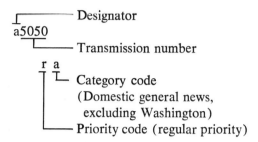

Keyword Slug Line

Immediately following the designator, transmission number, priority code, and category code, wire service copy will carry a cycle designator and keyword slug line and wordage count.

Cycle designators are always upper case and are always preceded by an upper rail, shown on many cathode ray tubes as ↑ or ∧.

There are three cycle designators:

AM—Indicates morning newspapers have first use of the copy.

PM—Indicates evening newspapers have first use of the copy.

BC—Indicates that the copy is for use by either AM or PM newspapers immediately if the item does not carry an advance slug, or on the publication date given if it does. This designation is used on all Sunday advances.

The keyword slug line immediately follows the cycle designator, separated only by a hyphen. This was simply called a "slug" in the past, but the new description was adopted because the line is the key that many newspaper computer systems use to link automatically any leads or other updates filed for a story.

The keyword itself is simply a descriptive word telling what the copy is about. Generally, the keyword should be a single word and it should be a word not likely to be used on any other story during the same cycle. The keyword, or keywords if more than one word is used, should not be longer than twenty-one letters and/or figures. It is followed by a comma and wordage count, rounded to the nearest ten, and then a flush left symbol, shown on many cathode ray tubes as either ← or <. The comma does not show up on high-speed circuits.

The keyword may consist of commonly used abbreviations and

acronyms, such as XGR for Legislature or *Scotus* for Supreme Court of the United States.

If there are several stories related to a single main topic on a given day, the same initial keyword should show on all copy. For example, on a day when the state legislature is involved in several major actions, the main story might be slugged: PM-XGR-General,450. The sidebars might be slugged: PM-XGR-Budget,200 and PM-XGR-Abortion,350. In each case, the numerals are the word counts for the given story.

The keyword slug line might include additional information if the story is a digest story on the particular cycle or if the story runs more than one take. No story on a slow-speed wire should run more than 450 words in a single take. Additional copy must be placed in a second take. On a high-speed wire the complete story may run in a single take.

If the main legislative story above is a budget item, running 800 words, the keyword slug lines on the two takes would look like this:

PM-XGR-General,Bjt-2 Takes,450-800
PM-XGR-General,Bjt, 1st Add,350

Note that the word count on the first example is in two parts, the first portion being the wordage of that take, the second portion being the total wordage of the two takes. The budget designation is separated from the main keyword by a comma but no space, and a hyphen separates the *Bjt* designation from the number of takes, again with no space. A comma always precedes the word count.

That portion of the keyword slug line noting *Bjt* or numbers of takes or the add is called the "version" section. It is intended to give newspaper computers and editors an easy indication of whether to place an item at the top, bottom or middle of previously sent material carrying the same main keyword. When more than one term is needed in the version section of a keyword slug line, the terms are separated by a hyphen with no spaces.

According to the Associated Press stylebook, only one of the following terms may appear in a version section (these terms are discussed in detail below):

Bjt
1st Ld, 2nd Ld, 10th Ld, etc.
Adv 01, Adv 15, etc.

Advisory
KILL
WITHHOLD
ELIMINATION

There is a second group of terms that may appear in a version section, but any of the terms from the second grouping must follow one of those listed above if any of the terms above are needed. The second group:

2 Takes, 4 Takes, etc.
1st Add, 3rd Add, etc.
Insert
Sub
Correction
Writethru
Box

It's possible that more than one of the above may be needed in the version section, in which case they can come in any order, but must be separated by a hyphen.

Format Identifiers

Two additional letters may show on copy moving on the wire. These letters, which immediately follow the priority and category codes and are on the same line, are limited to the following combinations: bt, bx, at, and ax. In this context, *b* means body type, *a* means agate type, *t* indicates the item contains tabular material, even if only one line of it, and *x* means that the entire item is in text, or non-tabular format.

Below are some samples of the information preceding a story on the wire:

a5050
u abx
↑ PM-Capitol,Bjt-2 Takes,400-800 ←

a6060
u wbx
↑ AM-Capitol,7th Ld-2 Takes,300-700 ←

j7070
a nbx
↑ BC-Rattlers,Adv 05-3 Takes,450-1100 ←

Terminology Dictionary

Many of the terms used on wire service copy have been covered in the preceding pages. There are others, however, with which editors should be familiar.

Here's a brief, alphabetical listing of various wire service terms and their meanings:

Add—An add is additional information on a story and is filed under the same keyword as the first take of material, with an add designation in the keyword slug line.

Advance slugs—Stories transmitted for future use carry an Adv and two-digit numeral in the keyword slug line. The line below that carries this coding—$adv 03—consisting of a "junk line" with the advance date to place the advance number in visible code in perforated tape. A third line carries the precise release information, such as "For Release Wed **PMS** June 9."

Bulletin—A bulletin contains at least one publishable paragraph and not more than two. It is used on top priority stories.

Bulletin matter—This slug may be used on no more than the first add to a particularly important story carrying a bulletin priority code.

Byline—The boldface, centered name of a writer and a second boldface centered line showing his designation.

Correction—Indicates that material corrects something in previously filed copy carrying the same keyword. An explanation of specifics is included; corrections always carry a *u* priority code.

Corrective—An item transmitted with a request to a newspaper to print the material if they carried a previous story on the subject. An explanation accompanies correctives. Normally correctives fix errors which reached print before they were discovered, usually on a previous day.

DataRecap—A high speed transmission pulling together various pieces of a single story into one more easily handled piece of copy.

Dateline—The designation of what community a piece of copy is filed from.

Dash lines—Three dashes, centered, are used to separate individual items sent under one transmission number and are used following a publishable editor's note. Dash lines also may be used on copy, such as election copy, so that material, generally background, can be set in type and will not have to be altered later.

Elimination—A bulletin elimination is filed when a story is offensive, untrue or inadequate, but not libelous. Stories eliminated must not be printed. If the material is libelous, a *Kill* is filed rather than an elimination.

Flash—A flash is used only to report a development of transcendent importance. It usually is only a few words following a dateline and is not in a complete sentence. It is followed immediately by a publishable bulletin. An example:

FLASH

DALLAS (AP)—Kennedy shot.

Hold-for release—Copy that is moved for release later in the same cycle carries a second line below the keyword slug line saying to hold for release at a given time, or saying to hold for release when an advisory moves to release the material.

Insert—An insert will carry the keyword, dateline, reason for insert and number of the paragraph in the previous copy that the insert is to follow.

Kill—A kill is moved on the wire when potentially libelous information has been sent in a story. A kill may pertain to an entire story or to a portion of a story. A kill moves on an *f* priority. A kill is followed immediately by an advisory explaining whether a substitute story, or a sub, will be filed.

Lead—A lead to a story provides new information and should always be used to update anything in the fourth paragraph or higher in a story.

Logo—A logo designates which wire service a story is from. Examples: (AP) or (UPI) or (Reuters). A logo follows the dateline and is followed by space-dash-space before the start of copy.

"More" lines—A slug of "more" at the conclusion of a take of copy tells newspapers that additional copy on that story is upcoming.

Nonpublishable editor's notes—Nonpublishable editor's notes are not indented, are sent boldface, and end with a flush left symbol.

Photo slug—A line after the keyword slug line may say that the story is accompanied by photos and gives the numbers of the photos.

Pickup lines—All leads, subs, corrections and inserts end with a pickup line. The exception is a *writethru* or a lead slugged "more" which need not carry a pickup line. The pickup line consists of the first two words of the paragraph into which the item picks up and gives the number of the paragraph as it existed before the lead was filed. Pickup lines also give the previous transmission number when available. An example:

a5130

  r w

PM-Kennedy Hearings,1st Ld,310

WASHINGTON (AP)—Handwriting analysts found no evidence supporting the theory that Lee Harvey Oswald had an imposter who either framed him or helped him in the assassination of President John F. Kennedy, the House assassinations committee was told today.

(Remainder of lead)

The panel's: 4th graf a5060

Precede—A precede line follows the keyword slug line and shows that a dateline is being changed.

Publishable editor's notes—Always begin with an indentation and the words EDITOR'S NOTE in all caps and are then separated from the text of the copy by a dash line.

Reference number—Used when possible with leads, inserts and the like and gives the number of the item as last transmitted.

Rerun—All stories being rerun on a circuit should carry a slug below the keyword slug line reading: REPEATING. The line may say what newspaper the repeat is for, such as: REPEATING for Greenville News.

Sidebar—A sidebar is a story to accompany a main lead on a subject. The sidebar keyword consists of the main story keyword followed by a hyphen and a second keyword.

Sub—A sub is a substitute paragraph for a story. The sub gives the reason for substituting and gives the number of the paragraph to be substituted, along with the first two words of that paragraph, an ellipsis, and the last two words of the graf being deleted. The new paragraph then is filed and ends with a pickup line. An example:

131

　r w

PM-Vance,Sub,60

WASHINGTON: To update with Vance-Carter meeting, sub for 3rd graf pvs. Vance, who . . . David accords.

Vance, who visited the heads of state of Jordan, Saudi Arabia and Syria, reported directly to Carter at an early-morning meeting today that was not announced in advance.

Vance's final: 4th graf pvs

Subheads—Not routinely used in news copy, but sometimes used to break up lengthy text or a sports results list. Subheads may be centered or flush left and are always boldface.

Supplementary slugs—These are slugs on the line below the keyword slug line, such as advance slugs, photo slugs, or the like.

Transmission number—The number assigned to a given piece of copy by a wire service computer.

Undated—A story without a dateline is undated. In place of a logo it will say: "By The Associated Press" or "By United Press International," etc. These are normally used on roundup stories, such as weather.

Urgent—An urgent is an important story which the wire service believes should move quickly. An urgent lead should not be more than 150 words long and an urgent add should not exceed 250 words. The urgent slug is on the line below the keyword slug line and is boldface, all caps.

Withhold—A withhold is filed when the information in a story has been questioned. It asks newspapers to withhold publication of the material pending further information. That information is filed as a kill, an elimination or an advisory releasing the story after the wire service has checked the accuracy of the story.

Word count—The last information on the keyword slug line is an estimate of the length of the story. This serves as a guide as to how much space the story will take when in print.

Writethru—A writethru is a complete rewrite of a story, incorporating all leads, adds, inserts and subs into one, completely rewritten story.

The Wires

While there are but two basic wire services in the United States, the Associated Press and United Press International, a host of supplementary wire services—such as the New York Times News Service, the Chicago Sun-Times News Service, and the Washington Star News Service—are available. AP and UPI attempt to provide a full spectrum of coverage of state, national and international news, along with complete coverage of sports, business, and other such fields. Supplementary services, by contrast, offer specialized reporting in certain fields, or general features and stories, but make no attempt to provide complete coverage of the state, nation or world.

Both AP and UPI offer a variety of wires to their respective members and clients. The primary national news wire of each service is called the "A" wire, often written as "AAA" or "Aye." A wire carrying national and international news of secondary importance is termed the "B" wire, also called the "BBB" wire.

Both AP and UPI offer financial wires, sports wires, state wires, stock market wires, and various regional wires. There are wires labeled SNO (state news only) and wires termed TTS, IB, or "single-circuit" wires which carry a complete basic news report for smaller newspapers.

Also, both AP and UPI offer broadcast wires which cover national news and news from a particular state or region in a fashion similar to the IB wires serving smaller newspapers. The style and format of broadcast wires differ considerably from that of newspaper wires. Essentially, copy is often repeated in rewritten form and stories are shorter. These wires also are moved in an all-caps format.

An example of the first paragraph of a story in newspaper style, then in broadcast style:

SAN DIEGO (AP)—A large jetliner approaching an airport crashed into a residential area Monday morning, police said. There were no immediate reports of casualties, but unconfirmed reports said up to 80 persons were aboard the plane.

(SAN DIEGO)—POLICE IN SAN DIEGO SAY A LARGE JETLINE APPROACHING AN AIRPORT CRASHED INTO A RESIDENTIAL AREA TODAY. THERE ARE NO REPORTS OF CASUALTIES AS YET, BUT UNCONFIRMED REPORTS SAY UP TO 80 PERSONS WERE ABOARD THE PLANE.

Slow-speed wires from both services generally provide copy at 66 words per minute, limiting a single slow-speed wire to a theoretical maximum of about 95,000 words per twenty-four-hour period. In practice, the volume is less since a wire seldom runs without pause. Slow-speed wires may run at speeds up to 100 words per minute.

High-speed wires run at 1,200 words per minute, boosting the theoretical maximum per twenty-four-hour period to about 1,728,000 words. That maximum is also unlikely to be reached. Generally, newspapers receive only selected portions of a high-speed wire, determined by coding done in selectors which sort the high-speed wire before it enters a newspaper computer.

The AP's high-speed wire, for example, carries numerous state wires, along with various national wires, in a given region. But, receiving newspapers in the region are interested only in copy from some of those wires and thus have selectors coded on the basis of designator letters to accept only those wires in their computers.

A second high-speed wire is available from the AP to carry various supplementary wires to which a member newspaper subscribes. Again, a selector is set up at the member newspaper to select out only those supplementary wires to which the individual newspaper subscribes. UPI carries these supplementary wires on its single high-speed circuit, along with its own variety of wires.

A third speed level is available from AP. Termed DigitalStocks, the wire provides computer-to-computer input on complete stock market tables from the AP to member newspapers at 12,000 words per minute, permitting newspapers to receive closing markets more quickly, thus enabling them to meet ever-tighter deadline schedules. No hard copy is available at the 12,000 words per minute speed.

Editing Wire Copy

Consideration number one in editing wire service copy is: Don't do anything to change the meaning or integrity of the copy as provided by the wire service. AP and UPI strive to provide impartial, balanced coverage of the news, with no political or other slants to color their reports. Regardless of the viewpoint of a given newspaper, wire service copy (or for that matter local copy) should never be edited or written in such a way as to give preferential treatment or coloring to a story.

With the exception of features, wire service copy is generally written in the inverted pyramid style. That is, with the most important information at the top and less important information as the text goes on. Generally, wire service copy can be cut most simply be removing paragraphs from the bottom up until achieving the desired length. In doing so, one should be careful not to remove any explanatory paragraph which is essential to convey the story accurately.

Due to the intensely competitive nature of the wire services and the need to get a story out as rapidly as possible, copy is not always edited as tightly as newspaper editors or the wire services might prefer. It is often possible to selectively edit wire service copy, removing excess verbiage.

For those newspapers continuing to use perforated tape to set their wire service copy, selective editing is a time-consuming and costly process. Each paragraph that is altered must be reset by hand in the newspaper composing room. For that reason, such editing is relatively uncommon. Corrections of typographical errors in such situations usually require resetting only a single line and are more routine than extensive in-copy editing.

For newspapers with the new electronic aides of cathode ray tubes (CRTs), or video display terminals (VDTs) as some prefer to call them, selective editing is a simple process, indeed. Since the wire copy is not being sent to the newspaper in justified perforated tape, an editor can freely edit the copy and then send it to his composing equipment from his screen with all corrections and deletions.

Occasionally, a wire service story will leave an unanswered question. When this happens, the editor must first be sure that the answer is not in some portion of the story that was edited out. He must then make sure that the question was not answered in a lead, add, sub, or correction filed by the wire service. If the question remains after checking carefully, the state bureau of either the AP or UPI must be called, told the transmission number and keyword of the story in question and asked for the information needed.

Normally, the wire service is able to provide a quick answer from its own source copy or from the editor's knowledge of the story. Sometimes the state wire service bureau will have to ask another bureau, where the story originated, for the information. That can take time, but usually can be accomplished in about an hour. Because of the time lag and upcoming deadlines, inquiries should be made as quickly as possible. It greatly enhances the chance that the wire service will be able to obtain the information in time for the next edition.

Frequently, newspapers receive copy from both AP and UPI and, perhaps, from a supplemental wire service on the same subject. There may be different details in the stories and the editor may wish to use some of the material contained in each of the two or more versions of the story.

He can.

But he should not leave the logo of any single wire service on the story. Most newspapers have developed a line they use on combination stories, such as "From Press Services," "From News Wires," or the like. On combination stories, attribution should be used internally.

For example, stories are received from both AP and UPI on one plane crash, and each contains different details that should be printed. The finished product might look like this:

> From News Wires
> ANYPLACE, State—Thirteen persons were killed in the crash of a commercial airliner today when the pilot died of an apparent heart attack, the Associated Press reported.
> Pilot Jim Williams, 57, had undergone a physical examination only two days before and was pronounced in excellent health by his physician, United Press International said.

All of the victims had boarded the plane at Someplace and were en route to Anyplace, the AP said.

Opinion in News

An editor should also be wary of opinion in wire service copy which is not labeled as such. The basic wire services serve a wide spectrum of newspapers with varying political and philosophical beliefs. The function of the services leaves no room for opinionizing.

Supplemental services may, on occasion, provide opinion in copy, and the UPI and AP wires may sometimes carry analysis pieces which the editor believes contain opinions. If this is the case, it is suggested that the story be preceded with an editor's note saying that the item contains opinions of the writer or the article should be internally labeled "analysis" or "opinion." For example, a newspaper which subscribes to the New York Times News Service might label a piece by Associate Editor Tom Wicker as follows:

> Swiftly moving events in Africa probably will produce strong new pressures upon President Carter to take more forceful action to counter the Soviet-Cuban presence on that continent.

News Analysis

> But what he should do is not so clear, except to those who always advocate military intervention.

If an editor comes across wire service copy that is represented as straight news material but contains obvious opinion, without being labeled "commentary" or "analysis," he should call his state wire service bureau and discuss it with the bureau chief or bureau manager. Usually, the wire service will gladly make a correction or justify the material as not being opinionated.

Chapter 12

The Editor
and the Law

MOST EDITORS HAVE experienced a sinking stomach feeling, weak knees, or outright panic when threatened with litigation. To compound this possibility, there are many ways an editor can be drawn into a courtroom. Areas in which the journalist is most likely to become involved include libel, fair trial/free press, contempt, privacy, and copyright.

Libel undoubtedly strikes the greatest fear into an editor. The reason is simple: astronomical damages are often sought. Large newspapers have legal staffs and resources to fight cases to their litigated conclusions. Widely circulated syndicated columnists such as Jack Anderson retain experienced counsel. Most newspapers, however, do not have vast financial and legal resources. It is important, therefore, that all editors have an understanding of communication law.

What, for example, does an editor do when Bill Green, a local merchant, threatens to cancel all his advertising and sue the paper if it prints his conviction for drunken driving? What options are open to to the editor when Mrs. Jones, eighty-year-old patron saint of the community, says she plans to sue the paper for libel because she was listed in the court news as being sentenced for contributing to the delinquency of a minor when, in reality, she was merely fined for running a stop sign? Or, what does an editor do when John Smith, who

221

is running for the state legislature, brings suit for a story that documented his bootlegging during the Depression?

Actually, there are ample precedents for editors confronted with these situations. The editor should not lose any sleep over Green and Smith; if Mrs. Jones is serious, however, he had better initiate overtures for an out-of-court settlement if he thinks that the newspaper was possibly negligent. Unfortunately, not all situations are as routine.

The Law of Libel

It is clear that editors must have a basic knowledge of law, particularly libel. Editors who touch base with attorneys each time a potentially sticky issue arises are likely to be editorially conservative and not report the news in the uninhibited, robust manner to which newspapers have a constitutional right.

Newspaper editors have a reasonable amount of protection when defending against libel suits—particularly if the plaintiffs are public officials or figures. Development of libel law, however, is an ongoing process. Though newspaper editors have a constitutionally-protected freedom to discuss public persons today, certain questions still have no concrete answers. How is a public figure defined? What constitutes "actual malice"? How far can newspapers go when reaching into the private lives of public officials?

Despite these complex questions, editors can have a working knowledge of libel. They should at least be able to recognize potentially libelous passages. According to the late Dean Prosser, defamation, made up of the twin torts of libel and slander, is generally held to mean "that which tends to injure 'reputation' in the popular sense; to diminish the esteem, respect, goodwill or confidence in which the plaintiff is held, or to excite adverse, derogatory or unpleasant feelings or opinions against him." Common law libel includes several classes of words: those which impute commission of a criminal offense; those which impute infection with a communicable disease which would exclude the victim from society; those which impute lack of integrity in the performance of employment; those which prejudice a particular party in his profession or trade; and those which impute immoral conduct.

Certain requirements must also be met before there is a cause for action. Robert Phelps and E. Douglas Hamilton, authors of a comprehensive book dealing with the subject, stress that there must be publication to a third party which has a damaging effect on an individual's reputation or good name; there must be identification of the person allegedly defamed; and there must be harmful effect. If one of these elements is missing, there is no libel.

Libel Defenses

If these conditions are met, however, the newsman is not automatically assessed damages. Before 1964, most libel actions were defended under statutory and common law provisions which varied widely among jurisdictions. It was in *New York Times Co.* v. *Sullivan* (1964) that the Supreme Court articulated the "actual malice" defense which could be utilized when public officials were the plaintiffs. (See below for a fuller explanation of the "actual malice" defense.)

Though the "actual malice" doctrine has become a primary post-1964 libel defense, common law defenses—used exclusively before the landmark decision—are also available if the newsman desires. Some of the defenses are absolute: consent or authorization; self-defense or right of reply; privilege of participant; and the statute of limitations. The remainder are conditional: truth; privilege of reporting; and fair comment and criticism. When utilizing a conditional defense, the defendant obviously must meet certain conditions for the defense to prove effective. If privilege of reporting is cited, for example, Phelps and Hamilton emphasize that it must be made clear that the article is a report, that it is fair and accurate, that there is no extraneous libelous matter, and that it is published without malice.

A summary of available common law defenses:

● *Consent or authorization.* When the plaintiff is aware a story is about to be printed and consents to its publication. This, obviously, is not likely to happen often.

● *Self-defense or right of reply.* If a victim of an attack in the press refutes the allegations, he must be careful not to overextend his protection; e.g., the reply must be related to the original publication and cannot be a separate personal attack.

● *Privilege of participant.* Protection given words spoken in legislative, judicial, or other official proceedings which are relevant to the role of the participant.

● *Statute of limitations.* This defense bars suits after a certain period of time. With only five exceptions—Arkansas, Delaware, Hawaii, New Mexico, and Vermont—the statute of limitations on libel is one, two, or three years.

● *Truth.* This is an absolute defense in a number of states, but in others only truthful statements which are published for "justifiable ends" or "good motives" are protected. Truth is not pervasively used as a defense. Critics of the Alien and Sedition Acts of 1798 were quick to learn that truth is often illusory and difficult to prove.

● *Privilege of reporting.* Since so much news evolves from governmental proceedings, this defense is commonly used. It gives the press a conditional privilege to make fair and accurate reports of what happens during public meetings and to report the contents of official reports.

● *Fair comment and criticism.* This defense gives the reporter or editor the right to articulate his *opinions* on matters of "public interest," e.g., reviews and editorials.

The "Actual Malice" Doctrine

Despite the common law defenses, threat of a libel action when discussing public officials (prior to 1964) continued to plague journalists. Newsmen who were guilty of small errors in reporting the activities of public officials were often faced with huge damage suits.

During the 1950s, a growing trend toward increased press protection developed, thus paving the way for the *Times* "actual malice" rule. The rule was adopted in a suit brought by L. B. Sullivan. Sullivan, one of three elected commissioners of Montgomery, Alabama, filed the action against the New York Times Company, alleging that he had been libeled by a *Times* advertisement published in 1960. The advertisement included statements, some of them false, about police action directed against students who participated in a civil rights demonstration and against a leader of the civil rights movement, Dr. Martin Luther King, Jr.

The rule of fair comment in Alabama was like that found in the majority of jurisdictions in America. It limited privilege to the expression of defamatory opinions based on facts that could be established as true. In *Sullivan,* the defendants were unable to establish the truth of several of the allegations. It was amid these circumstances that the U.S. Supreme Court held that a state could not, under the First and Fourteenth Amendments, award damages to a public official for defamatory falsehoods relating to his official conduct unless he proved "actual malice"—that the statement was made with knowledge of its falsity or with reckless disregard of whether it was true or false.

The "actual malice" defense obviously gave the press the constitutional privilege to discuss public officials engaged in "public conduct" without fear of libel suit damages unless the press acted with "reckless disregard" for the truth.

If a defendant is unable to utilize any of the absolute or conditional defenses, including the "actual malice" doctrine, there are mitigating factors he can cite to lower damages. Included are retraction, proof of previous bad reputation, or reliance on a usually reliable source. If a defendant cannot make use of any available defenses and is held liable for a defamatory publication, the types of damages which may be assessed against him are:

● *Special.* The tangible monetary loss, which must be established, suffered by the plaintiff as a result of a false statement.

● *Actual.* Allows for a broader possibility of harm than that required for special damages. This could include damages for personal humiliation, mental anguish, or loss of standing in the community.

● *Presumed.* Damages a plaintiff can collect without proof of harm. Since a 1974 libel decision, *Gertz* v. *Robert Welch, Inc.,* a plaintiff can collect presumed damages only if "actual malice" is proved.

● *Punitive or exemplary.* Used to punish libelous conduct and to discourage similar future attacks. This is sometimes called "smart money."

Sullivan and Its Aftermath

Though welcomed by the press, the historic *New York Times Co.* v. *Sullivan* decision did not put all libel law questions to rest. The majority opinion emphasized that the court had no desire to determine "how far down into the lower ranks of government employees the 'public official' designation would extend for purposes of this rule." The majority also made it clear that it would not specify "categories of persons" who would be included nor would it "determine the boundaries of the 'official conduct' concept." Thus, with so many unanswered questions, it was only natural that the High Court would be called upon to refine the opinion.

Newspaper editors, all of a sudden, had to keep pace with perpetual fluctuations in American libel law. After years of relatively little change in the common law, the constitutional privilege articulated in *Sullivan* was to be extended, refined, and eventually narrowed. Thus, a number of libel cases since 1964 have important ramifications for today's editor. The most important are discussed briefly below.

Garrison v. *Louisiana* (1964): The U.S. Supreme Court extended the "actual malice" doctrine to prosecutions for criminal libel.

Rosenblatt v. *Baer* (1966): The U.S. Supreme Court extended the *Times* standard to public employees who hold positions of responsibility for the control of public affairs. Frank P. Baer, a former supervisor of a county recreation area, was employed by and responsible to three county commissioners. This decision gave editors a better idea as to what types of persons would be categorized as public officials, a very important consideration when mapping defense strategies.

The Washington Post Co. v. *Keogh* (1966): The court of appeals for the District of Columbia held that newspapers could not be held legally responsible for writings by syndicated columnists about public officials unless the editors had reason to believe the facts in the column were false. Circuit Court Judge J. Skelly Wright emphasized that verification of syndicated columns would be a time-consuming process, a considerable burden in the day-to-day news operation. The court also stressed that extensive verification procedures would be extremely costly and could induce self-censorship. Though a circuit court ruling does not officially become the position of the U.S. Supreme Court by virtue of the latter's denial of *certiorari,* other lower courts often adopt new principles that are allowed to stand by the U.S. Supreme Court, as in this case. It is, of course, not known whether today's Supreme Court would accept this.

Keogh also has overtones for chain libel actions—suits brought against several newspapers based on the same defamatory statement. Chain suits can occur, for example, when hundreds of newspapers publish the same defamatory wire service story. Newspapers are responsible for stories they publish, though a few states place limitations on chain actions. The need for this is illustrated by an action brought in the late 1930s by Ohio Congressman Martin Sweeney against sixty-eight newspapers which published a Drew Pearson column.

It seems a bit stringent to hold individual newspapers responsible for passages written by the wire services or syndicated columnists—unless, of course, the local papers had reason to doubt their accuracy. In most instances, local newspapers have no means of checking the validity of all information received. Realistically, how could a small-town editor battling deadline pressures be expected to verify every sentence from the wire services or syndicated columnists? The *Keogh* decision indicates that economically devastating chain actions may be at an end, particularly when local papers have no practical way of checking every fact from outside sources. Also, in 1974 (see discussion of *Gertz* v. *Robert Welch, Inc.,* below) the Supreme Court held that in order to collect libel damages, a plaintiff must prove media negligence.

Curtis Publishing Co. v. *Butts* (1967): The U.S. Supreme Court extended the "actual malice" defense to defendants when the plaintiffs are public *figures.* Wallace Butts, athletic director at the University of Georgia, was deemed a public figure. This case is also important because it represented the first time the Supreme Court found a media defendant had acted with "actual malice"—in reckless disregard for the truth. The *Saturday Evening Post* had printed an article alleging that Butts and Paul Bryant, football coach at the University of Alabama, had conspired to "fix" a football game between the two schools. The magazine, though it had ample time to verify information supplied to it, published the article without reasonable attempts to determine its accuracy.

Associated Press v. *Walker* (1967): Circumstances in this companion case to *Butts* gave newspaper editors an indication as to what might constitute "actual malice." The case grew out of an erroneous Associated Press dispatch giving an eyewitness account of events on the campus of the University of Mississippi when a massive riot erupted because of federal efforts to enforce a court decree ordering the enrollment of a black, James Meredith, as a student in the University. The dispatch stated that Edwin Walker, a retired army general, had taken command against federal marshals. The article described Walker as giving rioters technical advice on combatting effects of tear gas. The court considered Walker a public figure, but it did not uphold his damage claim because the Associated Press had not departed "from accepted publishing standards" and that, because of deadline pressure, the news required "immediate dissemination." Thus, by 1967 it was clear that the Court, in applying the "actual malice" standard, would ascribe a different criteria to news which required rapid dissemination.

Monitor Patriot Co. v. *Roy* (1971): The U.S. Supreme Court held that a charge of criminal conduct, no matter how remote in time or place, could never be irrelevant to an official's or a candidate's fitness for office for purposes of application of the "knowing or reckless disregard" test. The suit grew out of a Pearson "Washington Merry-Go-Round" column in which the muckraker referred to a 1960 U.S.

Senate hopeful as a "former small-time bootlegger." The allegation referred to incidents which would have taken place some thirty years earlier.

Rosenbloom v. *Metromedia, Inc.* (1971): As expansion of the *Times* doctrine continued, the series of libel decisions favorable to the press reached its climax in this case. The U.S. Supreme Court made the "actual malice" rule applicable to "all discussion and communications involving matters of public or general concern, without regard to whether the persons involved are famous or anonymous." The public interest test laid down in *Rosenbloom* was open to extremely broad interpretation in the lower courts. A comment in the *San Diego Law Review* made the ramifications glaring: "It became clear that the media could fabricate their own privilege; most anything they published became a matter of public interest because of the publication."

Gertz v. *Robert Welch, Inc.* (1974): This case supplied the avenue for retrenchment of press protection. The U.S. Supreme Court partially reversed the *Rosenbloom* plurality when it held that a publisher or broadcaster of defamatory falsehoods about an individual who is neither a public official nor a public figure may not claim the *Times* protection on the ground that the statements concern an issue of public or general interest. The Court said one could become a public figure only by thrusting oneself "to the forefront of particular public controversies in order to influence the resolution of the issues involved." The Court went on to refute the *Rosenbloom* plurality in which it was left to judges to determine if an issue was of "general or public interest." The Court said that in defamation suits brought by private individuals, states could impose liability on a less demanding showing—presumably negligence— than that required by the *Times* doctrine. *Gertz* clearly placed the burden of formulating a negligence standard on individual states. Naturally, uniform definitions of negligence have not resulted. Basically, however, negligence is a failure to exercise "reasonable care." For example, a newspaper reporter might get his notes confused when writing a story; a defamatory hue could be placed over the wrong person as a result of failure to double check middle initials, e.g., improper identification in a court case or suicide story. Or, through a typographical error, a person could be defamed. Obviously, these situations would not involve "actual malice"—a reckless disregard for the truth—but rather a degree of carelessness or failure to exercise reasonable care.

Time, Inc. v. *Firestone* (1976): In an opinion which spread apprehension among editors who thought they knew "public persons" when they saw them, the U.S. Supreme Court defined as a private person a Miami socialite who was married to a member of a wealthy industrial family, was a party to a prolonged divorce trial which resulted in extensive media coverage, and whose appearances in the printed press were frequent enough to warrant subscribing to a press clipping service and to hold several press conferences in the course of the proceedings.

Herbert v. *Lando* (1979): The U.S. Supreme Court voted 6–3 that public figures suing for libel may inquire into a journalist's "state of mind" and the editorial process behind the allegedly libelous statement in order to help show that the defendant acted in reckless disregard for the truth. The suit, brought by Lt. Col. Anthony Herbert, sought $44,725,000 in damages from "60 Minutes" associate producer Barry Lando; correspondent Mike Wallace; CBS, Inc.; and the Atlantic Monthly Co. Herbert claimed that Lando had deliberately distorted the record (Herbert made national news headlines in 1971 when he publicly charged two superior officers with covering up Vietnam war crimes) through selective investigation, "skillful editing," and one-sided interviewing. During a one-year period, Lando responded to pretrial discovery questions that required twenty-six sessions. When asked questions relating to his beliefs, opinions, intent, and conclusions in preparing the program, however, Lando refused to answer. He cited the First Amendment. The Court of Appeals held for Lando, but the U.S Supreme Court reversed. In essence, the Court reasoned that since the *Times* decision makes it very difficult for a public person to prove actual malice, it is only logical that a plaintiff should be able to inquire into a defendant's state of mind to meet this burden.

The Editor and Libel Law Today

Essentially, three categories of libel actions exist today:

1. Public officials and public figures who fall under the *New York Times* standard;
2. Private plaintiffs who must merely show fault to receive actual damages and "actual malice" to receive presumed or punitive damages if the publication deals with a matter of general or public concern;
3. Private libels which continue to be dealt with under established common law principles of various states.

The difficulty in defining a "public" person is illustrated by the *Firestone* decision as well as by a number of lower court judgments. Though no single definition has emerged, an examination of lower court decisions shows:

1. Persons who actively seek publicity for themselves or their cases will be considered public figures.

2. Those who thrust themselves to the forefront of public controversies are public figures.

3. Those who accept a role in society where one can expect publicity are considered public figures.

Despite these general observations, the *Gertz* criteria remain muddled. The distinction between a private person and a public figure is still so loosely defined that the press cannot be sure in which categories their news subjects belong, thus casting doubts on the newsman's ability to utilize the *Times* "actual malice" defense. To further complicate matters, the negligence standard, presumably established in *Gertz*, has also received various interpretations from state courts.

At this point, it is safe only to conclude that the press, in regard to libel defenses, operates under a more liberal legal atmosphere than it did prior to nationalization of the law in 1964, but under more stringent conditions than it enjoyed during the late 1960s and early 1970s.

Fair Trial/Free Press

For nearly two hundred years, attorneys, judges, and media practitioners have struggled with the constitutional confrontation between the First and Sixth Amendments. The dilemma, of course, involves the freedom of the press to report judicial proceedings and the right of a defendant to a fair and impartial trial. Naturally, the press has long contended that it occupies a "preferred position" and that any prior restraint on it is unconstitutional.

The problem has been perpetual. Eminent Chief Justice John Marshall was faced in 1807 with the acute problem of selecting an unbiased jury in the trial of Aaron Burr. Burr was acquitted; thus, there was no appellate review to examine prejudicial pretrial publicity. The problem, however, persisted. In the 1960s, the U.S. Supreme Court became involved in a number of important fair trial/free press cases.

Irvin v. *Dowd* (1961): As a result of pervasive pretrial publicity in which Evansville, Ind., police told the press that "Mad Dog"

Leslie Irvin had confessed to six murders and subsequent intensely emotional news reports by Evansville area newspapers and radio and television stations, the U.S. Supreme Court reversed Irvin's conviction based on prejudicial publicity. Justice Tom Clark pointed out that, despite *voir dire* examination, eight of the twelve jurors thought the petitioner was guilty before the trial. Clark said: "With his life at stake, it is not requiring too much that petitioner be tried in an atmosphere undisturbed by so huge a wave of public passion."

Irvin was retried and again found guilty.

Rideau v. *Louisiana* (1963): The U.S. Supreme Court reversed and remanded the murder conviction of Wilbert Rideau, holding that it was a denial of due process of law to refuse the request for change of venue after residents of Calcasieu Parish, La., "had been exposed repeatedly and in depth to the spectacle of Rideau personally confessing in detail to the crimes with which he was later to be charged." A film with a soundtrack had been made of the "interview" between Rideau and the Calcasieu Parish sheriff and shown on television numerous times.

Estes v. *Texas* (1965): This case posed the question of whether Billie Sol Estes, Texas financier, had been deprived of his due process rights by the televising and broadcasting of his trial. The majority said Estes had been deprived of the "judicial serenity and calm" to which he was entitled. It was implied, however, that televised trials might some day be possible—when television equipment became more subtle and sophisticated.

Sheppard v. *Maxwell* (1966): Dr. Sam Sheppard, a Cleveland osteopath who had been convicted of second degree murder, was tried in a "circus atmosphere" after Cleveland newspapers had published emotionally charged editorials calling for Sheppard's conviction. Man-on-the-street interviews were held which sought opinions on Sheppard's guilt or innocence. The press was in such close proximity to the defendant and his attorneys during the trial that private conversations were nearly impossible. The U.S. Supreme Court reversed his conviction.

Murphy v. *Florida* (1975): The U.S. Supreme Court affirmed lower court convictions of Jack Murphy, who had been convicted in the Dade County, Fla., criminal court of breaking and entering a home, while armed, with intent to commit robbery, and of assault with intent to commit robbery. The robbery and arrest received extensive press coverage because Murphy, generally referred to as

"Murph the Surf," was a flamboyant, well-known figure. The Supreme Court said that the *voir dire* questioning did not indicate jury hostility. The majority said that Murphy had failed to show "inherent prejudice" in the trial proceedings. In other words, mere publicity about the trial and Murphy's prior criminal record was not sufficient to reverse.

These cases clearly illustrate that the fair trial/free press problem is one without simple answers. Though the press likes to regard itself as responsible, circumstances in cases like *Irvin, Rideau,* and *Sheppard* indicate that, on occasion, this is not so. With such blatant examples of press irresponsibility, the dilemma became one which press, bar, and bench could not ignore. In *Sheppard,* for example, the Court held that the accused had been robbed of a fair trial because of pervasive publicity and, in dictum, suggested that certain restrictions should be placed on extrajudicial statements made during the course of a trial. The American Bar Association's 1968 Reardon Report grew out of the *Sheppard* dictum. The 265-page report was directed mainly at the bench and bar, but indirect references were made to the press. From the Reardon Report there evolved bar-press agreements in more than twenty states. The agreements are, of course, voluntary.

The Nebraska Press Case

Focus of the fair trial/free press problem climaxed in June 1976 when the U.S. Supreme Court articulated its *Nebraska Press Association* v. *Stuart* decision. For the first time in the Court's history, it gave full-scale review to a direct judicial prior restraint (sometimes termed a "protective order" or "gag order") on press coverage of criminal prosecutions. Facts of the case which evolved from a mass murder in Sutherland, Neb., are well-known: Local police found the six members of the Henry Kellie family murdered in their home at Sutherland (a Lincoln County community of approximately 850 persons). Erwin Charles Simants was arrested and arraigned in county court the following morning. A "gag" order was issued, prohibiting, among other things, dissemination of testimony given in a preliminary hearing which was open to the public but subject to the order. The order also *required* members of the press to observe the "voluntary" Nebraska Bar-Press Guidelines.

In a unanimous decision, the Supreme Court ruled that the original county court "gag" and subsequent modifications issued by courts in the appeals process did not meet the "high constitutional barriers" imposed as a condition to securing a prior restraint. The Court held that the guarantees of expression are not an absolute protection under all circumstances, but barriers to prior restraint remain high.

As is often the case, the decision did not put all constitutional questions to rest; the dilemma remains. The boundaries were made clearer, but the problem was not eliminated. Chief Justice Burger's majority opinion contained the clear implication that under certain circumstances a judicial gag might be sustained. Justice William Brennan's strong concurring opinion was likely most pleasing to the press. Brennan said there should be no "prohibition on the publication by the press of any information pertaining to pending judicial proceedings or the operation of the criminal justice system, no matter how shabby the means by which the information is obtained." Brennan claimed that this did not imply any subordination of Sixth Amendment rights, for an accused individual still had several procedural safeguards available to him. In clear language, Brennan concluded: "The press may be arrogant, tyrannical, abusive and informative. But at least in the context of prior restraints on publication, the decision of what, when, and how to publish is for editors, not judges."

A circuit court of appeals judge said the decision would "make lower court judges think twice before attempting to gag the press and will make it difficult for any future type of press gag to hold up in court." A *Des Moines Register* editorial, however, most appropriately summarized the effects of the decision: "The victory [for the press] ended a battle, not the war."

Between *Sheppard* and *Nebraska Press,* one agency conservatively estimated there were 175 "gags" placed on the press in judicial proceedings. It was optimistically hoped that *Nebraska Press* would put an end to the issuance of prior restraints on the press when involved in coverage of litigation. This, however, has not been the case. Lower courts have continued to issue prior restraints on the press, despite the unambiguous language in the Nebraska decision. It is significant, however, that no appellate courts have upheld any orders which restrained the press from publishing information gathered in *open* court. Nevertheless, some judges have continued to seal records, have continued to issue exclusionary orders, and have continued to prohibit trial participants from speaking with the press.

A 1979 decision, in fact, opened the door to an increase in exclusionary orders. In *Gannett Co.* v. *DePasquale,* the U.S. Supreme Court upheld a lower court ruling that the public—which obviously includes the press—has no constitutional right under the "public trial" guarantee of the Sixth Amendment to attend pretrial hearings. Writing for the five-member majority, Justice Potter Stewart wrote that the Sixth Amendment's guarantee did not belong to the public—it belonged only to the accused. The case evolved out of New York where two men had been charged, in several counts, with second-degree murder, robbery, and grand larceny. Their attorneys had requested that the public and press be excluded from the hearing, claiming that the buildup of adverse publicity jeopardized the chances their clients could receive a fair trial. The judge granted the motion.

Stewart said he did not "disparage the general desirability of open judicial proceedings," but he also wrote that "closure of pretrial proceedings is often one of the most effective methods that a trial judge can employ to attempt to insure that the fairness of a trial will not be jeopardized" by news before the trial has begun. Chief Justice Warren Burger tempered the majority opinion with his concurring opinion. Burger emphasized that the ruling extended only to pretrial hearings. The thrust of the dissenting opinions was that the ruling would lead to a rash of lower court closures without sufficient reason to believe publicity would taint the proceedings. Justice Harry Blackmun said that an "inflexible rule" had been established that paid little attention to the importance of the public and press in open judicial proceedings.

On July 2, 1980, however, in *Richmond Newspapers, Inc.* v. *Virginia,* the U.S. Supreme Court relieved the press of some of its apprehension about *DePasquale.* The Court held that the media and public have a constitutional right to attend criminal trials—"absent overriding considerations"—even when defendants want to exclude them. The majority made it clear that judges could conduct portions behind closed doors only as a last resort to insure fairness to a defendant. The decision, of course, did not alter the primary thrust of *DePasquale,* which gave trial judges broad authority to exclude public and press from *pretrial* hearings in criminal cases.

Though it had long been assumed that the public and press had a constitutional right to attend public trials, *Richmond Newspapers* represented the first formal articulation of that right under the First Amendment. Floyd Abrams, a First Amendment lawyer, said the case was a "broad statement of the right of the press and public to gather information of a sort never before issued by the Court." In the majority opinion, Chief Justice Burger acknowledged that the press enjoyed "some rights" to gather information. He said: "The explicit, guaranteed rights to speak and to publish concerning what takes place at a trial would lose much meaning if access to observe the trial could, as it was here, be foreclosed arbitrarily."

Fair Trial/Free Press and the Editor Today

The constitutional battle between the First and Sixth Amendments continues. Only one point emerges clear: While reporting of *open* court testimony is upheld by the courts, indirect attempts to "gag" the press through secrecy orders imposed on trial participants (defendants, lawyers, and witnesses) and exclusionary orders are another matter.

Thus, the Court will continue to be called upon to consider individual circumstances. One thread, however, runs through many of the fair trial/free press cases; there are "alternative measures" which protect the Sixth Amendment rights of the accused while not trampling upon the First Amendment rights of the press. Chief Justice Warren Burger, in *Nebraska Press,* emphasized that these alternatives should be explored before judges issue prior restraints. These measures include:

● *Change of venue.* The trial is moved to another jurisdiction to relieve some of the prejudice and emotionalism often associated with major proceedings.

● *Change of venire.* Bringing in jurors from other jurisdictions.

● *Voir dire examination.* Use of searching questions for prospective jurors to determine if prejudice exists.

● *Sequestration of jurors.* Insulating jurors from television, radio, newspapers or any prejudicial source during the course of a trial.

● *Instructions from the presiding judge.* Use of emphatic and clear instructions on the sworn duty of each juror to decide the issues only on evidence presented in open court.

● *Normal appeal procedures.* Like Irvin, Rideau, and Sheppard, the accused would have the right to appeal his conviction based on grounds of prejudicial publicity.

Despite precedent cases, however, an editor who feels he is operating on safe constitutional ground during his newspaper's coverage—by words or pictures—of trial proceedings cannot be absolutely certain. Unanswered questions remain as to what constitutes an "acceptable" prior restraint on the press. The Supreme Court has refused to say that there could never be a constitutional prior restraint on media coverage of criminal proceedings. Though Chief Justice Burger made it clear in *Nebraska Press* that public trial proceedings are a matter of public record, editors and newsmen who, in the future, find themselves subjected to prior restraints must still obey the orders—or face contempt citations. Indeed, unanswered questions are many, but there is a need for editors to be familiar with the law—and to exercise common sense judgments.

Contempt/Newsman's Privilege

Journalists have found themselves in jail with increasing frequency during recent years for contempt of court. Contempt citations have been issued for a variety of reasons, including—

1. failure of a newsman to reveal the source of his information to proper authorities;

2. editorially criticizing judicial conduct or competence, particularly when a jury trial is pending.

3. printing articles which, in the opinion of the judge, affect the serenity of a courtroom;

4. refusal to abide by court-directed limitations ("gag" orders) during coverage of litigation;

5. blatant actions such as disturbing lawyers, judges or witnesses during court proceedings.

Black's Law Dictionary defines contempt of court as "any act which is calculated to embarrass, hinder, or obstruct [the] court in [the] administration of justice, or which is calculated to lessen its authority or its dignity."

The contempt power has, to some degree, always been part of the American judicial system. A federal contempt statute was passed in 1831 in an effort to cut down on liberties taken by some judges in issuing citations. The thrust of the 1831 law was that in order for one to be held in contempt, his action must be in the presence of the court or "so near thereto" as to obstruct the administration of justice. At the time, it was generally believed the "so near thereto" element meant that the questionable action must have been within the confines of the courtroom.

A decision by the Arkansas Supreme Court in 1855, however, took another view. The state court said that American courts had "immemorial powers" to try for contempt; it said state legislatures could not intercede. Other jurisdictions began to adopt this rationale, and in 1918 the U.S. Supreme Court articulated a similar stance in *Toledo Newspaper Co.* v. *United States.* In a ruling which was likely a product of the temper of the times, the majority reasoned that geographical considerations were not important; if a newspaper criticized a court, and if the criticism had a "reasonable tendency" to obstruct justice, the responsible individual could be held in contempt. Naturally, this causal interpretation placed pressure on newspapers which sought to criticize judicial proceedings or conduct. In effect, the ruling insulated judges from press criticism. Justice Oliver Wendell Holmes dissented, claiming that the "so near thereto" clause was a geographical dictate. Holmes felt judges should be strong in the face of criticism, that "misbehavior" on the part of the press had to mean something more than "adverse comment or disrespect" directed at the bench.

Twenty-three years later, in *Bridges* v. *California,* the U.S. Supreme Court applied the "clear and present danger" test to contempt citations. The majority, through Justice Hugo Black, said that in order for the "clear and present danger" test to be met, "the substantive evil must be extremely high before utterances can be punished." This decision has made it more difficult for judges to utilize indirect contempt citations to curb press criticism.

Dangers to Editors

Despite *Bridges* v. *California,* newspaper editors and reporters remain in constant danger of being cited for contempt. Judges are responsible for controlling their courtrooms; they must have methods at their disposal to do so. Journalists must obey judicial mandates even though, on their face, they are unconstitutional. This was emphasized by the Fifth Circuit Court of Appeals in 1972 in *United States* v. *Dickinson.* The circuit court held that apparent invalidity to a judicial mandate "is no defense to criminal contempt." The majority made it clear that, "Court orders have to be obeyed until they are reversed or set aside in an orderly fashion." This might be a few days; more than likely, however, it will be several months, or even years. The court emphasized that "newsmen are citizens, too" and that they "must sometimes have to wait" until litigation runs its course.

The Branzburg Case

Editors and reporters have found themselves in judicial hot water with increasing frequency during recent years for refusal to give names of their confidential sources. Journalists have contended they have a First Amendment privilege not to divulge news sources because it would drastically reduce the number of persons willing to provide information. Some sources, according to journalists, would be afraid to give information to a reporter without being guaranteed anonymity. Thus, in the ultimate crunch, the reporter or editor must decide whether to betray his promise of secrecy to his source or to face a fine and possible jail sentence for refusal to do so.

The U.S. Supreme Court, in *Branzburg* v. *Hayes* (1972), was asked to consider whether a journalist had a testimonial privilege not to reveal his source. Branzburg, a reporter for the Louisville *Courier-Journal,* had written two articles about drug use in Kentucky. A grand jury, looking into the state's drug problem, summoned Branzburg to testify. He refused. When the case reached the U.S. Supreme Court, Justice Byron White pointed out that a number of states had provided newsmen with a statutory privilege of "varying breadth" (see discussion of "shield laws" below). White continued: "Until now the only testimonial privilege for unofficial witnesses that is rooted in the Federal Constitution is the Fifth Amendment privilege against compelled self-incrimination. We are asked to create another by interpreting the First Amendment to grant newsmen a testimonial privilege that other citizens do not enjoy. This we decline to do." White said the Court could not "seriously entertain the notion that the First Amendment protects a newsman's agreement to conceal the criminal conduct of his source, or evidence thereof, on the theory that it is better to write about crime than to do something about it."

The majority made it clear, however, that "official harassment" of journalists merely to "disrupt a reporter's relationship with his news sources would have no justification." In a concurring opinion, Justice Lewis F. Powell said there was a "limited nature" to the Court's holding; he said courts would still be available to newsmen where "legitimate" First Amendment rights required protection. He also made it clear that government authorities were not free to make the press part of their normal investigation network. Despite efforts by some lower courts to recognize a conditional or qualified privilege in civil cases, *Branzburg* still carries ominous overtones for the press. As is the case with the editor who must decide who is or is not a public figure viewed against the *Gertz* criteria in libel actions, it is virtually impossible for the same editor to know with certainty whether the courts will extend a privilege to his refusal to release names of his sources.

In addition to claims of First Amendment protection, journalists have cited "shield laws" which have been formulated in more than half of this country's states. Shield laws are enacted by state legislatures to provide a specified level of protection to newsmen faced with the dilemma of revealing their sources. These laws, of course, attempt to establish what the privilege entails, who may use the "shield," and the circumstances under which it may be used. It is generally conceded that all shield laws have some loopholes, and that it is naive for journalists to rely exclusively on them. Branzburg, for example, was caught in a Kentucky shield law loophole—the law protected newsmen from revealing names of their sources—in this case, however, Branzburg was the source. He had witnessed the criminal activity and was therefore required to supply requested information.

Despite the apparent "no holes" appearance of some state shield laws, a number of universal problems must be considered. Don R. Pember, in *Mass Media Law,* lists five examples:

1. Lack of consistency in shield laws exists among states.
2. Members of the public and many journalists are not convinced of the merits of strong shield laws (reporters feel that the First Amendment provides them with all the protection they need; some members of the public look at shield laws as being beneficial only to the press, rather than a necessary avenue to insure continued flow of information).
3. Definitional problems are inherent in shield laws (e.g., What constitutes a news source? What is a newspaper?).
4. There are likely loopholes in even the so-called absolute shield laws.
5. Since some courts do not like shield laws, they can purposely interpret them narrowly.

Contempt, Newsman's Privilege, and the Editor Today

Editors and reporters have discovered that failure to obey judicial mandates often results in contempt citations—which normally translate into a fine and sometimes into jail time. Though the press enjoys considerable freedom under the First Amendment, in any direct confrontation between the press and bench, the press will find itself initially overmatched. If a judge instructs the press not to report certain open court proceedings, even though the order would likely not withstand appeal scrutiny by a higher court, reporters and editors are obligated to follow the judge's instructions—or face the very real possibility of going to jail. If an editor is summoned to reveal sources or information for a particular story, unless he works in a state with a strong shield law which *specifically* exempts him, he faces a fine or jail sentence if he refuses to cooperate. Shield laws can also, under judicial scrutiny, become terribly transparent and nonbeneficial to the journalist. All in all, state shield laws do not give journalists as much protection as they would like. Because of lack of uniformity in shield statutes now on the books, there have been several federal shield laws proposed in Congress during recent years. None, however, has received sufficient support to become law.

Journalists must generally abide by court mandates. Newsmen cannot escape such instructions simply by majestically pointing to the First Amendment or by quoting verbatim from state shield laws. On appeal, an editor might stand a good chance of gaining a higher court reversal of a judicial mandate—whether the mandate was in the form of an order to supply the name of a source, in the form of a contempt citation for articles critical of judicial conduct, or simply the failure of a reporter to abide by bench instructions not to print certain portions of public criminal proceedings. But in the months during which the appeal is advancing through the judicial process, the journalist is obligated to follow instructions which gave rise to the appeal.

In essence, the First Amendment does not give editors and reporters the right to disregard even the most atrocious court mandates. This was made clear in *Dickinson*.

Privacy

The right to privacy, a relatively recent legal phenomenon, has claimed the attention of reporters and editors who operate in an increasingly technological business. Cameras, an integral part of the newspaper process, also have great potential for invasion of privacy. Investigative reporting, a la Jack Anderson, Bob Woodward, Carl Bernstein, et al., is in vogue; this opens the door to potential conflicts between First Amendment sanctions of uninhibited, robust reporting and the private rights of individuals. Editors are constantly looking for that very special "rags to riches" feature story; conversely, the article's subject would often just as soon forget his past life.

Obviously, then, today's reporters and editors must contend with and respect the broad, often vague assertion that people have a right to privacy. Scholars trace privacy's roots to 1890 when attorneys Samuel D. Warren and (later U.S. Supreme Court Justice) Louis D. Brandeis contended in a *Harvard Law Review* article that there was a legal right to privacy. The lawyers claimed that increasing abuses by the press during the "yellow journalism" era made it mandatory that the courts or legislatures fashion a remedy for those whose privacy had been invaded.

Warren, member of a socially prominent Boston family, likely had a selfish reason for his then-bold legal assertion. Nevertheless, it captured the attention of bench, bar, and some state legislatures. Georgia, in 1905, first recognized a common law right to privacy in *Pavesich* v. *New England Life Insurance Co.* A gradual acceptance of a right to privacy—succinctly defined by Thomas Cooley as "the right to be left alone"—ensued in most American jurisdictions. Statutes have been adopted in a handful of states; common law recognition of a right to privacy has been articulated by courts in more than thirty jurisdictions. According to privacy scholar Pember, courts in Idaho, Maine, Minnesota, North Dakota, Washington, Vermont, and Wyoming have yet to declare whether a common law right to privacy exists. Courts in only one state—Rhode Island—have specifically held that there is no legal right to privacy in their jurisdictions.

Four Branches of Privacy

The late Dean Prosser once declared that the law of privacy "comprises four distinct kinds of invasion of four different interests of the plaintiff, which are tied together by the common name, but otherwise have almost nothing in common except that each represents an interference with the right of the plaintiff 'to be let alone.' " He divided privacy into four branches:

1. *Intrusion.* Intrusion into an individual's physical or mental solitude. This branch has become more paramount with the sophisticated eavesdropping devices of modern society and the upsurge in investigative reporting.

2. *Appropriation.* The area upon which the first New York

privacy statute was based. This occurs when the defendant appro-
priates, for his commercial gain, the name or likeness of the plain-
tiff. Prosser emphasized that the plaintiff's name is a symbol of
his identity, not the "mere name."

3. *Public disclosure of private facts.* When publicity of an objectionable kind, based exclusively upon purely private circumstances, is made public. This is hazy; courts have generally held
that "private facts" must be those which would be offensive or
objectionable to a "reasonable man of ordinary sensibilities"—
whatever that may be.

4. *False light in the public eye.* This privacy branch is closely related to libel. Articles which paint a false—though not necessarily defamatory—picture of a subject are often subject to invasion
of privacy charges.

Examples of cases which fit within each of these branches will
bring this broad legal area into sharper focus.

Intrusion

Damages for intrusion, unlike the other branches of privacy, are
not predicated upon publication. Though journalists generally do not
operate as detectives, utilizing purloined papers, and electronic surveillance equipment, today's investigative reporting methods often
bring writers and editors under—or dangerously near—this tort. Not
surprisingly, one frequently cited case in this area involved muck-
rakers Jack Anderson and the late Drew Pearson. Much of their
"Washington Merry-Go-Round" column material is gathered from
unauthorized sources. Anderson, in the 1950s, was once caught in a
Washington hotel room with a device for bugging a government-used
suite next door. No suit—only embarrassment—resulted; but two
cases with intrusion overtones were filed against Pearson and Anderson in the 1960s.

In *Pearson* v. *Dodd* (1969), Sen. Thomas Dodd of Connecticut
sued Pearson and Anderson for libel and invasion of privacy. During
the summer of 1965, some Dodd employees entered the senator's
office without authority, removed personal documents from his files,
made copies of them, replaced the originals, and gave copies to
Anderson. From this information, more than a hundred "Merry-Go-

Round" columns were published during an eighteen-month period. The columns charged among other things that Dodd had improperly diverted proceeds of fund-raising testimonial dinners to his personal use. Circuit Court Judge Wright, in denying Dodd's claim, emphasized that though the writers had knowingly received the material from an intruder, "injuries from intrusion and injuries from publication should be kept clearly separate." Thus, Pearson and Anderson were not held liable for damages.

There is one noteworthy case, however, in which the court held against a media defendant. In *Dietemann* v. *Time, Inc.* (1971), A. A. Dietemann sued Time, Inc., when two *Life* magazine reporters posed as husband and wife to seek advice from Dietemann who fashioned himself a "healer" by using clay, minerals, and herbs. The reporters, working in conjunction with Los Angeles law enforcement officials, carried hidden microphones and secretly photographed Dietemann, who was later charged with practicing medicine without a license. A lower court held that publication of the photographs did not invade Dietemann's privacy—but intrusion by means of concealed cameras and microphones did. Circuit Court Judge Shirley M. Hufstedler emphasized that the First Amendment "is not a license to trespass, to steal, or to intrude by electronic means into the precincts of another's home or office."

Appropriation

Though the media are not often sued for appropriation of an individual's name or likeness for personal profit, reporters and editors must be careful not to overstep their boundaries. Generally, when the news media write articles or display pictures of public performances, they are not subject to invasion of privacy suits. The media cover events because of their news value, not for personal profit at the expense of the subject. When the Georgia court, in *Pavesich,* held for the plaintiff who had sued a newspaper for publishing, without his permission, an insurance company advertisement which contained his photograph and laudatory remarks, the majority's intent was to protect persons from public exposure they did not want. Since then, this privacy branch has grown to include an individual's property right to publicity, as exemplified in a case brought by professional football player Joe Namath.

In *Namath* v. *Sports Illustrated* (1976), Namath brought suit against *Sports Illustrated* for use of his photograph in a magazine promotion without his consent. Obviously, the picture had been taken at a public event, with tens of thousands of spectators looking on. The New York Supreme Court reasoned that the "incidental" use of name or likeness in connection with advertising does not violate an individual's right to privacy. The court said that the First Amendment transcends the right to privacy, particularly when a petitioner seeks renumeration for a *property* right, not a *privacy* right.

Public Disclosure of Private Facts

To a large extent, the courts have been generous with the press in this sometimes hazy area. Though privacy suits are often brought under this branch, the defense of "newsworthiness" (to be discussed below) has proved to be an effective ally of the press. Still, reporters and editors must exercise common sense. Through the years, the courts have shown that they will bend to the First Amendment interests of the media, but they will not break. Two illustrative cases are discussed below.

In *Barber* v. *Time, Inc.* (1942), Dorothy Barber was awarded damages from Time, Inc. Mrs. Barber fell victim to a photographer who, without permission, took pictures of her while she was confined to a hospital bed. Mrs. Barber had a rare disease—her eating knew no bounds but she continued to lose weight. *Time* magazine labeled her the "starving glutton." This was, in the opinion of the court, going too far; it was apparently felt objectionable to reasonable men of ordinary sensibilities. The court said that *Time* could have written about the illness without mentioning the name.

In *Cox Broadcasting* v. *Cohn* (1975), the father of a young Georgia girl who had been raped and murdered sued a television station which had broadcast the deceased victim's name. A state statute made it a misdemeanor to broadcast the rape victim's name. The trial court granted summary judgment to the father. The Georgia Supreme Court denied appeal on the ground that a rape victim's name, under state policy, was not a matter of public concern and was therefore a legitimate limitation on the First Amendment. The U.S. Supreme Court reversed. The Court held that since the victim's name had been obtained from judicial records that were maintained in connection with a public prosecution and open to public inspection, the

First and Fourteenth Amendments protected the newsman. The Court said that the "interests of privacy fade when the information involved appears on public record." Thus, though the information was privately delicate and "embarrassing" to the father, the newsworthy public nature of the event precluded his collecting damages for invasion of privacy.

False Light

The false light branch of privacy is closely related to libel. Actions are based upon false information; the information, however, is not necessarily defamatory. Nevertheless, it places the plaintiff in a false light in the eye of the public. The most important case in this area was handed down by the U.S. Supreme Court in 1967. Its facts vividly illustrate the nature of this privacy branch.

The case is *Time, Inc.* v. *Hill* (1967). In 1952, the James Hill family was held hostage in its Pennsylvania home by three escaped convicts. No harm came to the family; under the tense circumstances, there were no acts of heroism or harsh treatment. A novel and Broadway play were later written about the incident. The family was portrayed as heroic. The family changed residence to discourage publicity about the incident. *Life* magazine described the play as a re-enactment and used photographs of scenes staged in the former Hill home as illustrations. Alleging that the article gave the knowingly false impression that the play depicted the Hill incident, Hill sued for damages under a statute providing a cause of action to a person whose name or picture is used by another without consent for purposes of trade or advertising. Time, Inc., maintained that the article concerned a subject of general interest. The Court reasoned that the subject of the *Life* article, the opening of a new play linked to an actual incident, was a matter of public interest. Thus, the U.S. Supreme Court applied the "actual malice" test utilized in libel decisions to the tort of "false light" invasion of privacy; it found that *Time* had not acted in "reckless disregard for the truth." This was the first case in which a mass medium was involved in a privacy suit which went to the Supreme Court.

Though the "actual malice" protection extends substantial protection to the media when involved in false light actions, as in libel, it is possible to go too far. This occurred in a case which evolved from an article published in the *Cleveland Plain Dealer*.

In *Cantrell* v. *Forest City Publishing Co.* (1974), suit was brought against a newspaper publisher and reporter for invasion of privacy based on a feature story which told, in graphic detail, the effects of the tragic death of a father on his surviving family. The poverty plight of the family was highly exaggerated; in fact, Mrs. Margaret Mae Cantrell was directly quoted, even though she had not been at home during the interview—the reporter had fabricated the quotes. The Supreme Court held that there was sufficient evidence to support the jury finding of publication of knowing or reckless falsehoods. The Court pointed to the use of "calculated falsehoods" to paint a more emotional and sympathetic picture of the family.

Defenses Against Privacy Actions

Some of the defenses against privacy actions have been mentioned in brief discussions of the cases. As a means of summary and elaboration, the following defenses are available:

1. *Appropriation.* Consent is the primary defense; it should be in writing. Also, it is possible for the subject to change his mind prior to publication.

2. *Intrusion.* As mentioned previously, newsmen have rarely been involved in privacy cases under this branch. With increasing technological advances and emphasis on investigative reporting, however, the possibilities are becoming greater. At present, there are no solid defenses for this prepublication tort. Newsworthiness is not sufficient, nor is publication even required.

3. *Public disclosure of private facts.* Newsworthiness is the primary defense. According to Pember, four elements are considered to determine whether newsworthiness is a viable defense—nature of the story, subject of the story, intimacy of the revelations, and degree of embarrassment. Newsworthiness has proved to be a solid—but obviously not absolute—defense for newsmen. After all, the mere decision to publish a story gives it a certain "newsworthy" credibility.

4. *False light in the public eye.* Newsworthiness, truth, and the "actual malice" test are primary defenses. Again, the "actual malice" test gives newsmen a certain degree of protection—though blatant circumstances such as those in *Cantrell* can defeat this defense.

Copyright

Editors who exercise good judgment need not be overly concerned about copyright law. Copyright, however, affects an editor from two viewpoints: (1) He wants to protect himself and his newspaper from infringement by others; and (2) he wants to make sure that he does not infringe upon the rights of others. Copyright is a somewhat fuzzy area of litigation, but a newspaper editor can generally be relatively certain about the status of his work in relation to the law.

As most are aware, the right to protect one's literary property evolves from the Constitution. Article I, Section 8, states that congress can "promote the Progress of Science and Useful Arts, by securing for limited Times to Authors and Inventors the exclusive Right to their respective Writings and Discoveries." The first copyright law in this country was enacted in 1790; there were a handful of revisions through 1909. A completely revised law was enacted in 1976; it took effect on Jan. 1, 1978. Under the new law, there is no longer common law protection for unpublished writings; all writings, whether published or unpublished, are now under protection of the new statute. Also, an author is protected for his lifetime, plus fifty years. Under the 1909 law, the original protection was twenty-eight years, with provision for a twenty-eight-year renewal.

Neither of these major changes is particularly relevant to newspaper editors. Only the most widely circulated newspapers in this country are copyrighted in their entirety. Thus, problems with infringement do not often occur. Newspapers, however, sometimes develop special enterprise stories which they copyright. Also, many newspapers subscribe to supplemental news sources, such as the *New York Times* or the *Washington Post* services, which are copyrighted. Newspapers which subscribe to these services place a copyright notice above the printed story.

Can a news story be copyrighted? Obviously, no. News events, in themselves, are not copyrightable, but the literary quality of the story and the organization and flow of sentences and phrases are. Thus, if the *New York Times* uncovered specific gross corruption in several government agencies, other news media would be able to report the highlights of the story. Newspapers should, however, preface it with, "In a copyrighted story today, the *New York Times* . . . ," or the attribution should be placed high in the story. The reporter doing the rewrite must be careful not to "borrow" the literary quality of the *Times* story, but references could be made to selected, small portions of the original report.

The Doctrine of Fair Use

Taken literally, the 1909 law meant that, under no circumstances, without permission from the owner, could the copyrighted material be utilized. The doctrine of "fair use," however, evolved. In essence, it holds that under certain conditions limited amounts of material can be directly quoted. As part of the 1976 revision, the fair use doctrine was made part of the statutory law. The new law specifies that the fair use of a copyrighted work "for purposes such as criticism, comment, news reporting, teaching (including multiple copies for classroom use), scholarship, or research, is not an infringement of copyright." Factors to consider in determining if fair use has been made of the appropriated material are:

● The purpose and character of the use, including whether such use is of a commercial nature or is for non-profit educational purposes;

● The nature of the copyrighted work;

● The amount and substantiality of the *portion used* in relation to the copyrighted work as a whole; and

● The effect of the use upon the potential market for or value of the copyrighted work.

Though these are only broad guidelines, it is apparent that newspaper editors and reporters can print, for the most part, extracts of copyrighted articles or books without fear of infringing upon someone's copyright. Copyrighted articles can also be used as a "tip" to further develop a related, but new, story. Newsmen must still, however, be careful not to print wholesale excerpts of copyrighted material. They might be safe in directly quoting up to two hundred or more words from a book or fifty words from an article. But two lines from a sixteen-line poem or one stanza of a song could be an infringement. Naturally, if an editor is not sure whether the material he plans to use falls into the category of fair use, he should consult an attorney who specializes in copyright law—or he could request permission from the owner of the copyright to reprint certain portions.

On the other hand, if an editor has a special story he would like to protect, copyright procedure is relatively simple. First of all, the story must be preceded with a © symbol, or "Copyright" is written. The date and holder of the copyright are also necessary, e.g., © 1978, New

York Times. Two copies of the material and $10 must then be sent to the Register of Copyrights, Washington, D.C.

All in all, copyright questions should not pose serious problems to a conscientious editor. For the most part, he and his reporters will be working with their own words. On those occasions, however, when copyrighted material is utilized, it is safest to quote only small portions. If the editor is still unsure of his legal standing, he should consult a knowledgeable attorney, apply for permission to reprint the material, or simply not use it.

Chapter 13

The Newspaper Hierarchy

J OURNALISTS WHO ASPIRE to editing positions quickly discover that they will be expected to do more than provide their readers with hard-hitting, responsible stories. Editors must also function within the newspaper chain of command, follow sound management techniques, deal with outside variables such as advertiser pressures, and follow newspaper policies—both written and assumed.

Editors, like reporters, feel pressure from superiors and must be prepared to deal with it. Publisher influence—whether perceived or real—stretches from the smallest weeklies and dailies to metropolitan newspapers like the *New York Times.* Author and former *Times* reporter Gay Talese recounted a tense scene at the newspaper prior to the Bay of Pigs invasion of Cuba. *Times* editors disagreed over how the pre-invasion story should be handled. Originally, the story had been scheduled for the lead position on page one. For a story of such gravity, publisher Orvil Dryfoos was consulted. Talese wrote in *The Kingdom and the Power* that Dryfoos "ordered the story toned down, moved to a less prominent place on the page, its headline minimized and any reference to the imminence of the invasion eliminated." Not all editorial decisions are of such magnitude. Publisher opinions, however, are often funneled to the newsroom. At some newspapers, the opinions might take the form of commands; at others, publisher mandates are more subtle.

Friction exists between executives and staff in most organizations. Newspaper operations are no different. This management-staff distinction, however, is not as apparent as in other industries. Though the line of authority in newspaper organizations is clearly defined, the nature of the work—finding truth and presenting objective news with balance—often leads to more informal management-staff interaction. Still, reporters and editors—whether or not they publicly admit it— often feel upper management pressure. Many publishers tell their editors that philosophies and personal interests of ownership should be ignored, but it is the rare editor who completely blocks from his mind the opinions of his publisher.

Warren Breed, in his classic study of socialization in the newsroom, found that newspaper staffers learn policy in a number of ways— through reading the newspaper daily; through staff meetings; through written policy statements; through blue pencil editing by superiors when a story concerns "special" people or issues; and, often, through gossip. Editors and reporters soon learn how their publishers or owners feel about certain issues; it is only natural that this influence is felt in the news columns.

Reporters and editors who perceive themselves as being responsible for getting the truth to the people are more likely to question— or sometimes ridicule—written and oral newspaper policy. In a *Social Forces* article Breed wrote:

> How is policy to be maintained, despite the fact that it often contravenes journalistic norms, that staffers often personally disagree with it, and that executives cannot legitimately command that it be followed? The first mechanism promoting conformity is the "socialization" of the staffer with regard to the norms of his job. When the new reporter starts work, he is not told what policy is. Nor is he ever told. This may appear strange, but all but the newest staffers know what policy is. Many reporters, on being asked, say they learn policy "by osmosis." Basically, the learning of policy is a process by which the recruit discovers and internalizes the rights and obligations of his status and its norms and values.

Norman E. Isaacs said the reality of publisher influence captured his attention during the depression. As a young reporter, he had difficulty understanding why stories about job layoffs were relegated to inside pages while glossy predictions by business spokesmen about possible economic upturns were almost certain to appear on page one.

With publishers or owners exerting a significant influence over news-editorial matters on many newspapers, editors must be aware of the middle-man status they occupy in the newspaper hierarchy. Editors must enforce newspaper or publisher policy—even when they personally disagree. Recognizing the role managing editors of most American newspapers play, Professor David Bowers surveyed editors of more than 600 dailies. He found, among other things, that publishers are often active in areas which conceivably could affect the newspaper's economic status directly or indirectly. Professor J. Edward Gerald, like Bowers, found that economic factors influence publishing policies. Gerald wrote: "When journalism abandoned politics for business as a way of making a living it switched its personality from that of a crusader trying to organize, teach, and change the people and the community to that of entrepreneuer, trying to make a good living with a minimum of trouble." Whether most newspapers take this approach is academic, but it is an assertion to seriously ponder.

A survey of Kansas and Nebraska daily newspapers showed that managing editors perceive little direct pressure from their publishers when making news and editorial decisions. Yet, the tendency of editors is to regard as influential the same persons based on occupation (bankers, merchants, lawyers, and public officials) that they perceive their publishers to hold in high esteem. This illustrates the possibility that editors do respond to subtle inferences from their superiors. Some 65 percent of the editors said they were expected to often or sometimes follow their publishers' recommendations on news-editorial matters—even if they disagreed. Only 9.4 percent said they were never expected to follow publisher recommendations. In the crunch, then, it is the publisher who usually makes the final decision in most controversial matters.

Obviously, publisher-editor-reporter relationships differ from newspaper to newspaper. But all aspiring editors must be aware of the compromising positions into which they will be cast. They have a responsibility to the public to produce the best possible editorial product; a responsibility to their staff to insure freedom to pursue robust, hard-hitting reporting; and a responsibility to their publishers to produce the best possible news product—within the publishers' guidelines. Outside pressures clearly influence news decisions, but an editor must make sure that these pressures do not interfere with responsible news reporting. Sometimes the pressures are in conflict; the editor is challenged to resolve the dilemma.

The Editors

To put the functions and responsibilities of newsroom editors in perspective, a review of their duties on a metropolitan daily with both morning and evening editions follows.

Executive Editor

The executive editor reports directly to the president or publisher. He is responsible for the news content of the paper. His duties and responsibilities include providing an efficient, cost-conscious operation of the news department; recruiting and training competent newsmen and developing potential news executives; assuring that all news department executives and other employees know what is expected of them and are given sufficient authority to meet their responsibilities; encouraging news staff members to suggest stories and offer proposals for improving the newspaper; negotiating necessary contracts with wire services and news syndicates; recommending to the publisher any changes in space allotted news; recommending public service and promotion programs which would enhance the newspaper's standing in the community and circulation area; and giving broad direction to editing through approval of style and headline rules and by frequent consultation.

Managing Editor

The managing editor reports to the executive editor. His duties and responsibilities include consulting with the paper's executive editor in regard to editing and display of news in evening editions; coordinating activities with night news; supervising training and upgrading of new and veteran copy desk personnel; and enforcing accuracy, balance, and fairness in editing and displaying news.

Night Managing Editor

The night managing editor reports directly to the executive editor. He is responsible for the direction of the nightside news and photo operations and is the top-ranking official during nightside hours in absence of the executive editor. His duties and responsibilities include overseeing the gathering of news, features, and pictures in the metropolitan area for morning editions; improving the gathering, interpretation, and illustration of news; consulting with sub-editors regarding coverage and display of news and features; supervising operation

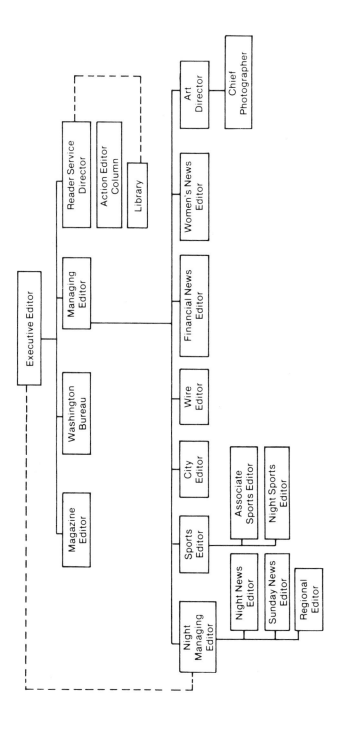

Fig. 13–1. The newsroom hierarchy of a metropolitan newspaper, with some variations depending on the individual publication, looks like this. This chart could apply to newspapers which circulate 100,000 copies and more.

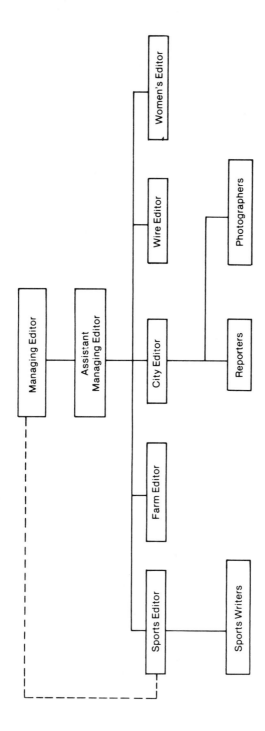

Fig. 13–2. The newsroom hierarchy of a medium sized newspaper, one that would circulate be-tween 15,000 and 100,000 copies, looks something like this.

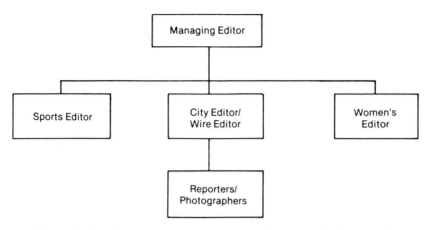

Fig. 13–3. The newsroom of a small sized daily, one that would circulate less than 15,000 copies, looks something like this.

of the night copy desk; and supervising contacts with state and national capital bureaus during night hours.

Night News Editor

The night news editor reports directly to the night managing editor. He is second in command on the night news staff. He consults with the night managing editor and carries out his instructions in regard to the layout and production of morning editions; confers with the night managing editor and makes staff assignments; supervises training for various copy desk, photo, and make-up positions; consults with the night managing editor on progress of new employees; and evaluates work of veteran staff members.

City Editor

The city editor reports directly to the managing editor. He is responsible for the operation of the day city desk, metropolitan photo operations, and special sections. He oversees the gathering of news, features, and pictures in the metropolitan area; provides reporting and photo assistance to the nightside, the regional desk, and the sports and women's departments in emergency situations; explains to other departments the significance of local and area news developments; consults on a continuing basis with the managing editor and night managing editor on common problems, advising them of upcoming news and pictures; consults with the Sunday editor on news and picture problems involving Sunday editions; supervises preliminary editing of news produced under his direction; and accepts responsibility of the accuracy of news that originates within his jurisdiction.

Assistant City Editor

The assistant city editor reports to the city editor. He supervises preliminary editing of all copy produced under his direction; consults with the Sunday editor on news and picture plans; originates picture and feature ideas; and supervises reporters and photographers in their daily assignments.

Sports Editor

The sports editor generally reports directly to the executive editor. He supervises the gathering, writing, editing, and design of sports news pages in daily and Sunday editions. He oversees the sports staff, including stringers; consults on a continuing basis with the city editor or other appropriate editors regarding news that is available for use in main sections; and writes a daily column.

Associate Sports Editor

The associate sports editor assists the sports editor in coordinating activities of the sports staff. He assists the sports editor with administrative duties; helps to coordinate the activities of the day and night sports personnel; and acts as a liaison with other members of the news staff.

Regional Editor

The regional editor reports to the managing editor or the night managing editor. He is responsible for the gathering, writing, and editing of general news and feature stories outside the metropolitan area. In addition, he works closely with the Sunday editor on development of weekend news, features, and photos; schedules and supervises the activities of roving reporters; and consults with the city editor or night managing editor in emergency situations for reporting and photo assistance.

Financial Editor

The financial editor reports to the managing editor. He supervises the gathering, writing, editing, and makeup of market pages as well as business news, features, and tables. He consults on a continuing basis with other editorial department heads regarding market-page coordination with the wire services and composing room.

Women's News Editor

The women's news editor reports to the executive editor or managing editor. The women's news editor oversees activities of the women's staff; writes a Sunday column and passes on Sunday color art suggestions; and works on a continuing basis with other editorial department heads regarding women's news available for main news section play.

Magazine Editor

The magazine editor reports to the executive editor. He supervises the assigning, gathering, writing, editing, and makeup of news and pictures appearing in the Sunday magazine. He deals on a continuing basis with the advertising department; consults with the art, photo, and mechanical departments regarding production problems; supervises buying of special features from syndicates and individual distributors; serves as a liaison between magazines and special local contributors; and maintains a liaison with the managing editor and other news departments to avoid duplication of articles scheduled for publication in the magazine.

These job descriptions vividly illustrate that newspaper editors do much more than assign, read, and edit copy. As is the case with other businesses, these middle-management editors supervise. A recent survey of 283 managing editors by James K. Gentry at the University of Missouri School of Journalism showed that 76 percent of the editors' time is spent managing—not working with news copy. In fact, 19 percent of the managing editors said they spend 99 to 100 percent of their time managing and some 42 percent spend 90 percent or more of their time on supervisory functions.

Obviously, the larger the newspaper, the more time editors spend on managing tasks. Gentry found that editors of newspapers which circulate more than 250,000 copies spend at least 90 percent of their time managing; editors engage in management chores 80 percent of the time if they work for newspapers that circulate 50,000 to 99,999 copies. Even at small dailies which circulate fewer than 15,000 copies, the survey showed that management time is some 59 percent of the total work load.

Gentry said the most encouraging aspect of the survey was the recognition among editors that improved management skills are needed. He also concluded that "careful planning can reduce and often prevent much of the chaos that prevails" in newsrooms. Though the newspaper chain of command is, in practice, likely a bit less formal than in many other industries, the fact is apparent that managerial concepts can be adapted from other fields.

Aspiring newspaper editors should be aware that management positions will indeed entail far more than rolling up shirt sleeves and digging into copy. Equally apparent is the fact that newspaper organizations should provide management training for supervisory personnel; being a good reporter is not sufficient background in many instances to function effectively in an editor's chair.

The Editorial Page Editor

One editor that does not appear on many newsroom hierarchy charts is the editorial page editor. The reason is simple: newspapers work hard to keep the news columns separate from editorial page views. Thus, most editorial page editors answer directly to the publisher. The editorial page editor (who likely doubles as the managing editor on small dailies) has a great responsibility to his newspaper and his readers.

An editorial page editor wears several hats. He is, of course, a working newsman. He writes editorials and chooses and edits syndicated columnists. This calls for sound judgment; when a newspaper takes a stand, all sides of the issue must be weighed before the editorial is written. This frequently includes painstaking research and, quite often, a conference with the publisher.

The editorial page editor must rapidly synthesize news from a variety of sources, isolate the essence of complicated information, and write an editorial which readers can easily and quickly grasp. Editorial page editors must also meet the public and withstand pressure from special interest groups and political figures. Naturally, not all editorials concern life-or-death matters; a good sense of humor is an asset to any editorial page editor.

In consultation with the publisher and possibly a few selected newsroom executives, an editorial page editor also selects syndicated columnists. This is a delicate task and one that should not be taken lightly. A variety of political pundits and humorists compete for space on editorial pages; media managers have a responsibility to choose from a broad philosophical spectrum.

Editorial page editors are also responsible for monitoring the letters column. They will often be called upon to decide whether certain letters will be printed. Considerations include available space, libel, obscenity, privacy interests, and the broad question of taste.

Editorial page editors are often criticized for failure to present a broad range of opinions. Unfortunately, the content of many editorial pages ranges only from ultra liberal to moderately liberal or from ultra conservative to moderately conservative. Newspaper critics contend that the editorial pages of some newspapers represent merely the narrow philosophies of newspaper management; the critics claim that nonmainstream ideas are not printed.

Jerome A. Barron, a law professor at George Washington University, is among those who feel that many editorial pages are closed entities controlled by media owners. Barron insists that the time-honored "marketplace of ideas" theory is unrealistic in present-day America. U.S. Supreme Court Justice Oliver Wendell Holmes said in 1919: "The ultimate good desired is better reached by free trade of ideas—that the best test of truth is the power of the thought to get itself accepted in the competition of the market, and that truth is the only ground upon which [such thoughts] safely can be carried out." According to Barron, newspapers are not doing their share to insure that truths will emerge from the "multitude of tongues" that Federal Judge Learned Hand envisioned in 1943 because of their refusal to publish unpopular ideas.

The social responsibility theory—that freedom of the press carries concomitant obligations to society—has gained acceptance by many press observers today. This responsibility presumably extends to making news columns available to those who have something to say —no matter how odious, irresponsible or juvenile their opinions might be.

Newspaper publishers and editors contend that they recognize their obligations to society. By such devices as letters-to-the-editor columns, locally written editorials, expanded reader viewpoint columns, and a variety of syndicated columnists, they insist they are fulfilling their obligation.

Obviously, the editorial page editor is charged with meeting this responsibility; it is he who determines whose ideas will be given access to the page. Although newspapers oppose any governmental attempt to assure accuracy or fairness, media executives are taking steps to be more accountable to their readers. In response to criticism that they do not provide enough diversity of opinion, many newspapers are giving more space to letters to the editor; some papers actively encourage readers to write letters expressing their opinions.

Research indicates that the letters column is the best-read entity on the editorial page. Most newspapers promote their letters column by printing open invitations to submit an opinion. Some newspapers also publish eye-catching advertisements in other parts of the newspaper encouraging readers to send letters.

Still, editors in smaller communities claim that they sometimes have difficulty finding local citizens with ideas that can be passed on to the public. A 1965 Gallup Poll supports this contention. The poll indicated that only 16 percent of those sampled had ever written a letter to the editor. Thus, despite efforts to open up editorial pages to average citizens, a large number of opinions continue to come from perpetual letter writers, professional writers, or experts in their particular fields.

Readers from nonmetropolitan areas are more likely to gain access to editorial pages. Readers naturally have the most difficulty getting their opinions printed in metropolitan newspapers. Former *New York Times* managing editor Clifton Daniel claims it is not possible for large metropolitan newspapers to print every letter sent in. He cites 1969 statistics when the *Times* received 37,719 letters to the editor. The *Times* was able to print only 6 percent of them. If it had printed them all—some eighteen million words—they would have filled up 135 complete weekday editions of the newspaper.

The National Conference of Editorial Writers is not unaware of the need to open up the editorial pages to the public. The group has consistently examined such issues as accessability of the editorial page to dissenting opinion and the presentation of local and syndicated columns whose views oppose those of newspaper management. The national organization has also criticized newspapers that rely too heavily on syndicated editorial columnists.

Generally, however, editors agree that syndicated columnists provide a broad spectrum of philosophies when conscientiously selected. Scores of American daily newspapers, realizing that a mixture of syndicated columns, locally written editorials, and reader opinions offer a solid "marketplace of ideas" forum have established op-ed pages. These pages appear opposite the editorial page and provide extra space for a variety of viewpoints. David Shaw, a *Los Angeles Times* reporter, said that his newspaper, after deciding that its op-ed page was "too dull, abstract, official, impersonal and predictable," extended the op-ed columns to the "common man."

Effective op-ed pages, coupled with a strong editorial page, potentially offer in this decade an equivalent of John Milton's basic concept of free speech. Newspapers that try to provide a wide variety of opinions on the editorial and op-ed pages rely heavily on the character and ability of their editorial page editors.

Chapter 14

Editing a Campus Newspaper

THE NUMBER OF campus newspapers in the United States now exceeds 2,500, more than the number of commercial dailies. College student newspapers have a combined circulation exceeding 10 million and claim a total annual operating budget of more than $75 million. A recent edition of the *Directory of the College Student Press in America,* compiled by Dario Politella, a journalism professor at the University of Massachusetts, lists 2,524 college newspapers on the basis of reports from 2,581 of the nation's 3,100 campuses. Projections based on averages determined by current listings may place the actual number of college newspapers as high as 3,038.

These newspapers, some in operation for more than a century, range from those with circulations of less than one thousand on small campuses to those in excess of thirty-five thousand. Their operating budgets range from a few thousand dollars annually to more than a million dollars.

The oldest surviving campus daily newspaper, the *Dartmouth,* dates back to 1839 at Dartmouth College. Dartmouth had earlier had a weekly newspaper, the *Dartmouth Gazette,* published between 1799 and 1820 and chiefly devoted to literary composition. Daniel Webster was numbered among its contributors. An interesting collection of personalities have written for or edited scholastic publications, one historian noted. The *Harvard Crimson,* for example, during its one hundred-year history, boasts of such notable student writers as Edward Everett Hale, William Faulkner, Franklin D. Roosevelt, James B. Conant, Gardner Cowles Jr., David Riesman, Cleveland Amory, and John F. Kennedy. The *College Star* at Southwest Texas State Teachers College claims Lyndon B. Johnson as a former contributing editor.

Role of the Campus Newspaper

A college student newspaper may serve a number of purposes. The primary purpose of a campus newspaper which is tied closely with a department or school of journalism, for example, may be to provide the opportunity for journalism students to develop their journalistic skills through practical on-the-job training. The primary purpose of a more independently-oriented campus newspaper, one more free of school control, may be to provide a vehicle for expression of vital student interests and concerns.

On the other hand, the primary purpose of a campus newspaper tied closely to the college or university administration may be to provide factual communication to better public relations among the various segments of the university—the administration, faculty, staff, students, and the community. One writer has correctly pointed out that only the last of these three purposes could be adequately fulfilled in other ways than through a campus newspaper. In fact, most professional journalists would argue that the function of a good newspaper should never be to serve as a public relations agency for the college or university. By the same token, the value of hands-on training for journalism students is viewed as invaluable by most prospective employers.

Herman A. Estrin, former chairman of the National Council of College Publications Advisers, in attempting to define the scope and purpose of a college newspaper more than twenty years ago, said:

> The objectives of the [campus] paper are to help the student and the college understand each other, to encourage greater cooperation between the faculty and the student body, to instill in each student a greater desire to participate in activities, and to promote a higher standard of journalism by learning and practicing its principles and ethics.

That list of objectives is still appropriate today. The campus newspaper should still be the arbitrator and the coordinator which strives to help the college, the faculty, and the students achieve those goals to which higher education is dedicated. By engaging in this cooperative effort, a college student newspaper, no matter how small or how large, can help to inculcate in its readers a love of learning and seeking for knowledge and, as Estrin puts it, "the courage to use this knowledge and to work for a better world for mankind."

While campus press scholars like Politella see the trend in campus journalism as being toward more professionalism, the student press is still viewed with alarm by many professional educators. The periodic eruption of student newspapers into one kind of controversy or another has almost become routine, as one educator noted a generation ago:

> It can raise more hell on a college campus than spiked punch at the Dean's reception for freshman women.
> It can make more errors of fact and judgment in a single four-page issue than a professional editor ever dreamed after a midnight snack of welsh rarebit.

There is sufficient evidence to indicate that the college press hasn't been entirely reformed. The *College Press Review*, for example, in its 1977–78 directory issue listing two hundred cases from its "Student Press Archives," notes the 1977 incident at the Massachusetts Institute of Technology involving two MIT coeds who named names and rated the sexual performances of thirty-six undergraduates they claimed they had slept with. The article was headlined "Consumer Guide to MIT Men." The report was published in the MIT campus weekly newspaper, *Thursday*. The executive committee of the student association voted to censure the newspaper, and a faculty committee met to consider discipline for the two women. The story, which apparently began as a joke, was called a "gross violation of our norms of tastes and regard for privacy" by MIT President Jerome Wiesner.

Responsible journalism? By professional standards, most would agree with the MIT president that such a publication was certainly not. Does the student press have the constitutional freedom to be so provocative, shocking, and even irresponsible? Can such publication be censored by a newspaper adviser, by the publications board, or by the college or university president prior to publication? How much freedom of expression does the college student and the college press have?

First Amendment Protection for the School Press

During the late 1960s and early 1970s, censorship of the school press became one of the most emotional issues in the controversy over student rights in the United States. Traditionally the public schools had been considered *in loco parentis* (standing in for the parent), temporarily exercising the mature judgment and authority of the parent. While such censorship existed on the college and university level, it was more prevalent in high schools, where censorship of journalism was often a matter of school policy, either stated or implied. The Commission of Inquiry into High School Journalism sponsored by the Robert F. Kennedy Memorial found, for example, that "Censorship and the systematic lack of freedom to engage in open, responsible journalism characterize high school journalism." Many student newspapers on college and university campuses also went through troubled times resulting in articles being censored, editions being confiscated, editors being fired, and even publications being suspended.

The efforts of school authorities to censor student expression and the student press during the 1960s resulted in numerous court actions. In a landmark case in 1969, the Supreme Court of the United States in *Tinker* v. *Des Moines Independent School District,* noting that it "can hardly be argued that either students or teachers shed their constitutional right to freedom of speech or expression at the schoolhouse gate," held that

> In our system, state-operated schools may not be enclaves of totalitarianism. School officials do not possess absolute authority over their students. Students in school as well as out of school are "persons" under our Constitution. They are possessed of fundamental rights which the state must respect. . . . In the absence of a specific showing of constitutionally valid reasons to regulate their speech, students are entitled to freedom of expression of their views.

The Supreme Court then went ahead to set out the justification for restriction of student expression:

> In order for the State in the person of school officials to justify prohibition of a particular expression of opinion, it must be able to show that its action was caused by something more than a mere desire to avoid the discomfort and unpleasantness that always accompany an unpopular viewpoint. Certainly where there is no finding and no showing that engaging in the forbidden conduct would materially and substantially interfere with the operation of the school, the prohibition cannot be sustained.

The lower courts repeatedly have applied the "material and substantial interference" test as a qualification for freedom of the student press, much as the "clear and present danger" test has been applied in regard to the commercial press. In numerous lower court cases, school administrators have been admonished that they are not the "unrestrained masters of what they create," and that they have no constitutional power to tell a student what thoughts to communicate either verbally or in the campus paper.

Freedom of the press, however, is not without restrictions in regard to the student press, just as First Amendment guarantees are not absolute in regard to the commercial press. School administrators, for example, are free to formulate reasonable regulations to control student behavior "which tends to impede, obstruct or threaten the achievement of educational goals." The forms of permissible administrative control may range from restriction of funds to disciplinary action against student editors. Attempts to control the press at North Carolina Central University, where school administrators withheld newspaper funds pending the working out of an agreement on editorial standards, was ruled constitutionally invalid by the U.S. Court of Appeals, Fourth Circuit.

Robert Trager, an authority on school press law (see bibliography for this chapter), notes that a more common form of administrative control is the refusal to print or distribute a particular offensive edition of a school paper. This often is easy to accomplish when the newspaper is published by the college or university. But, even if the newspaper is published off campus, the printer may be reluctant to offend school administrators, as it may mean the possible loss of other printing business.

While the courts generally have extended constitutional guarantees to student newspapers at public colleges and universities, student journalists and newspapers published at private schools may not have such First Amendment protection against censorship by school officials. The constitutional doctrine of "state action" holds that the First Amendment protects speech and press against abridgment by governmental action—federal, state, or local. When a school administrator at a public high school, college or university censors expression, that abridgment comes as the result of action by an agent of the state. The newspaper adviser or faculty representative in the newsroom, no matter what his title, may be the instrument of the state action at a public college or university, and the First Amendment protects against such censorship. There would likely be no state action involved, however, if such censorship were exercised by a school administrator at a parochial school or a private college or university. Before state action would likely be found under such circumstances, there would have to be a showing of a substantial financial tie between the state and the private school. After such a relationship has been established, it must then be determined whether or not the state itself had any part in formulating the rule under question or was involved with the specific form of censorship being used. Recent court rulings would indicate that, in most instances involving censorship at private schools, such a connection is unlikely to exist.

Prior censorship of news copy before publication by a representative of a public college or university would be an unconstitutional infringement of the rights of student journalists, just as prior censorship of a commercial newspaper by an agent of the state would be an unconstitutional prior restraint on the press. A student newspaper at Fitchburg State College in Massachusetts, for example, went to court when the college president, acting under state law, insisted that before he would release funds to pay for future issues, all materials to be printed in the newspaper would have to be approved by him or his representative. A federal district court, noting that it was doubtful that any procedural safeguards could be formulated which would support prior censorship, held that the state law giving the college president power to distribute student body funds "does not make him ultimately responsible for what is printed in the campus newspaper." A federal district court in Alabama, after holding that free press and free expression could be restricted only where the exercise "materially and substantially interferes with requirements of appropriate discipline," said that, "Boards of education, presidents of colleges, and faculty advisers are not excepted from the rule that protects students from unreasonable rules and regulations."

College journalists, like their professional counterparts off campus, are subject to subsequent punishment under the laws of libel, obscenity, and invasion of privacy and are liable for violation of other legal restrictions placed upon the press as discussed in chapter 12.

Types of Campus Newspapers

College student newspapers have been typecast in various ways. While the labels, which vary, are not important, the functions flowing from the various types of news operations are important. A panel discussion of how student newspapers might best be used in journalism education during an Association for Education in Journalism conference, for example, focused on three functional approaches. One speaker described what he labelled the "segregated approach," maintaining that the utilization of campus newspapers as laboratories for departments and schools of journalism was incompatible with the primary functions of the college press. Another discussed the "integrated approach," arguing that where college newspapers are published on campuses with a department or school of journalism, they should serve, at least in part, as a laboratory for the academic training of journalists. Then there was a "modified segregated approach," embracing various types of school control within the range marked by the other two functional types.

More recently, another panel, this one participating in a program of the Inland Daily Press Association, discussed four types of campus newspapers:

1. The laboratory newspaper, where students often participate in the newsroom for academic credit.

2. The so-called "independent newspaper," which usually retains some ties with the school, though at arm's length.

3. The off-campus "underground newspaper" with no university support.

4. The professional college newspaper, which the panelist described as an independent campus newspaper with professionally-oriented goals where students have the opportunity to learn and be responsible for all aspects of newspaper production—business and production as well as news.

From these and other classifications, it is clear that the campus press may be divided into at least three basic groups. Julius Duscha, co-author of *The Campus Press*, describes these three basic types in terms of their relationship to the college or university:

1. The student newspaper which can be directly controlled by the university administration or by faculty members responsible to the administration.

2. The student newspaper which can be placed in an amorphous situation by having it published by a publications board or a student governing body, and by having the newspaper financed, at least in part, with funds from the university or from a compulsory student activity.

3. The student newspaper which can be truly independent, operating with no direction from school administrators and with no funds from the university or student activity fees.

While there has been a move during the past decade toward the third type—that is, to newspapers with more editorial independence —few papers are truly independent, either legally or financially. A 1975 survey, for example, indicated that only 10 percent of the campus newspapers are editorially, financially, and legally independent. The survey found more independent student newspapers at private institutions (13 percent) than at public schools (7 percent). A lack of proper financing is usually given as the major reason for not having a totally independent status. While advertising is the largest source of income for most student newspapers, student fees and other school subsidies still provide an important part of the college press's operating budget. This is true of even some of the larger campus newspapers. The UCLA *Daily Bruin,* for example, with a circulation of 22,000 and an annual budget of $295,000, receives 75 percent of its income from advertising, 24 percent from school subsidies, and 1 percent from subscriptions. The *Iowa State Daily,* with a circulation of 14,700 and a budget of $276,000, gets 70 percent of its income from advertising, 27 percent from mandatory student fees, 2 percent from subscriptions, and 1 percent from school subsidies.

By contrast, the *Daily Illini* at the University of Illinois, with a circulation of 14,000 and a budget of $934,000, has achieved a high degree of financial and legal, as well as editorial, independence. Advertising revenue provides 77 percent of the *Illini*'s budget, 21 percent comes from subscriptions and 2 percent from other sources.

The *Daily Illini* is a five-day-a-week tabloid which averages thirty-six pages a day and employs a staff of ten full-time professionals and nearly two hundred fifty students in the business, circulation, advertising and editorial departments. Some are part-time hourly employees; some are news stringers or correspondents. The paper is published by the Illini Publishing Co., a nonprofit corporation under the direction of an eight-member board of directors appointed by the chancellor of the University. Four of the board members are faculty, and four are students, of which one may be a graduate student. The faculty members are usually from either the College of Communications or the College of Commerce and Business Administration. The board is also in charge of the student radio station, the yearbook, and a magazine. One of the board's major responsibilities is to appoint the editors and business managers of the various student media, according to Richard Sublette, publisher of the *Daily Illini.*

The organization and operation of the Illini Publishing Co. allows the newspaper to be independent from the university, Sublette argues. The financial arrangements assist in maintaining this independence. The *Daily Illini,* for example, does not receive rent-free housing, does not receive a bulk subscription rate or any kind of allocation, and, unlike many other campus publications, does not have university restrictions imposed concerning the spending of revenue. This arrangement, Sublette says, has helped to protect the First Amendment rights of students.

Sublette was quoted as saying recently in a *College Press Review* article: "I don't know of any time or have never heard of any time in the last 108 years where the university ever tried to stop something from being printed or insisted that something be printed on the editorial side of any of our publications or our radio station. We feel very immune from that sort of thing."

With this kind of independence, however, comes burdens and responsibilities, Sublette points out. Once the IPC board appoints student editors, for example, the board expects them to be responsible and to be accountable. The support of both the IPC and the full-time staff have helped students assume their responsibility, the publisher says.

Another campus newspaper falling into the independent category is the *Indiana Daily Student,* a broad sheet averaging eighteen pages, five days a week, with a circulation of 15,500 and with an annual budget of $630,000. The *Daily Student* receives 81 percent of its operating revenue from advertising, 14 percent from subscriptions and 5 percent from job printing. Except for payment of only token rent in Ernie Pyle Hall, the *Student* is almost totally financially independent of the university. But, those connected with the *Student* often refer to the paper as professional rather than independent.

Richard Gray, chairman of the Department of Journalism at Indiana University, sees such professionalism at Indiana growing out of a balanced plan which in essence makes the journalism department responsible for the business and publishing aspects of the newspaper and the students responsible for the editorial side. A board of publications, composed of three professional journalists, three faculty members, and three students, supervises the operation. Some one hundred fifty students are often involved in the *Daily Student* newsroom, eighty of those on the payroll of the newspaper. The charter setting up the board also provides for a code of ethics which staffers are required to abide by. Students within each department of the newspaper must also operate within their designated budget, affording another effective control approaching the responsible management required when students join newspapers off campus.

At the other end of the segregation-integration continuum is the *Columbia Missourian* at the University of Missouri, a unique campus newspaper in terms of the degree to which the newspaper is integrated into the educational program of the School of Journalism. Published daily except Mondays, the *Missourian* is also professionally oriented in that it covers city and county news much more extensively than most campus newspapers. It has a paid circulation of eight thousand and an operating budget in excess of $1 million. It is printed offset in a modern plant on campus, averaging twenty-four broad sheet pages daily.

But the *Missourian,* unlike the *Daily Illini* and the *Indiana Daily Student,* is a laboratory newspaper for the hundreds of news-editorial students in the School of Journalism. The publisher, J. Robert Humphreys, is an associate professor on the faculty of the school. Roy M. Fisher, dean of the school and teacher of the editorial writing class, heads the editorial board which determines the editorial page policy of the newspaper. Both faculty and students make up the editorial board.

The *Missourian,* however, in contrast to the so-called independent campus newspapers, has no general publications board or hierarchy of student editors. The news-editorial faculty are, in effect, the policy makers for the *Missourian.* Students taking reporting courses are assigned to cover live beats downtown and throughout the county as a part of their class work. The editing class, under the supervision of the instructor and with the aid of teaching assistants, edit the copy for the newspaper. Advertising classes use the newspaper as their laboratory. The production department, in contrast to many other student newspapers, is staffed by full-time nonstudent professionals from the various craft unions. The *Missourian,* by tradition and design, is a laboratory newspaper—a teaching newspaper. This does not mean, however, that it is not professional. In many ways it is more professional, competing with the commercial press for off-campus news to a greater degree than the majority of campus newspapers. Two other campus student newspapers at Missouri, the semi-weekly *Maneater* and the *Campus Digest,* both with circulations of 3,250, cover the campus news.

In between the *Daily Illini*'s segregated, independent position and the *Columbia Missourian's* integrated, school-oriented approach, there are hundreds of variations on the theme. In fact, except for the off-campus underground-type newspapers, the majority of campus newspapers, while striving for editorial independence, often find it necessary to retain some financial ties with the university. Many campus newspapers also find it advantageous to maintain some professional relationship with the department or school of journalism on campuses where one or the other exists. The *Daily Egyptian* on the Southern Illinois University campus falls somewhere along this continuum.

The *Egyptian,* a five-day, tabloid newspaper with a circulation of 25,000 and a budget of $405,000, has many of the characteristics of an independent newspaper, but the *Egyptian* also has close ties with the school of journalism. The newspaper is largely self-supporting, receiving 90 percent of its revenues from advertising, 5 percent from subscriptions, and 5 percent from printing and other miscellaneous sources. But the *Egyptian,* as many campus newspapers, occupies rent-free space in the school of journalism wing of the communications building and receives various other subsidies, such as janitorial service. In fact, the *Daily Egyptian* is an arm of the university. The board of trustees of the university is the publisher.

The newspaper serves as both a laboratory for the news-editorial sequence of the school of journalism and as a newspaper for the campus community, covering news both on campus and off. As a laboratory, students in reporting, editing, and practicum receive on-the-job training as a part of their class work. More advanced students compete for some thirty paid positions on the news staff. An additional eighty students from throughout the university are employed in other departments of the newspaper. Educational opportunities in the newsroom are viewed as being further enhanced by the presence in the newsroom of a faculty managing editor who teaches the editing course. Another faculty member serves as business manager of the newspaper. The director of the School of Journalism is the chief fiscal officer of the newspaper and chairs a policy and review board, an advisory body made up of faculty, students and professional members. The board, established in 1974, is viewed as a buffer between the university administration and the newspaper.

The content of the *Egyptian* is generally the responsibility of the student staff, headed by the student editor-in-chief named by the director each semester with the advice of the policy and review board. Editorial page policy is determined by an editorial committee made up of the faculty managing editor, the student editor-in-chief, the editorial page editor, a student selected from the news staff, and the instructor of the editorial writing class. The 1974 reorganization which provided for a student editor-in-chief was designed to allow more student participation in policy decisions and to encourage responsibility for those decisions.

There are various methods of organizing, financing, and operating a campus newspaper, as the above examples suggest. Which one method is best is a question upon which neither journalism educators nor student journalists are likely to agree. Editorial independence during the past decade is definitely on the upswing, largely because the courts have mandated such freedom for students. Financial independence has both advantages and disadvantages. Close ties with departments or schools of journalism provide opportunities for journalism students and often bring subsidies from the university, but such ties are sometimes viewed with suspicion by the rest of the student body.

The Role of the Student Editor

It is important that student editors and staffers alike understand the organization, structure, goals, and policies of the newspaper for which they work. Official guidelines of one type or another usually exist for communications and publications boards, or in the absence of such groups, for established campus newspapers. These guidelines define the rights, restrictions, and responsibilities of the school administration, the faculty adviser, and the student journalist. Such guidelines, based upon legal, professional, and economic concerns, as well as on day-to-day operational problems, form the basic ground rules for everyone involved in the publication of campus newspapers, particularly newspapers on public school campuses. These guidelines generally remain in effect from year to year with modifications as required by new legal rulings or where changes are needed to make the guidelines work more efficiently.

Student editors are vitally interested in such guidelines for a number of reasons. In the first place, they generally set out the qualifications for the various editorial positions, listing the duties involved and explaining the relationship of the editor with various other departments and members of the newspaper's staff.

Student editors must also be aware of the editorial policy of the newspaper for which they work. Editorial policy, in contrast to the official guidelines, is usually formulated by the newspaper staff in conjunction with the adviser and the publications board, if one exists. Editorial policy may deal with questions involving the purpose of the newspaper and its content; with stylistic and usage concerns; with readability, fairness, ethics, and accuracy; and with other policy goals. Policy statements are usually directed toward greater professionalism. Policy describes the paper's conduct, determines its personality and character, and provides for uniformity and continuity under changing personnel. The canons of journalism formulated by the American Society of Newspaper Editors is often a part of the policy guidelines.

One thing which guidelines and policies cannot legally do, however, is to forbid student journalists from writing on controversial topics which may invite or stimulate heated discussion or debate among students. Nor can criticism of school officials be forbidden. In writing and editorializing about controversial issues, however, the student journalist must observe the same legal responsibilities imposed upon the conventional news media.

Once the newspaper's guidelines and policies are formulated, it is the responsibility of the student editor to see that they are observed. Unless the policies are followed, the purpose of the newspaper to serve as a forum for the exchange of student opinion, concerns, and viewpoints will not be fully realized. The student editor is primarily responsible for the general news side of the newspaper, and he sees to it that established news policies regarding both the coverage and editing of news are carried out in a responsible way. He is usually responsible for the editorial pages, although an editorial page editor or an editorial assistant may actually supervise editing the page. The editor's overall responsibility toward the editorial page usually includes selecting of materials to be published, determining the position which the paper will take on various public issues, setting the policy governing letters to the editor, and encouraging fairness and balance in dealing with controversial issues, both in the news columns and on the editorial page.

As the newspaper's leader and manager, the editor is also responsible for promoting a feeling of understanding and encouragement among his staffers. He is responsible for training new reporters and copy editors. He must keep the staff informed of changes in editorial policy and involve them in long-range planning toward future changes in policy. Indeed, the student editor has the same responsibility as his counterpart in the commercial press, a responsibility which he must often meet with a minimum of experience and with a staff which is part-time and constantly changing.

The Role of the Adviser

While the role of the student editor is closely related to the duties of the conventional editor, the campus newspaper adviser often plays an amorphous role. On a more independent campus newspaper controlled by a publications board or committee, there may be no faculty adviser. On newspapers at smaller schools the adviser may act as publisher as well as adviser. On a few laboratory newspapers, as noted above, the faculty member may be the editor. In a few instances, even where the newspaper has a hierarchy of student editors, the adviser may be a supervisor with the authority and responsibility for everything which gets published in the newspaper.

Whatever role the adviser may occupy, however, he does not have the legal authority to institute a system requiring prior approval of all student expression before publication. The adviser, even at public schools, does have the authority to censor expression which threatens "to materially and substantially interfere with the requirements of appropriate discipline in the operation of the school," as the U.S. Supreme Court states in *Tinker*. Moreover, other courts have held that libelous statements, obscene materials, so-called fighting words which are to cause readers to breach the peace, and speech which threatens national security are subject to censorship because they are without First Amendment protection. Other courts have stated, however, that the faculty adviser should counsel against publication of such expression, but that the adviser does not have the legal authority to forbid its publication. Without doubt, the adviser's role as censor has been greatly diminished by the courts during the past decade.

An adviser's role normally should be primarily one of counseling and teaching. A recent symposium of views published in *College Press Review* focusing on the question of what advising the school newspaper means brought various responses. Evelyn A. Jez of Averett College wrote:

> I view publications work and the positions held by students as leadership positions—training grounds, where those who are ready may test and expand their capabilities to perceive this campus community accurately, to learn and work with others in an atmosphere

of mutual respect and to project their abilities to inform, to entertain, and to persuade with a sense of purpose and style.

William J. Rushimann of Suffolk University discussed his role as a counselor, rather than editor: "If I were to censor the newspaper, I would become in effect the editor—a practice that would at once rob and absolve the students of their own responsibility." Warren A. Mack of DeAnza College views the adviser as needing "professional newspaper experience, a large measure of empathy and patience, a thick skin, and academic training—in that order."

These are expressions of advisers reflecting the classic and traditional approach. Even advisers who have the power of supervisors, however, often do more counseling than giving orders. Faculty supervisors strive for professionalism also, but they may see more faculty input as the way of getting a more professional product than a hands-off policy.

Weaknesses and Virtues of the Campus Press

The campus newspaper is beset with many problems which make the role of the student journalist and student editor difficult and frustrating, but there is much evidence that the quality and professionalism of campus journalism is on the upswing.

One of the primary problems in editing the campus newspaper is the lack of continuity of student personnel. No sooner does a beat reporter, a department editor, or a news editor become proficient at his job than he graduates and the arduous training process must begin once again. Even with a more experienced news staff which is striving toward greater proficiency, the fact that staffers are part-time journalists and full-time students poses additional problems. For one thing, there are twice as many reporters which the student editor must supervise than there would be to do the same work on a commercial newspaper with a full-time news staff. Also, the student editor whose task it becomes to supervise the part-time staff is himself a part-time editor. Since most schools require that candidates for the position of editor be full-time students, arguments that the student editor should be full-time, cutting back or cancelling class for a semester or year, are usually doomed from the beginning.

Aside from personnel problems, it is often more difficult to define, gather, and edit the news for a campus newspaper than for a commercial paper. There may be a problem of defining what is news. Should news for the campus newspaper be limited to events and issues which center on the campus, or should the newspaper cover city, county, and even regional events of interest to students? The more widespread the area of news responsibility, the more difficult it is to recruit student editors who know the territory, who are aware of the news sources, and who understand the functioning of the administrative and political organizations and governmental bodies involved. Even on campus, the adviser's view of what is news may differ from that of a student journalist. Once the news role is defined and the news is gathered, it is usually more difficult to edit student-written copy than it is to edit the copy of professional journalists. A student copy editor may lack the expertise to bring the story into focus and write an intelligent headline which avoids ambiguity, editorializing, and double-meanings.

Besides all these problems, a student editor may have problems in assuming the authoritative role of editor and taking the responsibility for everything which goes into the newspaper. He may have difficulty, for example, in saying "no" to pressure groups in student government or to other peer groups. Such peer pressures upon a student editor in a campus environment may lead to inaction on his part and to letting problems grow for a lack of editorial decision.

The attitude of many faculty and townspeople also may make it more difficult for student journalists to operate in a responsible, professional manner. For example, student editors are sometimes reminded that they are only students, reminded that their tenure on the newspaper is limited, and told that they shouldn't become involved in various issues because of their long-term consequences. An adviser can help compensate for some of these limiting factors placed upon the student press, but an adviser is too often asked to share his knowledge with too many inexperienced staffers.

While a campus press may be beset with many problems not faced by the commercial press—at least not in the same degree—a student editor needs the freedom to experiment and to innovate. A campus press can benefit from the editing principles set out in the various chapters of this book as much as can a professional editor on a commercial newspaper.

The student editor is editing a newspaper for a different audience—one made up largely of students. He needs and generally has the freedom to adapt his approach to meet their needs. But he must use that freedom in a responsible manner.

Chapter 15

Editing a Weekly Newspaper

The weekly newspaper press in the United States has played an important informational role longer than any other communications medium. During the colonial period, every newspaper was published at weekly or even greater intervals. It wasn't until 1783 that Benjamin Towne established the *Pennsylvania Evening Post* in Philadelphia, which one journalism historian has called a "shoddy little daily." It survived for only seventeen months.

The weekly press has a long history, but it is also important because it is so pervasive. From its humble beginnings, the number of weekly newspapers of general circulation grew throughout the nineteenth century, reaching 14,000 in 1910. That same decade saw the number of English-language daily newspapers reach a high mark of 2,200. Economic pressures during World War I and the decades which followed, however, had a marked effect on newspaper publication. The 1978 *Ayer Directory of Publications* listed 1,765 dailies— 1,414 evening and 351 morning publications. In 1978 there were 8,617 nondaily newspapers, according to Ayer. The total included 7,980 weekly, 569 semiweekly, and 68 triweekly publications. While the ratio differential between the number of daily and nondaily newspapers has decreased since 1910, the weekly press still outnumbers the daily press by almost four to one. In some states the ratio is even greater. In Illinois, for example, which boasts the largest state press association in the United States, there are some 745 newspapers, only 94 of them dailies.

The weekly press, since it is so massive and pervasive, offers an excellent training ground for the beginning journalist. Kenneth R. Byerly, author of *Community Journalism* and a former journalism teacher at the University of North Carolina, once asked students in his community newspaper class to list and explain why they might desire a career in community journalism. Some students viewed the weekly newspaper as an opportunity to gain needed experience before moving on to the daily newspaper field. Others saw the community newspaper as offering more job satisfaction, more freedom to exercise individual judgment, and more opportunity to work toward owning their own newspaper. To own a community newspaper is also the dream of many established journalists.

With increasing competition for daily newspaper jobs, a journalism student might also add to Byerly's list that in today's market the community press is where the jobs are. The pay might not equal that of the medium-size or big-city daily, but the challenge and opportunity to work at various aspects of newspaper publishing—reporting, advertising sales, photography, editing, and even printing—is unequaled.

Diversity of the Weekly Press

To classify a newspaper as being published weekly, without knowing more, is of little help in understanding the great diversity and ubiquitousness of the weekly press. One needs to know something of its circulation, its ownership, its geographic location, its community orientation and various other publication characteristics. The journalism student from a small town, for example, may immediately think of the weekly as a small-town community newspaper. Such a newspaper, historically referred to as a "country weekly," may be a marginal operation published in a letterpress plant with few resources and edited by a printer or publisher with little skill in news gathering or editing. But a small-town weekly may also be a quality newspaper published by a highly respected writer and skillful editor, such as the *Martha's Vineyard Gazette* published for many years by Henry Beetle Hough and recently purchased by James Reston of the *New York Times.*

Thousands of weekly newspapers are published in small towns throughout the United States ranging in size from only a few hundred residents to communities of ten thousand population and in suburban areas many times larger. Whether such newspapers are performing successfully or whether they are struggling to survive, they may be the sole news medium serving that community. Economic pressures and the shift of population from the small town to the city since World War I have brought hard times to many of these country weeklies. Hundreds have gone out of business; others have consolidated in order to survive in the face of dwindling advertising revenue—the lifeblood of any newspaper. The story of the courage displayed and economic hardships faced by some of these editors is told in a recently published book, *Main Street Militants,* edited by Howard R. Long, a journalism educator and secretary of the International Society of Weekly Newspaper Editors (ISWNE) for many years. The problems and successes of the small town newspaper press are reported and discussed in a quarterly magazine, *Grassroots Editor,* published by the ISWNE, now located at Northern Illinois University.

The journalism student from the city, on the other hand, may be thinking of his suburban newspaper when he makes reference to the weekly press. In contrast to the small-town weekly, which often lacks the resources needed to gather, edit, and publish the news of its community, the suburban weekly is more often than not printed in a modern central printing plant, often equipped with video display terminals on-line to computerized phototypesetting equipment and with the latest in offset printing facilities. While the competition in the suburban press field may be fierce, both from weekly competitors and from big city dailies with their suburban sections and zoned editions, the necessary potential advertising revenue is there for the aggressive entrepreneur.

The movement of urban residents from the core city to the suburbs has helped to foster the growth of the suburban press since World War II. In the early 1970s, more than half of all families living within the major metropolitan areas of the United States resided in the suburbs. The general prosperity of suburbia is reflected in its newspapers which have grown in number, in circulation, and, more often than not, in quality. In the Los Angeles metropolitan area, for example, the *Los Angeles Times,* which has news bureaus in seven American cities and sixteen foreign countries, leaves most of the routine local reporting to community newspapers—some 300 community weeklies and 19 community dailies. This "remarkable sociological phenomenon," according to David Shaw, a press critic for the *Times,* has resulted because of the increasing appetite of suburban readers for news of their individual suburban communities—about municipal controversies, social affairs, high school athletic news, and even PTA and school news. The community press as a social element of suburban life is discussed by Morris Janowitz in *The Community Press* and Hal Lister in *The Suburban Press*. (See bibliography.)

A scientific attempt to profile weekly newspapers was undertaken by two researchers at California State University at Long Beach in 1977. In a report published in *Grassroots Editor* by Gerald C. Stone and Chris Gulyas based upon a national random sample of 763 weekly newspapers, three community newspaper types were identified. The largest group (54 percent) was found to be published in agricultural-industrial communities—the small-town weeklies. Of these, about 40 percent were reported to be published in county seat towns, primarily in the Southeast and Midwest. The second largest group (35 percent) were the suburban weeklies found primarily in the metropolitan centers of the North Atlantic and Midwestern states. A third category (11 percent) was made up of weeklies published in resort communities.

The majority of the weeklies in each of the three categories (58 percent) are published on Thursday. The majority of all weekly newspapers (62 percent) were found to be eight-column format with the number of tabloids greatest (35 percent) among the suburban weeklies. The average paid circulation was largest for the suburban weeklies (5,117), lowest among the agri-industrial weeklies (2,892). Competition was highest among the suburban weeklies (50 percent), lowest among the county seat weeklies (30 percent).

While one can generalize about the differences between the small town (agri-industrial) and the suburban weekly, there are other factors than geography which add to the diversity of the weekly press. One such factor is ownership. Chain ownership and the economic advantages which such joint operation often brings is affecting the weekly press as it has the daily press. Standardization of the editorial product which chain ownership may bring and other fears which press critics have voiced about the continuing growth of newspaper chains and its effect on the family-owned weekly and the so-called market-place of ideas apply also to the operation of the weekly press, though perhaps to a lesser degree than the daily press, in part because of the greater number of weekly newspapers.

Chain ownership is reflected, however, by the fact that the twenty-five largest daily newspaper chains, which own a total of 419 daily newspapers, also own 232 weeklies. Harte-Hanks, which owns 26 dailies, owns the largest number of weekly newspapers—61. Gannett, which owns the largest number of dailies—78—owns 19 weekly newspapers as well. Weekly newspaper chains, often operating in the suburbs, also produce scores of newspapers, usually from a central printing plant. In Chicago, for example, a dozen or more chains publish the majority of the suburban weeklies, offering combination rates to advertisers to provide maximum coverage in a given area. Lerner Newspapers publishes more than 40 weeklies with a combined circulation of 350,000. Paddock Newspapers publishes 9 dailies and 6 weeklies which circulate in thirty suburban communities. Williams Press publishes 15 semiweeklies with a combined circulation of 95,000. The Barrington Press publishes 5 magazine-format weeklies with a total circulation of 69,000. The Illinois advertising rate book and newspaper directory is a maze of group newspaper cross-listings, combinations offering special rates, and a compendium of information demonstrating the variety of publication dates, deadlines, and page sizes of the 745 newspapers published in the state.

A distinctive new type of citizen-developed, issue-oriented urban press—some published weekly, some less frequently—has also developed in cities such as New York, Chicago, Boston, Minneapolis, Detroit, Washington, D.C., and St. Louis. While most of these papers are initiated and financed by local residents and citizens groups, a few are financed by government agencies. They are generally distributed free to neighborhood residents—door-to-door or through the mail— or they are distributed through local businesses or community centers. Most are nonprofit.

Another factor fostering diversity in the weekly press is the need for orientation of each weekly newspaper to its audience. The general assumption, of course, is that the weekly newspaper is carefully edited for a local audience—for a rural or city dweller—about issues relevant in a small town or suburban setting. But a weekly newspaper need not necessarily be community oriented. Dow Jones, publisher of the *Wall Street Journal,* launched a general weekly, the *National Observer,* in 1962 and the circulation reached a half-million before the paper was forced to close in 1977 because of a lack of advertising. Most weekly newspapers, however, do have a distinctive community orientation and are edited under a carefully considered set of assumptions regarding what local readers are interested in and want to be informed about. But a daily newspaper published in a small town or in a suburban area may also be community oriented. Many of the problems discussed below in regard to the community weekly would apply equally as well to many small town dailies. The primary difference in content between the two types is that a small city daily, while emphasizing local news and issues, would usually carry wire news of state, national, and international events. The community weekly almost never uses wire news, although an occasional semiweekly or triweekly looking toward daily publication might do so.

Editing a Community Weekly

The weekly newspaper has been called a social institution which provides the communications system needed to orient individuals toward group action and to provide social cohesion grounded in local community integration. This is the scholarly view of Morris Janowitz, a professor of sociology and author of *The Community Press,* who also notes that the content of community newspapers is generally low in controversy, affording a contrast to the "noise" of the daily press. The community press is viewed also as a means of extending prestige to hundreds of persons who are without influence or reputation beyond their own community and who, by their sheer numbers, are largely excluded from the columns of the daily press. But, Janowitz argues:

> The extensive reader interest in the community press is related to family attributes and community orientations, and trends in these factors are certain to influence the viability of the community. . . . Moreover, the impact of the community press is conditioned by the imagery of its audience which sees the contents in non-commercialized, non-partisan perspective. This imagery contributes to a willingness to accept the validity and trustworthiness of its message. Careful management by community newspaper publishers can help maintain this audience perspective.

A growing problem for the small-town or suburban newspaper editor in the 1980s may be to determine what the family attributes and community orientations of a given newspaper's readers actually are. Recent research has questioned the traditional journalistic stereotype of readers as a fairly homogeneous group with shared interests and common preoccupations which have somehow been molded by an intense sense of community identity. Daniel Riffe and Eugene F.

Shaw, two researchers from the University of Tennessee college of communications, discussing this stereotypical view of community newspaper readers, noted:

> Their [the readers] primary focus is stipulated to be in the immediate environment, and their great interest in civic and social events locally is nourished by their regular exposure to the "news minutiae" of their local newspaper, which they read carefully and thoroughly. The small-town newspaper, which assumes the public role of the community's voice, is the principal purveyor of this parochial information to its residents and leaves the presumably less salient non-local news and information to be supplied by national and metropolitan media to the deviant few with their eccentrically more cosmopolitan outlook.

Based upon their study of two community daily newspapers in Tennessee, Riffe and Shaw warn that if community newspapers are to continue to serve as the traditional "voice of the community," they must recognize that community newspapers readers are not the homogeneous group they are often assumed to be. Small towns, like suburban communities, vary in both size and character. Many communities are more cosmopolitan than others. Minority groups and social problems differ from town to town. The history and cultural heritages of communities differ. The residents of some communities are more mobile than others, resulting in less community integration and orientation. Other demographic factors, such as age, education, income, etc., may vary greatly among residents from one community to another as well as within a given community. Since every community is different in many respects, the newspaper serving that community should be different if it is to serve the needs and preferences of its readers.

Edward DeCourcy, editor and publisher of the *Newport* (N.H.) *Argus-Champion,* a weekly newspaper which has won more than one hundred fifty state, regional, and national awards for journalistic excellence, is one editor who recognizes the problems facing the community editor. In a lecture at Southern Illinois University in March 1979, DeCourcy noted that the changing lifestyle in which people move more frequently from one community to another requires that the community editor must work harder to create informed readers which, in turn, will help to foster the roots of democracy and make self-government work. But the decisions which the community editor must make are becoming tougher, DeCourcy argues, and community editors, as well as newspaper readers, need more information to make political decisions wisely. DeCourcy said:

> We need to know about the, communications explosion that is making it possible for a person to live in the New Hampshire mountains and manage a business in Mississippi.
>
> We need to know why the school board thinks it needs a new school, or why it does not if a vocal group of people think it does, and we need to know why they think it does.
>
> That is what our community newspapers should be reporting.
>
> We report the community's plans for building housing for the elderly, where the state intends to run a superhighway through our town, what the recreation department is doing to give our kids wholesome fun, what our churches are doing to provide spiritual nourishment, what the arts center and the library are doing to challenge us intellectually and culturally.
>
> We report the selectmen who overspent their budget, the landlord who gouged his tenants, the high school students who sold marijuana, the kids who stayed home from school because they had no shoes.
>
> We report the accidental spilling of thousands of gallons of concentrated sulphuric acid into our river, and the killing of fish and plant life, and the leaking of millions of gallons of drainage water into aging sewer lines.
>
> All this is essential information the people must have in order to govern themselves.
>
> We report who we are, because a community is more than a few hundred acres of real estate. A community is people who want to live together in peace and harmony and—if possible—prosperity.
>
> So we report who has been born, who has died, who is engaged and who has been married. We report who has graduated and who has been promoted and who has been honored.
>
> We report our efforts for community betterment—or mere social pleasure—as people join together in the Grange or the Odd Fellows or the Masons or the Knights of Pythias or the Elks or the Moose or the Eagles or the Owls or the Knights of Columbus or the Jaycees or the Rotary Club or the Lions Club or the Kiwanis Club.
>
> We report people's activities as they pursue their interests in the Garden Club or the Home Demonstration Club or the Organ Club or the Ladies' Aid or the CB Club or the Snowmobile Club.
>
> All this is part of the fabric of the community.

We even report Uncle Herman's trip to Burlington to visit his cousin.

Knowledge essential to self-government?

Hardly!

Uplifting for the community?

Absolutely.

Every person is important, and when our newspaper reports Uncle Herman's trip, he perceives the newspaper as representing the community and, if we think he is important enough to have his name in the paper, it lifts him up. He thinks he counts, and in a democracy he does.

We report the names of those who donate blood at the Bloodmobile. This is probably the most encouraging news in our paper, not because we have reached our quota. We seldom do. It's important because those names represent a cross section of the community. Whatever it is that moves men and women to give their blood to heal or save the life of somebody they will never know, it cuts across the whole community. There is no common bond of social standing, politics, religion, economic position, education, national origin or sex, and the only age limitation is the one set by the Red Cross.

This strengthens the fabric of the community, and the people are able to recognize it because they know who these people are, at least partly because of what they have read about each other in our newspaper.

We report the impact of nature, storms, disasters and bounty on the community and how our people deal with that.

We report the impact of state and national government and how our people deal with that.

The newspaper plays a vital role in the economy of our community. We report the events and the forces that affect it and how the people trade with each other. Our advertising columns are the fertilizer that nourishes the economy.

It is not enough, however, as we report the information the people need to govern themselves, that we cover merely events and trends.

If self-government is to succeed, we need to know what our neighbors are thinking. The newspaper is the medium through which the people expound their ideas and the debating platform on which they challenge the ideas of their neighbors. We report what they say in public meetings and we print their letters.

Newspaper work is fun. There is satisfaction in knowing we are an essential part of what makes self-government possible.

After eighteen years as the editor and publisher of the *Argus-Champion,* that's the formula which Edward DeCourcy has arrived at for meeting the needs of his readers. In Newport, New Hampshire, population 3,800, that editorial policy has worked exceedingly well in making the *Argus-Champion* the voice of the community. But, without modification, such a policy might not be right for a small town in the Midwest or for a suburban weekly in the Los Angeles–Orange County metropolitan area in California. The midwestern editor or the suburban editor in California should be the first to know whether or not DeCourcy's formula needs modification in his community. One of the distinctive characteristics of the community newspaper is its nearness to its readers, which can be both a strength and a problem. Before the community newspaper can help readers understand their environment, the editor himself must understand that environment. That is the real challenge of editing the community newspaper.

Common Editing Problems

What do editors regard as the biggest, most troublesome problem facing them in editing and publishing a weekly newspaper? This question, along with a series of related queries, was asked of a sample of weekly newspaper editors and publishers in Nebraska and Illinois in 1978. Fifty weekly newspapers were contacted in Nebraska with twenty-five replying. A purposive sample of seventy-five newspapers, divided between small towns and suburban publications, all with circulations of 3,000 or more, was surveyed in Illinois with thirty-six editors responding. The open-ended answers from editors to the above question identify a number of basic problems common to most community publishers.

One of the most frequently mentioned problems troubling editors was the lack of an adequate staff. Here are two representative responses:

> The principal problem is the lack of an adequate staff brought about by the size of the newspaper which limits the size of the payroll. Because most of the news staff has been trained on the job, competence varies drastically from person to person. Maturity compensates, thank God, for book learning to a degree, but the degree of excellence that we attempt to maintain requires constant vigilance.
> Marion E. Best, editor, *Moultrie County* (Ill.) *News*

The biggest problem is probably staff. It is difficult to find good trained employees who will stay at the job more than a year or two.
Bob Pinkerton, publisher, *Western Nebraska Observer.*

Another related problem identified by weekly editors was a lack of time—a lack of time to do as good a job as the editor would like to do and frustration over the demands on the editor's time by the public. Here are two representative replies:

Probably the biggest problem in publishing is the fact there are just not enough hours in the day. Today we are expected to be at each and every function: city council, school board, all athletic events, and on call 24 hours each day for pictures.
Loren C. Fry, editor, *Neligh* (Neb.) *News and Leader*

Time management is the biggest single problem for a weekly. On a daily, the week is broken into six or seven blocks, but not so on a weekly. The buildup to publication day is akin to a weekly roller-coaster with enormous peaks and valleys. If intermediate deadlines are not established and met, we cannot meet our production schedule.
Drew Davis, managing editor, *Barrington* (Ill.) *Courier-Review*

A third common problem, related to both a lack of time to perform editorial work adequately and the lack of sufficient staff, according to a few Nebraska and Illinois weekly editors, is an inadequate financial base—a lack of advertising revenue. While few answers were focused specifically on financial problems, here is one which did:

Money is probably the largest problem. When a small town starts getting smaller, as ours is, advertising revenue does too. The solution is to establish a larger market area, but to get other area businessmen to advertise you need to cover news in their area. That would mean more employees and more payroll.
Wendy Martin, editor, *Fulton* (Ill.) *Democrat*

These problems of lack of time, insufficient staff, and lack of revenue seem to cut across all segments of the weekly press, from the small-town weekly printed in a letterpress shop to the suburban weekly printed in a modern plant in combination with other community newspapers. As noted above, among the sample newspapers in Illinois, all had circulations in excess of 3,000. Hundreds of weeklies published in small towns in Illinois, as well as in other states, have fewer than 3,000 subscribers. Many have even smaller staffs and less advertising revenue to work with than do the sample editors heard from in the two-state survey.

One of the survey questions specifically asked about the size of the newspaper's staff and the duties of each employee. The responses indicated that some small-town weeklies are husband-wife or family operations. Or, if the head of the family is solely involved in the newspaper, his duties may include not only reporting and editing but advertising sales and business management as well. Wayne Lingg, editor of the *Harlan County* (Neb.) *Journal,* for example, publishes the 2,400 circulation weekly with the assistance of only one reporter; his wife, who sets type, lays out the pages, and keeps the books; his son, who does the job printing and sets type; and one part-time employee who assists in the typesetting.

Newspapers in the 3,000 circulation range may have a more varied staff, but the number assigned to the news operation may still be small. The *Mason County* (Ill.) *Democrat,* with a circulation of 3,800, has seventeen full-time employees. Yet only three persons— the publisher, who is a jack-of-all-trades, including the day-to-day manager of the newspaper; an editor, who has the responsibility for all editorial material; and a part-time reporter assigned to sports and school news—are involved in the news operation.

Larger community newspapers have larger news staffs, but the staff is usually viewed as being too small in relation to its responsibility. The triweekly *Salem* (Ill.) *Times-Commoner,* circulation 5,800, has an editorial staff of three full-time and four part-time persons, plus a number of country correspondents. The *Fox Lake* (Ill.) *Press,* circulation 4,784, one of eleven newspapers and three special military base papers published by the Lakeland Newspaper group, presents a different type of news operation. The newspapers, which have a combined circulation of 36,587, are edited from a central news desk which has the responsibility for all local news, including departments such as sports and women's news. The central desk is staffed by nine editorial personnel and a full-time photographer, plus various part-time correspondents.

It has been said that every weekly newspaper is a unique business operation. Some, for example, are printed in plants with complete production units—either letterpress or offset. Some weeklies with production plants publish other newspapers or do extensive commercial printing. But more and more of the smaller weeklies are being printed in central publishing plants, some long distances from the town where the newspaper is published. Some supply the central printing plant with camera-ready pages; a few use the facilities of central plants for all the typesetting and production operations. It is difficult, therefore, to compare staffs among newspapers, but it is clear from the responses above that most community newspaper editors think that their staff is too small in relation to the news and editorial responsibilities which they face.

The Editor as Generalist

Weekly newspaper editors in Illinois and Nebraska were also surveyed to learn what skills and qualities they look for in a new reporter-editor. Predictably, a majority of those responding emphasized that a mastery of the basic language skills was of utmost importance —spelling, punctuation, English usage, the basics of news style, and the ability to write clearly and concisely. But a majority of the editors also emphasized the need for generalists with knowledge about a wide range of topics—local government, economics, accounting, and press law—as well as a willingness to perform many noneditorial duties. Still others were concerned with such attributes as personality, attitude, flexibility, enthusiasm and various other personal traits.

When asked what skills he would look for when hiring a new reporter-editor, C. D. Beaver, editor, *Burt County* (Neb.) *Plaindealer,* said, "(1) The ability to spell, (2) the ability to spell, and (3) the ability to spell." Robert D. Hastings, editor, *Tuscola* (Ill.) *Review,* said he looked for "someone with the ability to write, use the camera, and talk intelligently about advertising." The need for all-round skills was also emphasized by David L. Volz, editor, *Highland* (Ill.) *News Leader:* "Good grammar and spelling are musts. Camera skills are also helpful, and a person must be prepared to take on duties such as page layout or ad selling. The ability to work closely with people in the community would also be important." And, though skills are essential, Marlin G. Waechter, editor, *Stanton* (Neb.) *Register,* cited the need for enthusiasm. "Without it," he said, "no employee—or employer—is any good to himself or his organization."

The representative responses make clear why the community press affords such a good training ground for those entering journalism. While the skills required in gathering and writing the news are often just as demanding on the weekly newspaper as they are on the daily, the weekly newsman's duties seldom are limited to just writing or editing. The weekly reporter-editor often has the opportunity to perform a multitude of challenging tasks—in page makeup, photography, production, and even advertising sales. If he desires, he may truly become a jack-of-all-trades. If one hopes to become a weekly newspaper publisher, one must become a generalist, learning all aspects of newspaper editing and publishing.

Future of the Weekly Newspaper

The future of the community newspaper is both clouded and bright. For many small-town publishers, shrinking population figures and dwindling advertising dollars only increase the problems which the country weekly already faces. Even in small towns where the population is holding its own and advertising revenue remains fairly constant, the weekly publisher may still face difficulties imposed by inflation and the growing cost of production. To support a weekly newspaper financially in today's economy, it requires a larger town and trading zone than it did even a decade ago.

Recent statistics indicate, however, that for some small towns, especially those within commuting distance of metropolitan centers, the future may look brighter. A University of Illinois geography professor, Curtis Roseman, for example, believes that fundamental changes are occurring in society which makes small towns and rural life more desirable than was true twenty or thirty years ago. Roseman pointed out in a 1979 interview that every town of ten to fifteen thousand today has franchised motels, supermarkets, fast food outlets and other modern conveniences which were nonexistent in most small towns a generation ago. Young people who used to leave for college and never return are now finding jobs after college in industry which is relocating more and more in small towns. With small-town life becoming more attractive, it is not unusual, Roseman said, to find towns located sixty to seventy miles from metropolitan areas to be growing for the first time in years. The fuel shortage, however, may temper this trend during the 1980s.

In the suburbs, the picture is more encouraging for the community publisher. As a supplier of local news which urban dailies and television usually cannot afford to gather and disseminate, a suburban newspaper fills an immediate informational need, especially in localities where residents have a strong sense of community identification and orientation. Not only have the suburbs continued to grow during the past decade, the trend toward decentralization of downtown business has tended to strengthen the economic base supporting the suburban press. Competition for the advertising dollar in the suburbs may be keen, but for the suburban publisher-businessman-entrepreneur, the challenge and the opportunity are there.

The future of the community press, however, is not just a matter of finding the financial support to remain in business. The newspaper will ultimately fail or succeed as a communications medium on the basis of its editorial content. A shopper can garner advertising from hundreds of businesses and remain only a throw-away shopper. A community newspaper must first succeed as a business and have the financial backing required to meet the day-to-day bills. Nevertheless, if profits are maximized to the extent that the news staff must continue to operate as a skeletal force, the primary news and leadership function of the community press will continue to be thwarted, and the newspaper will ultimately fail.

On the other hand, a community newspaper which is news oriented, which is carefully edited to meet the unique needs and interests of residents of the community it serves, which isn't fearful of commenting upon important issues, and which strives to provide the editorial leadership needed to orient readers toward desirable community action will not only continue to be a sound business venture, it will serve the community in a way no other business has the opportunity to do. The content of such a newspaper may be as unique as the community it serves; it certainly should not attempt to imitate or emulate area or regional dailies. The urban newspaper cannot compete with what the community weekly does best—gathering and disseminating local news, and providing the editorial leadership needed both to foster social cohesion within the community and to provide the impetus toward community action in areas where social change is needed.

The American Newspaper Publishers Association has supported a number of research studies regarding newspaper readership and newspaper use. More and more, the studies have found that media use is related to a set of psychological needs that newspaper reading satisfies. In a study reported in March 1979, conducted by Robert L. Stevenson, an assistant professor of journalism at the University of North Carolina, surveying how community ties lead to various psychological needs which are motivations for newspaper reading, three distinct audience segments were identified:

    1. The traditional newspaper audience, with strong, permanent

bonds to the community, whose need for information, guidance
and community surveillance leads to reading hard news, editorials
and background features.

2. More mobile readers, less tied to the community, who use the
newspaper for entertainment and as a guide to leisure opportunities.

3. Peripheral readers, with few contacts to the community, who
use the newspaper to maintain vicarious links with the community
and to fill time which is not taken up by demands of family, job
and community activities.

If a community editor is lucky, the majority of his readers will fall
under the first grouping. But the needs of readers in the other two
areas must also be satisfied if he is to reach a maximum number of
residents in the community.

The format and design of a community newspaper likewise should
reflect the community the newspaper serves. The bold, innovative,
and sometimes personal approach taken by the *Village Voice,* a singu-
larly successful New York City weekly, might not be an appropriate
format and approach for every community newspaper. But a community tabloid needs to have a distinctive look and character of its
own. It can be bold and striking, as is the *Village Voice,* without taking on the sensational characteristics of a *National Enquirer.* Nor
would the weekly *Chronicle of Higher Education,* with its conservative headlines and traditional, though prestigious, format necessarily
be a good model for every community newspaper, even though it
apparently is appropriate for the scholarly readers which the *Chronicle* serves—the nation's college and university teachers. But the careful attention which the *Chronicle* gives to layout and design, and the
appearance of quality and orderliness which the newspaper conveys,
might well be imitated by community publishers in communities
where such qualities would be appreciated.

Above all, a community newspaper should strive to meet the
opinion function of the nation's press. John Cameron Sim, in *The
Grass Roots Press,* estimates that more than half of the community
newspapers contain little or no editorial commentary and few letters-
to-the-editor columns. A small-town newspaper may not be able to
afford a full-fledged editorial page each week free of all advertisements; but every community editor can find the time to write a
personal column where he can comment on the news, illuminating

those issues which need explanation, analyzing problems and examining questions facing local residents, and providing guidance in the formulation of public policy affecting the community.

If an editor fails to provide such editorial leadership, he is missing an opportunity which no other person in the community is in a position to exercise. Such an opinion column does not have to be critical, nor does the opinion expressed need to be shrill or antagonistic, but it does need to be forthright and honest. Such an editorial voice will enhance the public's view of the newspaper. It may also jar readers out of their reveries from time to time and remind them that they cannot take local government and services—or the newspaper—for granted.

Chapter 16

News Editing: Ever Expanding Horizons

THE IMAGE IS more romantic legend than contemporary fact:

The editor—Hard smoker, rough talker, excessive drinker. Wears baggy pants, a coffee-stained, wrinkled shirt, and green eyeshade.

His power—Gets results when he screams, "Stop the presses!" or "Copy boy!"

His equipment—Beat-up manual typewriter, soft-lead pencil, scissors, and paste pot.

His domain—Ink-spotted wooden or tile floors, clanking Linotype machines, pervasive odor of printer's ink.

Widespread adoption of offset printing and electronic copy-processing has altered these late-night television movie stereotypes at most American newspapers. The image of newspapers and their editors is being revised, just as the perceptions held by editors about themselves, their products, and their readers are continually being re-evaluated. Indeed, editors realize that their philosophies and methods change with such speed that a discussion of the present or conjecture about the future are soon outdated. Nevertheless, it is safe to say that newspaper editors are now more conscious of the role of their readers. At a 1978 American Newspaper Publishers Association conference for young newspaper men and women, considerable discussion focused on the important role of the reader and the growing realization that the paper belongs to him. In an outline for the discussion, Tom Schumaker, managing editor of the *Grand Forks* (N.D.) *Herald,* and Rich Oppel, executive editor and vice president of the *Tallahassee* (Fla.) *Democrat,* wrote that, "We're getting closer to the reader. Listening to him. Encouraging him to talk and write. Telling the news in terms of people he knows or has heard about. Devising special participation features for him. We're asking ourselves how well our content relates to individuals: Big names, making news; little people whose experiences bring events to life."

Responsibility, credibility, and innovation are prime ingredients in the success of a newspaper. Thus, Schumaker and Oppel reasoned that it will be essential to "publish a lively, easy-to-read, vital newspaper, without stinting the prime duty of informing, where proper, instructing; and, as part of our journalistic heritage, entertaining." In addition, newspaper editors must strive for an effective content blend, realizing that the total package includes not only news but opinion and analysis, service information, entertainment, comics and features, illustration and advertising. "Useful tidbits," like meeting times and public notices, Schumaker and Oppel said, must be presented in such a way that enough room is left to present the major news of the day. Other probable developments include:

1. The trend will continue toward more thorough, in-depth coverage, an outgrowth of tailoring the news to avoid duplication of other media.

2. Editors will strive to make aesthetically pleasing pages—more emphasis will be placed on graphics, design and artwork.

3. Newspapers will come to life by active media promotion of editors and reporters who, before personality-oriented television journalism, remained virtually unnoticed, performing their daily duties in anonymity.

4. National and international news, growing in volume, will be condensed, packaged and presented to readers in terms they can readily comprehend.

5. People profiles and feature stories will likely be published with more regularity.

6. Consumer-oriented features, "how-to" articles, and entertainment news will continue to grow.

7. Technological advancements will help make possible superior editorial products.

Schumaker and Oppel summarized the qualities necessary to make the newspaper of today and tomorrow effective. It must be diverse in subject matter, stimulating in impact, satisfying in reading material, people-oriented, and one that serves its home community best while trying to relate the world and the nation to main street.

Newspapering in this electronic age is exciting. But, before an individual can play a role in shaping the newspapers of the future, he must have a job. A report issued by Worldwatch Institute, a Washington, D.C., think tank, concluded that the most difficult technological problem of this century may be how to create one billion new jobs worldwide by the year 2000 to deal with unemployment caused by the population growth expected in the Third World. Though this report centered upon worldwide employment, the nation's journalism school graduates must ponder their situations.

Newspaper Employment Opportunities

Gloomy reports have been issued about the difficulty in finding jobs for the country's aspiring journalists. Journalism school enrollments are at record levels, but the number of daily newspapers is declining. A jointly sponsored survey completed in 1979 by the Association for Education in Journalism and the American Newspaper Publishers Association Foundation (AEJ-ANPA) Cooperative Committee on Journalism Education found, however, that there was no shortage of newspaper jobs for journalism school graduates.

The S. I. Newhouse School of Public Communications at Syracuse University surveyed forty-six of the nation's accredited journalism schools. All reported placement of graduates in newspaper jobs was "good to excellent." At least 25 percent reported more jobs available than there were students to fill them.

Record numbers of the nation's 1978 journalism school graduates, according to The Newspaper Fund, Princeton, New Jersey, were hired by daily newspapers. The majority of those hired prepared specifically for news work as news-editorial college journalism majors. The Fund's study showed that 71 percent of the daily newspaper jobs were offered to news-editorial majors. The remaining jobs were taken by those with majors in other speciality areas such as broadcasting, public relations, and advertising. Two-thirds of the news-editorial majors were offered media-related jobs, including daily newspaper positions, less than one month after graduation or before they graduated, according to the Newspaper Fund. The survey also showed that jobs were most abundant in the Midwest and South. Jobs on the nation's more than eight thousand nondaily newspapers are also available to graduates who would like to report for or edit weekly, semiweekly or triweekly publications.

The survey cited above should not, of course, be interpreted to mean that all journalism school graduates can select any newspaper they would like to work for and then instantly be hired. The survey does, however, illustrate that if a journalism school graduate really wants to find a job on a daily or weekly newspaper, chances are good that he will be able to.

Once graduates obtain reporting or editing jobs on newspapers, they quickly learn that more responsibility is being demanded of journalists than ever before. These mandates for increased professionalism and responsibility come from both internal and external sources.

The Press, Society and the Courts

The Commission on Freedom of the Press concluded shortly after World War II that since the media enjoys a privileged position under the First Amendment, it should be more responsible to the American people. From this report there emerged a new interest in press responsibility. Among other things, the commission said that the media should insure that divergent views—not just those philosophically compatible with management or ownership—should be aired. The commission's views form the basis for much of the inner-ranks policing of newspapers today. Development of codes of ethics, appointment of ombudsmen to act upon complaints directed at newspapers, formulation of press councils to involve the community in press evaluations, and an increasing emphasis on articles dealing with government malfeasance and social injustices are but a few of the ways America's editors are attempting to meet their responsibility to society.

Despite these inner-industry efforts, the press remains under criticism from private and public sectors. Vice President Spiro T. Agnew, in November of 1969, criticized the Eastern establishment press and complained that there was too much media power in the hands of a few. Agnew's speech marked the start of an era in which the press would find itself under increasingly intense external scrutiny. Others quickly jumped on the bandwagon. Cries erupted from many quarters that the press should become increasingly responsible and that it could not operate in a vacuum—reacting only to its internal needs and philosophies. Though the courts in the 1960s and early 1970s extended greater protection to the press than ever before, a contraction of these liberal court interpretations began in the middle and latter years of the decade of the 1970s. These decisions have spurred many journalists to conclude that, because of fear of huge damage payments as a result of litigation, publishers and editors could shy away from the aggressive reporting that was on the upsurge in the 1960s and 1970s.

David Shaw, a reporter for the *Los Angeles Times,* wrote that "many editors and publishers—especially those in smaller towns—will become overly cautious practitioners of what *Miami Herald* attorney Dan Paul terms 'economic censorship'—an unwillingness to publish important but controversial stories that could result in long, costly lawsuits." The fear is well founded. Newspapers like the *New York Times* and *Washington Post* have the financial resources and the knowledgeable legal staffs to see litigation through, in most cases, to a successful conclusion. But smaller dailies and weeklies cannot afford costly law suits. To them, it could mean the difference between profit and loss, or even the ability to continue publishing.

One of the 1978 suits involved Myron A. Farber, a reporter for the *New York Times.* It spread apprehension throughout the nation's press. In 1976, Farber had written two three thousand-word articles about the deaths of thirteen patients in a suburban New Jersey hospital. The deaths had occurred in 1965 and 1966. The state reopened an investigation. During a trial, Farber was subpoenaed and asked to turn over his notes. The reporter refused. He and the *Times* were held in contempt. The newspaper paid more than $250,000 in fines. Troubling to the press was the fact that the defense asked for *all* notes, pictures, memos, and the like—some five thousand items in all —which Farber had gathered while researching his articles. The subpoena—which the press viewed as a poorly disguised fishing expedition—was indeed broad. But the trial judge contended that Farber should comply. The natural fear among journalists is that news sources will begin to dry up as courts repeatedly fail to recognize the confidentiality of the reporter-source relationship. This, of course, could have far-reaching effects on the aggressive press that blossomed in recent decades.

In a suit which reached the U.S. Supreme Court in 1978, the justices held that neither the First nor the Fourteenth Amendments were violated by the issuance of a warrant to search for criminal evidence believed to be in the offices of the *Stanford* (University) *Daily,* even though no individual at the paper was suspected of involvement in a crime. The student paper brought an action against law enforcement and district attorney personnel, claiming that the search for photographs of an altercation between police and demonstrators at the Stanford University Hospital, although conducted persuant to the warrant, violated the newspaper staff's constitutional rights. Writing for the majority, Justice Byron White said the court declined to reinterpret the First Amendment "to impose a general constitutional barrier against warrants to search newspaper premises, to require resort to subpoenas as a general rule, or to demand prior notice and hearing in connection with the issuance of search warrants."

Justice Potter Stewart assumed a position in dissent which more clearly reflected the thinking of many journalists. Stewart said it was "self-evident that police searches of newspaper offices burden the freedom of the press . . . [and would] inevitably interrupt its normal operations, and thus impair or even temporarily prevent the processes of newsgathering, writing, editing, and publishing." Stewart also pointed to the "possibility of disclosure of information received from confidential sources." He said the protection of these sources was "necessary to ensure that the press can fulfill its constitutionally designated function of informing the public, because important information can often be obtained only by an assurance that the source will not be revealed."

Jerry W. Friedheim, executive vice president and general manager of the American Newspaper Publishers Association, said court decisions in *Farber* and in *Stanford Daily* were indications that the nation's judges appeared to be moving in the direction of an "imperial judiciary." However, Congress approved legislation to take the impact from *Stanford Daily.* To be sure, newspaper editors in the 1970s found themselves and their publications the subjects of intense scrutiny from a reading public who demanded fairness and accountability and a court system which put a halt to the liberal legal pendulum swings initiated by the Warren Court of previous decades.

In yet another case in 1979, the U.S. Supreme Court refused to review a ruling by a lower court that held that news media are not entitled to prior notice, even when the subpoenaed records may identify confidential sources. The case evolved from a suit filed by the Reporters Committee for Freedom of the Press, Dow Jones & Co., Knight-Ridder Newspapers, and twelve individual journalists, including Jack Anderson. The plaintiffs challenged the practice of the American Telephone & Telegraph Co., which made available to government agencies the long-distance telephone filing records of its subscribers without notice to those whose records were to be released. A brief for the plaintiffs claimed that the Bell System made records available to government agencies on thirty-two thousand occasions from March of 1974 through June 1975.

Shaw, during interviews with scores of journalists, found that newsmen "regard the . . . decisions challenging the confidentiality of news sources as perhaps the single most ominous aspect" of the trend toward conservative First Amendment judgments. Though most journalists reacted with fear or indignation to the court decisions, William Rusher, publisher of the *National Review,* evaluated the situation differently. He told Shaw:

> The impression is widespread that we are witnessing a judicial attack upon essential privileges and immunities conferrred upon the press by the First Amendment. The truth is precisely the reverse: We are witnessing a brand-new bid by an aggressive and highly politicized press for privileges and immunities which it has never previously had, which it neither needs or deserves and which it would be dangerous to confer upon it.

The New Technology

Though editors must be concerned with their responsibilities to society and with the impact of court decisions, they must also be increasingly cognizant of the rapid technological improvements which affect their jobs. Advancement by the wire services is a case in point. Delivery of news in the twentieth century has taken quantum leaps forward from the day when telegraphers forwarded a limited news report from wire service offices to their counterparts in newspaper offices across the land. At the receiving newspapers, other telegraphers interpreted the morse code signal and typed the stories. Then came radio, Teletype, television, and, finally, electronic news editing. What does the future hold in, say, the next decade?

Already, the clack, clack of wire service printers has disappeared from the majority of newspaper offices nationwide. Instead, the reports from the Associated Press, United Press International and many supplementary news services are delivered directly to a newspaper computer. Only tiny flickering red and yellow lights indicate the movement of copy—and they are in the computer room, not in the newsroom. In a growing number of cases, these wire service reports are being delivered at a speed of twelve hundred words per minute—a long leap from the old sixty-six words per minute Teletype printers. But, in many smaller newspapers, delivery continues to be made at sixty-six words per minute, even though the copy is flowing from computer to computer, rather than to clacking printers.

It seems likely that sometime in the 1980s, all newspaper copy will be delivered at high speed, twelve hundred words per minute as the minimum. Already, there is consideration of doubling that rate and there are stock tables being moved on AP circuits at twelve thousand words per minute—ten times the current high-speed news-story delivery rate. What's more, the flow of wire service copy, long physically accomplished via telephone lines, is likely to be done by way of outer space. Instead of having a massive nationwide network of telephone lines leased by the wire services, the AP and UPI reports will be beamed to one or more satellites and the signals bounced back down to receiving dishes installed at every newspaper and broadcast station. In some communities, the various media may jointly own a single receiving antenna, with phone lines linking the receiver to the individual media operations.

It's widely anticipated that satellite delivery will reduce or at least help hold the line on increasing delivery costs for wire service reports. In broadcast stations, where there has been only a limited movement toward computers in the news rooms, the clacking printers will be replaced, at the least, by modern, nearly silent units which produce a low buzz rather than the loud clacking sounds. In addition, these printers are more than likely going to operate at a speed of a hundred or more words per minute, rather than the current day sixty-six words per minute.

The computer era brings with it another major change in the relationship of newspapers and their wire service reports. The Associated Press already has installed "electronic carbon" systems in some major metropolitan newspapers and on a statewide basis in Nebraska. The electronic carbon system permits AP member newspapers to send locally-originating news copy directly from the newspaper computer to the nearest AP regional computer. In turn, AP bureau personnel then call the stories to their VDT screens and process the stories, sending back rewritten and edited material on the general news circuits for all members to see.

The advantages are many, but most important is that the electronic carbon system permits newspapers much more easily to share current cycle news with fellow newspapers. Without electronic carbons, news printed in afternoon newspapers does not normally reach the state AP bureau until late in that day's PM cycle and thus doesn't reach other evening newspapers in time for that day's publication deadline.

With electronic carbons, which eliminate the need for time-consuming dictation from a newspaper office to an AP bureau, a newspaper can in a matter of seconds transmit its copy to the wire service at the same time it sends the story to its own composing room. This speeds the delivery to fellow newspapers by hours, allowing all members in a given region to share in today's news today. The electronic carbon system is likely to expand nationwide.

In the 1940s, the wire services began providing justified tape to newspaper members and clients. This meant that copy had to be set only once in proper column-width measure for all newspapers to use, thus eliminating the justification step at each individual newspaper. But, as newspapers took on a more modern appearance, the standard 11-pica column began to disappear, and the justification codes placed on news copy being transmitted from the wire services became a burden rather than a help at many newspapers. Incoming wire service copy had to have the justification coding stripped from the copy and then the newspaper computers had to rejustify the copy in the proper measure.

Already, the wire services are delivering nonjustified copy to those newspapers wanting it, thus eliminating the justification stripping step at individual newspapers. It's likely that justified tape will go the way of the morse code delivery of wire service copy.

The technology of the 1970s also permitted good advancement in the quality of photographs delivered by wire to newspapers and television stations. But, photos from foreign lands still often lost much of their resolution and quality when transmitted by radio or telephone to the United States for relay to individual newspapers. The development of the "electronic darkroom" has helped to overcome some of this problem. The AP began testing the electronic darkroom in the late 1970s. Essentially, incoming photo copy is broken into millions of bits of information and stored in a bank of computers. From there, AP photo technicians call the picture to VDT screens, where contrast, resolution, and detail can be electronically enhanced. Photos can be cropped, blown up, rearranged or altered in a variety of ways on the VDT screen, then caption information can be written beside or beneath the photo and the photo technician can transmit the picture to member newspapers with a command to the VDT.

It seems likely that electronic darkrooms will at some point become standard equipment at most newspapers, perhaps being used to receive wire service photo reports and probably to process photos taken by the newspapers' own staff photographers. The system will give editors in newspaper newsrooms the same flexibility to edit photos that they now enjoy with the electronic editing of news copy.

Portable news transmitting devices are already available, permitting wire service and newspaper personnel alike to file copy over ordinary telephone lines from remote locations directly into computers at wire service or newspaper offices. It is possible that similar lightweight devices will be brought into play for the transmission of photos or, perhaps, even of a photographer's negatives.

Obviously, there have been tremendous technological advances made by the wire services, but the electronic revolution extends to the nation's weekly and daily newspapers as well. Electronic copy-processing systems are common in many newspapers. As is the case with the wire services, breakthroughs are expected to continue. Joseph M. Ungaro, vice president and executive director of Westchester Rockland Newspapers Inc., White Plains, New York, said on the eve of the decade of the 1980s that the newspaper industry is "in a period of stability and maturity. Users are developing a more realistic appraisal of what a front-end system can and cannot do. If we have learned one lesson, it is that computers have limitations, and the smaller the computer the more limitations. On the vendors' side, the level of promises has dropped. That doesn't mean that every statement from a salesman is the Gospel truth, but at least they are no longer promising the moon."

With so many rapid technological strides made during the past decade, it is dangerous to predict the future. A study by Benjamin M. Compaine, chairman of the Department of Marketing and Management at the Community College of Philadelphia, showed that "the rate of introduction and widespread use of much of the new production technology has proceeded at a pace much faster than had been anticipated as recently as 1970." Compaine's study showed that technological developments had moved at a rate from five to fifteen years faster than had been anticipated. Thus, before the ink is dry on a page, the prediction could become a reality. Nevertheless, Ungaro sees two possible approaches to the electronic newspaper of the future.

One approach would be the implementation of a big computer that would serve all functions—creation of display and classified advertising; storage of ads; billing of ads; creation of news; editing and layout of pages with input of pictures; storage of stories for library purposes; creation of printing plate and control of the press; total list of subscribers and nonsubscribers on a data base; plus a host of business office functions. According to Ungaro, this approach was the goal of the Newspaper System Design Group—seven newspapers working with IBM. The project was given up as too complex and too costly. Still, it may become possible as computer science becomes more sophisticated.

The second approach is to divide the tasks and attack them in a series of subsystems, installing them one at a time, tailoring to each paper's need. This is the direction most papers are taking. The smaller the paper, the more functions the paper will combine. Ungaro breaks the functions down:

Display ads. Creating them, making proofs, storing the ads, billing the customers, scheduling the ads for the paper, and laying out the paper.

Classified ads. Creating the ads, making credit checks, billing, sorting and merging the ads, creating the section daily.

News. Creating stories, editing stories from reporters and wire services, writing headlines, laying out pages including pictures, outputting completed pages to the typesetter or platemaker.

Photo-Graphics. This subsystem would have a means to input negatives and/or half-tones (for both news and ads). It would then store them, until called up on a VDT screen for editing and cropping and output to the typesetter or platemaker.

Circulation. This would be a subsystem to include subscribers or nonsubscribers, demographic information, prepaid information if necessary, starts, stops, etc., and would each day prepare a manifest for the carrier and an order for the pressroom. It might even be linked to the press to automatically control the press order.

Business. This would be a subsystem to do all the traditional business office jobs.

All these systems would be linked together to create an all-electronic newspaper. Ungaro envisions it as looking something like this:

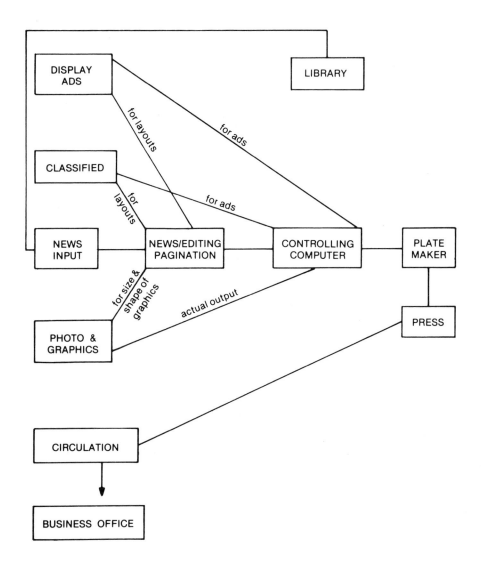

Fig. 16–1. As newspaper technology advances, the all-electronic newspaper will likely combine these systems.

310

Where does the new technology fit into the educational picture? An Associated Press Managing Editors survey drew responses from twenty-six educators and thirty-three newsmen. Abe Rosenthal, executive editor of the *New York Times,* said it was "absolutely essential for journalism students to master the new technology while they are in school." Albert Fitzpatrick, executive editor of the *Akron Beacon Journal,* said that students should "get as much exposure as possible to the new technology. While they will run into different systems when they finally land a job, a basic understanding of the new technology is helpful."

The managing editor of the *Des Moines Register and Tribune,* Drake Mabry, said students should become familiar with VDTs "so they are not afraid of them." Donald Duncan, managing editor of the Tacoma (Wash.) *News Tribune* and *Tribune & Ledger,* said journalism schools should emphasize a "very broad general education, and a thorough grounding in the fundamentals of the craft. I don't expect them (students) to be VDT experts. We can teach that in a few days. In fact, we'd probably have to unteach what they've already learned."

The nation's college and universities are taking various approaches to the introduction of electronic editing into their curriculums. George W. Ridge Jr. of the University of Arizona said that students can learn "the mechanics of operating a VDT in a few minutes, but it takes a long time to become fast and efficient. We think that having electronics is a plus as long as it doesn't take away from teaching the basics of good reporting and editing." John B. Adams of the University of North Carolina said his school has "enough equipment now to provide the essential ingredient—a hands-on experience to overcome initial trauma at the thought of using new technology."

This initial familiarization with electronic equipment is important. Gerald M. Sass Jr., who as a graduate student worked with reporting classes at the University of Kansas, said: "Reporters and copy editors often don't trust their new sophisticated equipment. I've seen copy editors who probably wouldn't be afraid to correct copy written by God become totally overawed by an editing terminal." In the end, then, it still takes confident, skilled journalists to operate the machines. Dolph C. Simons Jr., president and publisher of the *Lawrence* (Kan.) *World,* said that "equipment is of the utmost importance to the future of newspapers. Press design and full-functioning electronic display terminals are important. Just as crucial, however, are news people who are knowledgeable and *properly motivated.*" Simons said no matter how many technological advances are made, "if we don't have skilled people, I think we're dead."

Indeed, while continuing advancements in computer technology will permit ever quicker and more efficient production of photos and news, some elements will remain stable: good reporters, able to dig out the stories and write them in clear, crisp, concise fashion, will still be the heart of any newsgathering system. Good editors, able to improve, correct and enhance the stories and photos, will never be replaced by computers which, after all, can do only what they are instructed to do.

Bibliography

Chapter 1. NEWS EDITING IN CONTEMPORARY AMERICA

BOOKS

DeFleur, Melvin L., and Ball-Rokeach, Sandra. *Theories of Mass Communication*, 3d ed. New York: David McKay, 1975.

Dennis, Everett E. *The Media Society: Evidence About Mass Communication in America*. Dubuque, Iowa: William C. Brown, 1978.

Halloran, James D. *The Effects of Mass Communication*. Leicester, England: Leicester University Press, 1965.

Hovland, Carl I., Janis, I.L., and Kelley, H.H. *Communication and Persuasion*. New Haven, Conn.: Yale University Press, 1953.

Hulteng, John L. *The Messenger's Motives*. Englewood Cliffs, N.J.: Prentice-Hall, Inc., 1976.

Kraus, Sidney, and Davis, Dennis. *The Effects of Mass Communication on Political Behavior*. University Park, Pa.: Pennsylvania State University Press, 1976.

Merrill, John C. *The Imperative of Freedom: A Philosophy of Journalistic Autonomy*. New York: Hastings House, 1974.

Nimmo, Dan. *Political Communication and Public Opinion in America*. Santa Monica, Cal.: Goodyear Publishing, 1978.

Peterson, Theodore, Schramm, Wilbur, and Siebert, Fred S. *Four Theories of the Press*. Urbana: University of Illinois Press, 1956.

Rubin, Bernard, ed. *Questioning Media Ethics*. New York: Praeger, 1978.

Stonecipher, Harry W. *Editorial and Persuasive Writing: Opinion Functions of the News Media.* New York: Hastings House, 1979.

Shaw, Donald L., and McCombs, Maxwell E. *The Emergence of American Political Issues: The Agenda-Setting Function of the Press.* St. Paul, Minn.: West Publishing, 1977.

Swain, Bruce M. *Reporters' Ethics.* Ames: Iowa State University Press, 1978.

ARTICLES

Anderson, Douglas. "Editors Applaud Electronic Editing." *Associated Press Managing Editors News* (March 1979):11.

Comment. "New Challenges to Newspaper Freedom of the Press— The Struggle for Right of Access and Attacks on Cross-Media Ownership." *DePaul Law Review* 24 (Fall 1974): 165–84.

Healey, Gerald B. "Ethics Codes Working, Reporter Tells Colleges." *Editor & Publisher* 109 (Dec. 11, 1976):40.

Hill, I. William. "Code of Ethics Adopted by AP Managing Editors." *Editor & Publisher* 108 (April 19, 1975):11.

Meloon, Bob. "Our Accountability Extends to the Public." *Associated Press Managing Editors News* (August 1978):15.

Rupp, Carla Marie. "AP Sports Editors OK Standards of Ethics." *Editor & Publisher* 108 (June 7, 1975):11,38.

Smedley, Gene. "Ethics Moves into the Curriculum." *Associated Press Managing Editors News* (October 1977):13.

Chapter 2. THE COPY EDITOR
Chapter 3. EDITING COPY
Chapter 4. NEWS STYLE AND READABILITY

BOOKS

The Associated Press Stylebook and Libel Manual. New York: The Associated Press, 1977.

Barzun, Jacques. *Simple and Direct: A Rhetoric for Writers.* New York: Harper & Row, 1975.

Berner, R. Thomas. *Language Skills for Journalists.* Boston: Houghton Mifflin, 1979.

Bernstein, Theodore M. *The Careful Writer: A Modern Guide to English Usage.* New York: Atheneum, 1965.

———. *Dos, Don'ts and Maybes of English Usage.* New York: Times Books, 1978.

Callihan, E. L. *Grammar for Journalists.* Radnor, Pa.: Chilton, 1969.

Copperud, Roy H. *A Dictionary of Usage and Style.* New York: Hawthorn Books, 1964.

_____. *American Usage: The Consensus.* New York: Van Nostrand Reinhold, 1970.

_____. *Words on Paper: A Manual of Prose Style for Professional Writers, Reporters, Authors, Editors, Publishers, and Teachers.* New York: Hawthorn Books, 1960.

Evans, Bergen, and Evans, Cornelia. *A Dictionary of Contemporary American Usage.* New York: Random House, 1957.

Flesch, Rudolf. *The Art of Readable Writing,* 25th Anniversary Ed. New York: Harper & Row, 1974.

Follet, Wilson; Barzun, Jacques; et al. *Modern American Usage: A Guide.* New York: Grossett & Dunlap, 1966.

Fowler, H. W. *Modern English Usage,* 2d ed. New York: Oxford University Press, 1965.

Gunning, Robert. *The Technique of Clear Writing,* Rev. Ed. New York: McGraw-Hill, 1968.

Jordan, Lewis, ed. *The New York Times Manual of Style and Usage.* New York: Quadrangle/The New Times Book Co., 1976.

Klare, George R. *The Measurement of Readability.* Ames: Iowa State University Press, 1963.

Morris, William, ed. *The American Heritage Dictionary of the English Language.* Boston: Houghton Mifflin, 1969.

Nicholson, Margaret. *A Dictionary of American-English Usage.* New York: Oxford University Press, 1957.

Nickles, Harry G. *The Dictionary of Do's and Don'ts: A Guide for Writers and Speakers.* New York: McGraw-Hill, 1974.

Strunk, William, Jr., and White. E. B. *Elements of Style,* 3d ed. New York: Macmillan, 1979.

United Press International Stylebook. New York: United Press International, 1977.

Webb, Robert A., ed. *The Washington Post Deskbook on Style.* New York: McGraw-Hill Book Co., 1978.

Zinsser, William. *On Writing Well.* New York: Harper & Row, 1976.

Chapter 5. THE NEW TECHNOLOGY

ARTICLES

Anderson, Douglas. "Editors Applaud Electronic Editing." *Associated Press Managing Editors News* (March 1979):11.

Barnes, Andrew. "Technical Equipment for Use by Nontechnical

People." *American Newspaper Publishers Association Research Institute Bulletin* (Dec. 7, 1978):491–93.

Blasko, Lawrence G. "Fifteen Years of Technology." *The AP World* 34 (December 1977):3–16.

Eary, Ralph E. "How Computers Will Affect Mass Communications." *Editor & Publisher* 111 (Oct. 14, 1978):30–32.

Kurtz, Larry. "Study Examines Impact of Electronic Newsroom." *Editor & Publisher* 111 (Sept. 23, 1978):28,32.

Lupo, J. M. " 'Digitalizing' of Electronic Technology Has Had Impact." *Publishers' Auxiliary* 113 (Aug. 28, 1978):7.

Randall, Starr D. "Effect of Electronic Editing on Error Rate of Newspaper." *Journalism Quarterly* 56 (Spring 1979):161–65.

"Newsroom Joins Computer Age." *Omaha* (Neb.) *World-Herald* 113 (June 18, 1978):10-A.

"Readers to Benefit From Later News, Improved Editing." *Omaha* (Neb.) *World-Herald* 113 (June 18, 1978):10-A.

"Retrieval System Speeds Research." *Editor & Publisher* 109 (Nov. 13, 1976):50.

Shoquist, Joseph W. "Metro Paper Adapts Newsroom to VDTs." *Editor & Publisher* 109 (Aug. 28, 1976):36–37.

Taylor, Heber. "Texas Editors Like New Technology." *Editor & Publisher* 111 (Nov. 19, 1978):35.

Trawick, Jack. "SNPA Workshop Examines New Technology Impact." *Editor & Publisher* 109 (Nov. 13, 1976):52.

"Video Display System Installed in 4 Months." *Editor & Publisher* 109 (Oct. 9, 1976):34.

Chapter 6. NEWS JUDGMENTS

ARTICLES

Carter, Roy E. "Newspaper 'Gatekeepers' and the Sources of News." *Public Opinion Quarterly* 22 (Summer 1958):133–44.

Dimmick, John. "The Gatekeeper: An Uncertainty Theory." *Journalism Monographs* (November 1974):1–39.

Gieber, Walter. "How the 'Gatekeepers' View Local Civil Liberties News." *Journalism Quarterly* 37 (Spring 1960):199–205.

Lewin, Kurt. "Frontiers in Group Dynamics: II." *Human Relations* 1(1947):143–53.

Liebes, B. H. "Decision-Making by Telegraph Editors—AP or UPI?" *Journalism Quarterly* 43 (Autumn 1966):434–42.

Nicolai, Richard N., and Riley, Sam. G. "The Gatekeeping Function from the Point of View of the PR Man." *Journalism Quarterly* 49 (Summer 1972):371–73.

Snider, Paul B. "Mr. Gates Revisited: A 1966 Version of the 1949 Case Study." *Journalism Quarterly* 44 (Autumn 1967):419–27.

Temple, Wick. "The New Sports Writing is Seeing the World in a Microcosm." *The AP World* 33 (1976):2–9.

Uchitelle, Lou. "The New Business News." *The AP World* 35 (1978): 11–15.

White, David M. "The Gatekeeper: A Case Study in the Selection of News." *Journalism Quarterly* 27 (Fall 1950):383–90.

Chapter 7. HEADLINES

BOOKS

Arnold, Edmund C. *Ink on Paper*. New York: Harper & Row, 1972.

Evans, Harold. *News Headlines*. New York: Holt, Rinehart and Winston, 1974.

Garst, Robert E., and Bernstein, Theodore M. *Headlines and Deadlines,* 3d ed. New York: Columbia University Press, 1961.

ARTICLES

Everett, George. "Printing Technology as a Barrier to Multi-Column Headlines, 1850–95." *Journalism Quarterly* 53 (Autumn 1976): 528–32.

Haskins, Jack B., and Flynne, Lois P. "Effects of Headline Typeface Variation on Reading Interest." *Journalism Quarterly* 51 (Winter 1974):677–82.

Steigleman, Walter A. "Do Newspaper Headlines Really Promote Street Sales?" *Journalism Quarterly* 26 (Summer 1949):379–88.

Chapter 8. PHOTOS AND CUTLINES

CASES

Channel 10, Inc. v. *Gunnarson*, 337 F. Supp. 634 (Minn. 1972).
Galella v. *Onassis*, 487 F.2d 986 (2d Cir. 1973).

BOOKS

The Associated Press Stylebook and Libel Manual. New York: The Associated Press, 1977.

Edom, Clifton C. *Photojournalism.* Dubuque, Iowa: William C. Brown, 1976.

Fox, Rodney, and Kerns, Robert. *Creative News Photography.* Ames: Iowa State University Press, 1961.

Geraci, Philip C. *Photojournalism: Making Pictures for Publication,* 2d ed. Dubuque, Iowa: Kendall/Hunt, 1976.

Hicks, Wilson. *Words and Pictures.* New York: Harper and Brothers, 1952.

Ingle, Robert D., ed. *The Miami Herald Stylebook.* Miami: The Miami Herald, 1970.

Kalish, Robert D., and Edom, Clifton C. *Picture Editing.* New York: Rinehart, 1951.

MacLean, Malcolm S., Jr., and Kao, Anne Li-An. *Editorial Predictions of Magazine Picture Appeals.* Iowa City: School of Journalism, University of Iowa, 1965.

Webb, Robert A., ed. *The Washington Post Deskbook on Style.* New York: McGraw-Hill, 1978.

Rhode, Robert B., and McCall, Floyd H. *Press Photography.* New York: Macmillan, 1961.

Sidey, Hugh, and Fox, Rodney. *1000 Ideas for Better News Pictures.* Ames: Iowa State University Press, 1956.

BOOKLETS

The Associated Press. *Factbook of Wirephoto.*

The Associated Press. *Picture Talk.*

Jones, Jenk, Jr. *Laserphoto: How it Works.* A report of the Associated Press Managing Editors Photo and Graphics Committee, 1979.

ARTICLES

"AP's Digital Darkroom Breaks Ground." *Editor & Publisher* 110 (June 11, 1977):15.

Blake, Donald P. "The Editor vs. The Photographer." *Quill* 53 (December 1965):18–20.

Copperud, Roy H. "Words and Pictures—I." *Editor & Publisher* 97 (Dec. 19, 1964):26.

———. "Words and Pictures—II." *Editor & Publisher* 98 (Jan. 2, 1965):37.

"Electronic Darkroom Tests are Successful." *AP Log* (April 10, 1978):1.

Friedman, Rick. "Study Examines Role of Picture Editor." *Editor & Publisher* 102 (Feb. 15, 1969):32.

————. "Study Examines Role of Picture Editor." *Editor & Publisher* 102 (Feb. 22, 1969):42,44.

Kerrick, Jean S. "Influence of Captions on Picture Interpretation." *Journalism Quarterly* 36 (Spring 1959):183–88.

————. "News Pictures, Captions and the Point of Resolution." *Journalism Quarterly* 36 (Spring 1959):183–88.

MacLean, Malcolm S., Jr., and Hazard, William R. "Women's Interest in Pictures: The Badger Village Study." *Journalism Quarterly* 30 (Spring 1953):139–62.

MacLean, Malcolm S., Jr., and Kao, Anne Li-An. "Picture Selection: An Editorial Game." *Journalism Quarterly* 40 (Spring 1963): 230–32.

"Reporting With a Camera." *The AP World* 28 (Winter 1971):32–37.

Singletary, Michael W. "Newspaper Photographs: A Content Analysis." *Journalism Quarterly* 55 (Autumn 1978):585–89.

Stephenson, William. "Principles of Selection of News Pictures." *Journalism Quarterly* 37 (Winter 1960):61–68.

Trayes, J. Edward, and Cook, Bruce. "Picture Emphasis in Final Editions of 16 Dailies." *Journalism Quarterly* 54 (Autumn 1977): 595–98.

Warner, Bob. "Good Photographers Sour on Bad Editing." *Editor & Publisher* 94 (Aug. 12, 1961):42,44.

Witwer, Bruce. "Laserphoto Hailed Despite Problems." *Editor & Publisher* 111 (Nov. 12, 1978):54.

"Who's Editing the Pictures?" *Editor & Publisher* 94 (July 15, 1961):15,38,40,42.

UNPUBLISHED MATERIALS

Arnold, George. "A Theory of Picture Editing." Master's thesis, School of Journalism, University of Missouri, 1974.

Hall, Don Alan. "A Survey of Picture Editing Procedures and Their Effects Upon American Daily Newspapers." Master's thesis, Department of Journalism, Indiana University, 1968.

Kadrmas, Kathleen H. "Perceptions of News Photographs as Invasions of Privacy." Master's thesis, School of Journalism, University of Iowa, 1977.

Chapter 9. NEWSPAPER PAGE DESIGN

BOOKS

Arnold, Edmund C. *Ink on Paper*. New York: Harper & Row, 1972.
——. *Modern Newspaper Design*. New York: Harper & Row, 1969.
Babb, Laura Longley, ed. *The Editorial Page*. Boston: Houghton Mifflin, 1977.
Cincinnati Enquirer Design Stylebook. Cincinnati: Cincinnati Enquirer, 1977.
Evans, Harold. *Editing and Design*. New York: Holt, Rinehart & Winston, 1972.
Hutt, Allen. *Newspaper Design*, 2d ed. London: Oxford University Press, 1967.
——. *The Changing Newspaper: Typographical Trends in Britain and America, 1622–1972*. London: Gordon Fraser, 1973.
Turnbull, Arthur T. *Practical Exercises in Typography, Layout and Design*. New York: Holt, Rinehart & Winston, 1972.

ARTICLES

Arnold, Edmund C. "Aiming for Visual Excitement." *Masthead* 30 (Summer-Fall 1978):29–30.
Belden, Joe. "A New Front Page." *Editor & Publisher* 107 (Nov. 30, 1974):12,13.
Berner, R. Thomas. "The Golden Rectangle in Newspaper Page Design." *Editor & Publisher* 109 (Aug. 21, 1976):30,31.
Huenergard, Celeste. "Editorial Page Seen as 'Graphically Dull.'" *Editor & Publisher* 111 (Dec. 2, 1978):15,22.
Janecke, Ron. "Format Tips Suggested by Max McCrohon." *Editor & Publisher* 107 (May 25, 1974):10,44.
Moen, Daryl. "Four Elements in Good Newspaper Design." *Editor & Publisher* 111 (Sept. 23, 1978):15,50.
——. "How to Handle Multiple Picture Pages." *Editor & Publisher* 111 (Dec. 9, 1978):22,24.
——. "Proper Packaging is the Answer." *Editor & Publisher* 111 (Oct. 28, 1978):32.
——. "Using Artwork Effectively." *Editor & Publisher* 111 (Dec. 23, 1978):12.
"Mod Layout Encourages Readership." *Editor & Publisher* 111 (Dec. 9, 1978):24,42.

"New Haven *Journal-Courier* Uses 'Ragged Right' Format." 112 *Editor & Publisher* (April 21, 1979):72,78.

"No 'Yawn' Heads, Larger Pictures Attract Readers." *Editor & Publisher* 109 (Dec. 4, 1976):12.

Ramage, Dick. "Tips on Nifty Page Designs." *Editor & Publisher* 109 (Dec. 11, 1976):12,14.

Siskind, Theresa G. "The Effect of Newspaper Design on Reader Preferences." *Journalism Quarterly* 56 (Spring 1979):54–61.

Sissors, Jack Z. "Do Youthful, College-Educated Readers Prefer Contemporary Newspaper Designs?" *Journalism Quarterly* 51 (Summer 1974):307–13.

Chapter 10. THE WIRE SERVICES
Chapter 11. PROCESSING WIRE COPY

BOOKS

The Associated Press Stylebook and Libel Manual. New York: The Associated Press, 1977.

Cooper, Kent. *Barriers Down.* New York: Farrar & Rinehart, 1942.

———. *Kent Cooper and the Associated Press.* New York: Random House, 1959.

———. *The Right to Know.* New York: Farrar, Straus & Cudahy, 1956.

Desmond, Robert W. *The Information Process.* Iowa City: University of Iowa Press, 1978.

Emery, Edwin, and Emery, Michael. *The Press and America,* 4th ed. Englewood Cliffs, N.J.: Prentice-Hall, 1978.

Gramling, Oliver. *AP: The Story of News.* New York: Holt, Rinehart & Winston, 1940.

Morris, Joe. *Deadline Every Minute: The Story of the United Press.* New York: Doubleday, 1957.

Mott, Frank Luther. *American Journalism: A History: 1690–1960,* 3d ed. New York: Macmillan, 1962.

Rosewater, Victor. *History of Cooperative News-Gathering in the United States.* New York: Appleton-Crofts, 1930.

ARTICLES

Schwarzlose, Richard A. "Early Telegraphic News Dispatches: Forerunner of the AP." *Journalism Quarterly* 51 (Winter 1974): 595–601.

―――. "Harbor News Association: The Formal Origin of the AP." *Journalism Quarterly* 45 (Summer 1968):253–56.

UNPUBLISHED MATERIALS

Schwarzlose, Richard A. "The American Wire Services: A Study of Their Development as a Social Institution." Ph.D. dissertation, College of Communications, University of Illinois, 1965.

Chapter 12. THE EDITOR AND THE LAW

CASES

Associated Press v. *Walker*, 388 U.S. 130 (1967).

Barber v. *Time, Inc.*, 159 S.W.2d 291 (1942).

Branzburg v. *Hayes*, 408 U.S. 665 (1972).

Bridges v. *California and Times Mirror Co.* v. *Superior Court*, 314 U.S. 252 (1941).

Cantrell v. *Forest City Publishing Co.*, 419 U.S. 245 (1974).

Cox Broadcasting Co. v. *Cohn*, 420 U.S. 469 (1975).

Curtis Publishing Co. v. *Butts*, 388 U.S. 130 (1967).

Dietemann v. *Time, Inc.*, 449 F.2d 245 (9th Cir. 1971).

Estes v. *Texas*, 381 U.S. 532 (1965).

Gannett v. *DePasquale*, 443 U.S. 368 (1979).

Garrison v. *Louisiana*, 379 U.S. 64 (1964).

Gertz v. *Robert Welch, Inc.*, 418 U.S. 323 (1974).

Herbert v. *Lando*, 441 U.S. 153 (1979).

Irvin v. *Dowd*, 366 U.S. 717 (1961).

Liberty Lobby, Inc. v. *Pearson*, 390 F.2d 489 (1968).

Miami Herald Publishing Co. v. *Tornillo*, 418 U.S. 241 (1974).

Monitor Patriot Co., v. *Roy*, 401 U.S. 265 (1971).

Murphy v. *Florida*, 421 U.S. 794 (1975).

Namath v. *Sports Illustrated*, 39 N.Y.2d 897 (1976).

Nebraska Press Association v. *Stuart*, 423 U.S. 1327 (1976).

New York Times Co. v. *Sullivan*, 376 U.S. 254 (1964).

Pavesich v. *New England Mutual Life Insurance Co.*, 122 Ga. 190 (1905).

Pearson v. *Dodd*, 410 F.2d 701 (D.C. Cir. 1969), *cert. denied*, 395 U.S. 947.

Rideau v. *Louisiana*, 373 U.S. 723 (1963).

Rosenblatt v. *Baer*, 383 U.S. 75 (1966).

Rosenbloom v. *Metromedia, Inc.*, 403 U.S. 29 (1971).

Sheppard v. *Maxwell*, 384 U.S. 333 (1966).

The Washington Post Co. v. *Keogh*, 365 F.2d 965 (D.C. Cir. 1966), *cert. denied*, 385 U.S. 1011 (1967).

Time, Inc. v. *Firestone*, 421 U.S. 909 (1976).

Time, Inc. v. *Hill*, 385 U.S. 374 (1967).

Toledo Newspaper Co. v. *United States*, 247 U.S. 402 (1918).

United States v. *Dickinson*, 465 F.2d 496 (1972), *cert. denied*, 414 U.S. 665.

BOOKS

Anderson, Douglas. *A "Washington Merry-Go-Round" of Libel Actions.* Chicago: Nelson-Hall, 1980.

Black, H.C. *Black's Law Dictionary,* 4th ed. St. Paul: West Publishing Co., 1968.

Devol, Kenneth S., ed. *Mass Media and the Supreme Court,* 2d ed. New York: Hastings House, 1976.

Francois, William E. *Mass Media Law and Regulation,* 2d ed. Columbus, Ohio: Grid, 1978.

Franklin, Marc. *The First Amendment and the Fourth Estate.* Mineola, N.Y.: The Foundation Press, 1977.

Gillmor, Donald and Barron, Jerome. *Mass Communication Law: Cases and Comment,* 3d ed. St. Paul: West Publishing Co., 1979.

Lawhorne, Clifton. *Defamation and Public Officials: The Evolving Law of Libel.* Carbondale: Southern Illinois University Press, 1971.

Nelson, Harold L. and Teeter, Dwight L., Jr. *Law of Mass Communications,* 3d ed. Mineola, N.Y.: The Foundation Press, 1978.

Nimmer, Melville B. *Nimmer on Copyright.* New York: Matthew Bender and Co., 1963.

Pember, Don R. *Mass Media Law.* Dubuque, Iowa: Wm. C. Brown Company Publishers, 1977.

———. *Privacy and the Press.* Seattle: University of Washington Press, 1972.

Phelps, Robert H. and Hamilton, E. Douglas. *Libel: Rights, Risks, Responsibilities.* New York: Macmillan Press, 1966.

Prosser, William. L. *Handbook of the Law of Torts,* 4th ed. St. Paul: West Publishing Co., 1971.

Siebert, Fred S., Peterson, Theodore B., and Schramm, Wilbur. *Four Theories of the Press.* Urbana: University of Illinois Press, 1956.

Zuckman, Harvey, L. and Gaynes, Martin J. *Mass Communications Law.* St. Paul: West Publishing Co., 1977.

ARTICLES

Comments. "The Law of Libel—Constitutional Privilege and the Private Individual: Round Two." *San Diego Law Review* 12 (March 1975):455–74.

Jenkins, John A. "Ask and You Shall Receive." *Quill* 63 (July-August 1975):22.

Pember, Don R. and Teeter, Dwight L. "Privacy and the Press Since *Time, Inc.* v. *Hill.*" *Washington Law Review* 50 (1974):57–91.

Warren, Samuel and Brandeis, Louis D. "The Right of Privacy." *Harvard Law Review* 4 (1890):193–220.

Stonecipher, Harry W. and Trager, Robert. "The Impact of *Gertz* on the Law of Libel." *Journalism Quarterly* 53 (Winter 1976): 609–18.

Trager, Robert and Stonecipher, Harry W. "Gag Orders: An Unresolved Dilemma." *Journalism Quarterly* 55 (Summer 1978):231–40, 268.

Chapter 13. THE NEWSPAPER HIERARCHY

BOOKS

Barron, Jerome A. *Freedom of the Press for Whom?* Bloomington: Indiana University Press, 1973.

Gerald, J. Edward. *The Social Responsibility of the Press,* Minneapolis: The University of Minnesota Press, 1963.

Rucker, Frank W., and Williams, Herbert Lee. *Newspaper Organization and Management,* 5th ed. Ames: Iowa State University Press, 1979.

Siebert, Fred S., Peterson, Theodore, and Schramm, Wilbur. *Four Theories of the Press.* Urbana: University of Illinois Press, 1956.

Stonecipher, Harry W. *Editorial and Persuasive Writing: Opinion Functions of the News Media.* New York: Hastings House, 1979.

Talese, Gay. *The Kingdom and the Power.* New York: World Publishing, 1969.

ARTICLES

Anderson, Douglas. "Managing Editors Perceive Little Pressure."

Nebraska Newspaper (March 1976):4,27,28.

Anderson, Douglas, and Murdock, Marianne. "External and Publisher Influences on News-Editorial Decisions." *Graduate Communication Studies* 1 (Spring 1977):12–16.

Bagdikian, Ben H. "Right of Access: A Modest Proposal." *Columbia Journalism Review* 8 (Spring 1970):10–18.

Bowers, David R. "A Report on Activity by Publishers in Directing Newsroom Decisions." *Journalism Quarterly* 44 (Winter 1967): 43–52.

Breed, Warren. "Social Control in the News Room." *Social Forces* 33 (May 1955):326–35.

Daniel, Clifton. "Right of Access to Mass Media—Government Obligation to Enforce First Amendment." *Texas Law Review* 48 (March 1970):783–90.

Donohew, Lewis. "Publishers and Their 'Influence' Groups." *Journalism Quarterly* 42 (Winter 1965):112–13.

"Eight Million Write Letters to the Editor." *Editor & Publisher* 107 (Jan. 26, 1974):30.

Gentry, James K. "How Can the Managing Editor Manage?" *Associated Press Managing Editors News* (September 1978):6–7.

Gissler, Sig. "A Better Forum for the Readers." *Masthead* 23 (Spring 1971):32–33.

Isaacs, Norman E. "Why We Lack a National Press Council." *Columbia Journalism Review* 8 (Fall 1970):16–26.

Stencel, Sandra. "Access to the Media." *Editorial Research Reports* (June 21, 1974):449–67.

Chapter 14. Editing A Campus Newspaper

BOOKS

Captive Voices: The Report of the Commission of Inquiry Into High School Journalism. New York: Schocken Books, 1974.

Clay, Roberta. *The College Newspaper*. New York: Pageant Press, 1965.

Dusha, Julius, and Fischer, Thomas. *The Campus Press: Freedom and Responsibility*. Washington, D.C.: American Association of State Colleges and Universities, 1973.

Estrin, Herman A., and Sanderson, Arthur M. *Freedom and Censorship of the College Press*. Dubuque, Iowa: William C. Brown, 1966.

Politella, Dario, ed. *Directory of the College Press in America, 1977–78.* New York: Oxbridge Communications, Inc., 1977.

Stevens, George E., and Webster, John B. *Law and the Student Press.* Ames: Iowa State University Press, 1973.

Trager, Robert. *Student Press Rights.* Urbana, Ill.: ERIC Clearinghouse on Reading and Communication Skills and Journalism Education Association, 1974.

Trager, Robert, and Dickerson, Donna L. *College Student Press Law,* 2d ed. Urbana, Ill.: ERIC Clearinghouse on Reading and Communication Skills and National Institute of Education, 1979.

ARTICLES

Applegate, Phyllis. "Providing Editorial Experience." *College Press Review* 17 (Spring 1977):14–15.

Brasler, Wayne. "1977 Pacemakers: The New Simplicity." *Scholastic Editor* 57 (March 1978):8–15.

Deaver, Frank. "Independence for College Newspapers?" *College Press Review* 16 (Spring 1977):18–21.

Good, Sherrie. "Editorials Studied in Selected Indiana College Newspapers." *College Press Review* 16 (Winter 1976–77):18–19.

Hartman, Mary. "Official Guidelines and Editorial Policies: Remedying the Confusion." *Scholastic Editor* 57 (April–May 1978):4–8.

Hunt, Todd. "Learning to Edit . . ." *College Press Review* 14 (Fall 1974):27–29.

Mencher, Melvin. "Casting Out Stereotypes." *College Press Review* 16 (Spring 1977):5–7

————. "Teaching Reporting Without a Student Newspaper is Like Teaching Swimming Without Water." *Community College Journalist* 6 (Summer 1978):4–6.

Sessler, Michael. "Communication Boards Create Atmosphere of Professionalism." *Scholastic Editor* 57 (October 1977):18–19.

Trager, Robert. "The College President Is Not Eugene C. Pulliam: Student Publications in a New Light." *College Press Review* 14 (Spring 1975):2–5.

————. "Freedom of the Press in College and High School." *Albany Law Review* 35 (Winter 1970–71):161–81.

Upah-Bant, Marilyn. "Maintaining Independence." *College Press Review* 17 (Summer 1978):16–21.

Chapter 15. EDITING A WEEKLY NEWSPAPER

BOOKS

Barnhart, Thomas F. *Weekly Newspaper: Makeup and Typography.* Minneapolis: University of Minnesota Press, 1949.

————. *Weekly Newspaper Writing and Editing.* New York: The Dryden Press, 1949.

Byerly, Kenneth R. *Community Journalism.* Philadelphia: Chilton, 1961.

Editors of the *Harvard Post. How to Produce a Small Newspaper: A Guide for Independent Journalists.* Harvard, Mass.: Harvard Common Press, 1978.

Hough, Henry Beetle. *Country Editor.* Riverside, Conn.: Chatham Press, 1940.

Janowitz, Morris. *The Community Press in an Urban Setting: The Social Elements of Urbanism,* 2d ed. Chicago: University of Chicago Press, 1967.

Johnston, J. George. *The Weeklies: Biggest Circulation in Town.* Bolton, Ontario, Canada: The Bolton Enterprise, 1972.

Kennedy, Bruce M. *Community Journalism: A Way of Life.* Ames: Iowa State University, 1974.

Lister, Hal. *The Suburban Press: A Separate Journalism.* Columbia, Mo.: Lucas Brothers, 1975.

McKinney, John. *How to Start Your Own Community Newspaper.* Port Jefferson, N.Y.: Meadow Press, 1977.

Romano, Frank J. *How to Build a Profitable Newspaper.* Philadelphia: North American Publishing, 1973.

Rucker, Frank W., and Williams, Herbert Lee. *Newspaper Organization and Management,* 5th ed. Ames: Iowa State University Press, 1979.

Shaw, David. *Journalism Today: A Changing Press for a Changing America.* New York: Harper's College Press, 1977.

Sim, John Cameron. *The Grass Roots Press.* Ames: Iowa State University Press, 1969.

Turnbull, Arthur T., and Baird, Russell N. *The Graphics of Communication,* 3d ed. New York: Holt, Rinehart and Winston, 1975.

ARTICLES

Anderson, Douglas. "The Good Life of Small Town, Family Tradition, Incentives for Entering Weekly Field." *Nebraska Newspaper* 30 (December 1978):7.

Bogart, Leo, and Orenstein, Frank. "Mass Media and Community Identity in an Interurban Setting." *Journalism Quarterly* 52 (Spring 1975):179–88.

Brovald, Walter. "Controversy Rare Topic." *Grassroots Editor* 19 (Spring 1978):6,10.

Edelstein, Alex, and Larsen, Otto. "The Weekly Press's Contribution to a Sense of Urban Community." *Journalism Quarterly* 37 (Autumn 1960):489–98.

Friedman, Rick. "Why Own a Weekly?" *Grassroots Editor* 18 (Summer 1977):3–6.

Gaziano, Cecilie and Ward, Jean. "Citizen-Developed Neighborhood Press." *Mass Comm Review* 5 (Spring 1978):14–17.

Stone, Gerald C., and Gulyas, Chris. "Weekly Papers Profiled." *Grassroots Editor* 19 (Fall 1978):9–12.

Ward, Jean, and Gaziano, Cecilie. "A New Variety of Urban Press: Neighborhood Public–Affairs Publications." *Journalism Quarterly* 53 (Spring 1976):61–67.

Chapter 16. NEWS EDITING: EVER EXPANDING HORIZONS

ARTICLES

"Electronic Carbons Replace Dupes." *AP Log* (April 9, 1979):1.

Feck, Luke M. "Keys to Success With Remote Terminals." *American Newspaper Publishers Association Research Institute Bulletin* (Dec. 7, 1978):489–91.

King, Blaine. "Handling the Wire Services." *American Newspaper Publishers Association Research Institute Bulletin* (Nov. 22, 1978): 478–80.

Lawrence, David, Jr. "It's a Different World With Cold Type." *American Newspaper Publishers Association Research Institute Bulletin* (Nov. 22, 1978):472–75.

"Pictures Enter the Computer Age." *The AP World* 34 (December 1977):10,11,13.

Shaw, David. "Journalists Fear Impact of Court Rulings." *Associated Press Managing Editors News* (March 1979):5–10.

Simons, Dolph C., Jr.; Jones, Jenkin L., Jr.; Sass, Gerald M., Jr.; Brooks, Brian S. "Future Journalists and New Technology." *Amer-*

ican Newspaper Publishers Association Research Institute Bulletin (Dec. 7, 1978):502–7.

Sizemore, H. Mason. "Moving to a New General System." *American Newspaper Publishers Association Research Institute Bulletin* (Dec. 7, 1978):500–501.

Ungaro, Joseph M. "State of the Art." *American Newspaper Publishers Association Research Institute Bulletin* (Nov. 22, 1978): 469–72.

Wilt, Bill. "The Electronic Makeup Editor." *Editor & Publisher* 111 (Aug. 12, 1978):12.

UNPUBLISHED MATERIALS

Stricklin, Michael. "The New Printing Technology and Journalism Education: Toward a Paradigm." Ph.D. Dissertation, School of Journalism, University of Iowa, 1977.

Index